I

Michelin Scenic Drives

Experience the thrill of the open roads of North America with these great Scenic Drives from Michelin. The famous star ratings highlight natural and cultural attractions along the way.

   ★★★   **Worth a special journey**
   ★★   **Worth a detour**
   ★   **Worth a visit**

ABBREVIATIONS

N	North	NM	National Memorial/
E	East		National Monument
S	South	NMP	National Military Park
W	West	NP	National Park
NE	Northeast	NPR	National Park Reserve
NW	Northwest	NRA	National
SE	Southeast		Recreation Area
SW	Southwest	NWR	National Wildlife
Hwy.	Highway		Refuge
Pkwy.	Parkway	PP	Provincial Park
Rte.	Route	SHP	State Historical
Mi	Miles		Park
Km	Kilometers	SHS	State Historic Site
Sq Ft	Square Feet	SP	State Park
NHS	National Historic Site	SR	State Reserve
NL	National Lakeshore	VC	Visitor Center

For detailed coverage of the attractions, and for where to dine and stay overnight, see Michelin's North America **Regional Atlas Series**, designed for the way you drive, and Michelin's **Green Guide** and **Short Stays** collections, the ultimate guidebooks for the independent traveler.

NORTHWEST

Anchorage/Fairbanks/Denali★★★
892 miles/1,436 kilometers   Map 74
From **Anchorage★**, Alaska's largest city, take Rte. 1 (Glenn Hwy. and Tok Cutoff) N and then E through the broad Matanuska Valley to the small town of **Tok**. The route passes agricultural communities, the **Matanuska Glacier** and the Wrangell Mountains before heading up the Copper River Basin. From Tok, take the Alaska Hwy. (Rte. 2) NW to **Fairbanks★**, a friendly town with a frontier feel. The road passes the **Trans-Alaska Pipeline** and **Big Delta SHP** then parallels the Tanana River. From Fairbanks, opt for Rte. 3 W which crosses the river at Nenana, then veers S to **Denali NP★★★**, home of spruce forests, grassy tundra, grizzlies, moose and North America's highest peak, **Mount McKinley** (20,320ft). Return S to Anchorage via Rtes. 3 and 1.

Mount McKinley, Denali NP

Badlands★★★
164 miles/264 kilometers   Maps 22, 23
From **Rapid City★**, South Dakota, drive SE on Rte. 44 through Farmingdale and Scenic, then east to Interior to enter **Badlands NP★★★**. Take Rte. 377 NE 2mi to Cedar Pass and stop at the park's Ben Reifel VC. From there, Cliff **Shelf Nature Trail★★** (.5mi) is popular for its shady juniper trees; **Castle Trail★★★** (4.5mi) is spectacular in early morning when the moonscape valley and pointed spires get first light. Turn left onto Rte. 240, **Badlands Loop Road★★★**, along the northern rim, where prairie grasslands give way to buttes and hoodoos. **Pinnacles Overlook★★** is a sweeping viewpoint to the south. Drive N to I-90, and cross the Interstate N to Wall. On Main St. visit **Wall Drug★**, a "drug store in name only" with over 20 shops filled with historical photos, 6,000 pairs of cowboy boots, wildlife exhibits and Western art displayed in five dining rooms. In the backyard a roaring, 80ft **Tyrannosaurus** sends toddlers running. Leave Wall on I-90, driving W. Take Exit 67 to Ellsworth Air Force Base, where the **South Dakota Air and Space Museum** displays stealth bombers and other aircraft. Continue W on I-90 back to Rapid City to conclude the tour.

Badlands NP

Black Hills★★
244 miles/393 kilometers   Map 23
From **Rapid City★**, drive S on US-16 then US-16A S past Keystone. Take Rte. 244 W to **Mount Rushmore NM★★★**. Continue W on Rte. 244 to the junction of US-16/385. Enroute S to Custer, **Crazy Horse Memorial★** honors the famous Sioux chief. From Custer, head S on US-385 through Pringle to the junction of Rte. 87. Take Rte. 87 N through **Wind Cave NP★★** and into **Custer SP★★★**. Follow **Wildlife Loop Road★★** (access S of Blue Bell, across from Rte. 342 junction) E and N to US-16A. Then travel W to join scenic **Needles Highway★★** (Rte. 87) NW to US-16/385 N. Where US-16 separates, continue N on US-385 to **Deadwood★★**, a former gold camp. Turn left onto US-14A, driving SW through **Lead★**, site of the former **Homestake Gold Mine★★**, to Cheyenne Crossing. Drive N on US-14A to I-90, turning SE back to Rapid City.

Mount Rushmore NM

Columbia River Gorge★★
83 miles/134 kilometers   Map 8
From **Portland★★**, Oregon's largest city, take I-84 E to Exit 17 in Troutdale. There, head E on the winding **Historic Columbia River Highway★** (US-30), which skirts the steep cliffs above the river. For great **views★★**, stop at **Vista House at Crown Point**. You'll pass the 620ft **Multnomah Falls★★** and moss-draped **Oneonta Gorge**. At Ainsworth State Park (Exit 35), rejoin I-84 and travel E to Mosier (Exit 69), where US-30, with its hairpin turns, begins again. Continue E on US-30, stopping at **Rowena Crest Viewpoint★★** for grand vistas—and wildflowers. Just past the Western-style town called The Dalles, take US-197 N to conclude the tour at **The Dalles Lock and Dam VC★★**.

Mount Moran, Grand Teton NP

Grand Tetons/Yellowstone★★★
224 miles/361 kilometers   Maps 20, 21
Note: parts of this tour are closed in winter.
From **Jackson★★**, drive N on US-26/191/89 to Moose. Turn left onto Teton Park Rd. to access **Grand Teton NP★★★** and **Jenny Lake Scenic Drive★★★**. From Teton Park Rd., drive N to the junction of US-89/191/287 (**John D. Rockefeller Jr. Memorial Pkwy.**) and follow the parkway N into **Yellowstone NP★★★** to **West Thumb**. Take Grand Loop Rd. W to **Old Faithful★★★**, the world's most famous geyser. Continue N on the Grand Loop Rd., passing **Norris Geyser Basin★★** en route to **Mammoth Hot Springs★★★**. Turn E on Grand Loop Rd. to Tower Junction, then S into **Grand Canyon of the Yellowstone★★★**. Continue S from Canyon Village through **Hayden Valley★★** to Yellowstone Lake. Head SW, back to West Thumb, to conclude the tour.

Pacific Coast/Olympic Peninsula★★★
419 miles/675 kilometers   Map 8
From the state capital of **Olympia**, drive N on US-101 to Discovery Bay. Detour on Rte. 20 NE to **Port Townsend★★**, a well-preserved Victorian seaport. From Discovery Bay, head W on US-101 through **Port Angeles** to the **Heart O' the Hills** park entrance for **Olympic NP★★★** to see **Hurricane Ridge★★★**.
Back on US-101, head E then S to the park entrance that leads to **Hoh Rain Forest★★★**. Follow US-101 S, then E after Queets to **Lake Quinault**, home to bald eagles, trumpeter swans and loons. Continue S on US-101 to Aberdeen, taking Rte. 105 to the coast. At Raymond, return to US-101 heading S to **Long Beach**. Follow Rte. 103 N past the former cannery town of **Oysterville** to **Leadbetter Point★** on Willapa Bay, where oysters are still harvested. Return S to **Ilwaco** and drive E and S on US-101 to Astoria, Oregon, to end the tour.

The Oregon Coast★★★
368 miles/592 kilometers   Map 17
Leave **Astoria★**, Oregon's first settlement, via US-101, heading SW. **Fort Clatsop National Memorial★★** recalls Lewis and Clark's historic stay. **Cannon Beach★** boasts a sandy beach and tall coastal rock. At the farming community of **Tillamook★**, go west on 3rd St. to **Cape Meares** to begin **Three Capes Scenic Drive★★**. Continue S, rejoining US-101 just beyond Pacific City. Drive S on US-101 through **Newport★**, then **Yachats★**, which neighbors **Cape Perpetua Scenic Area★★**. From **Florence** to **Coos Bay★** stretches **Oregon Dunes National Recreation Area★★**. At Coos Bay, take Cape Arago Hwy. W to tour the gardens of **Shore Acres State Park★**. Drive S on the highway to rejoin US-101. Pass **Bandon★**, known for its cheese factory, and Port Orford, with its fishing fleet. Farther S, **Boardman State Park★** shelters Sitka spruce, Douglas fir and **Natural Bridge Cove**. End the tour at **Brookings**.

Cannon Beach, Oregon Coast

SOUTHWEST

Big Bend Area★★
581 miles/935 kilometers   Maps 58, 59

Head S from **El Paso★** via I-10, then E to Kent. Take Rte. 118 S to Alpine, passing **McDonald Observatory★** (telescope tours) and **Fort Davis NHS★★**. Continue S to Study Butte to enter **Big Bend NP★★★**, edged by the Rio Grande River and spanning 1,252sq mi of spectacular canyons, lush bottomlands, sprawling desert and mountain woodlands. The park has more species of migratory and resident birds than any other national park. Travel E to the main VC at Panther Junction in the heart of the park (US-385 and Rio Grande Village Dr.). Then take US-385 N to Marathon. Turn E on US-90 to Langtry, site of **Judge Roy Bean VC★**. Continue E to **Seminole Canyon SP★★**, with its 4,000-year-old pictographs. Farther E, **Amistad NRA★** is popular for water sports. Continue on US-90 to conclude the tour in Del Rio.

Canyonlands of Utah★★★
481 miles/774 kilometers   Map 34

From **St. George★**, drive NE on I-15 to Exit 16. Take Rte. 9 E to Springdale, gateway to **Zion NP★★★**, with its sandstone canyon, waterfalls and hanging gardens. Continue E on Rte. 9 to Mt. Carmel Junction, turn left onto US-89 and head N to the junction with Rte. 12. Take Rte. 12 SE to **Bryce Canyon NP★★★**, with its colored rock formations. Continue SE on Rte. 12 to Cannonville, then S to **Kodachrome Basin SP★★**, where sandstone chimneys rise from the desert floor. Return to Cannonville, and drive NE on Rte. 12 through Boulder to Torrey. Take Rte. 24 E through **Capitol Reef NP★★**—with its unpaved driving roads and trails—then N to I-70. Travel E on I-70 to Exit 182, then S on US-191 to Rte. 313 into **Canyonlands NP★★★** to Grand View Point Overlook. Return to US-191, turning S to access **Arches NP★★★**—the greatest concentration of natural stone arches in the country. Continue S on US-191 to **Moab★** to end the tour.

Canyonlands NP

Central Coast/Big Sur★★★
118 miles/190 kilometers   Map 31

From **Cannery Row★** in **Monterey★★**, take Prescott Ave. to Rte. 68. Turn right and continue to Pacific Grove Gate (on your left) to begin scenic **17-Mile Drive★★**, a private toll road. Exit at Carmel Gate to reach the upscale beach town of **Carmel★★**, site of Carmel **mission★★★**. The town's Scenic Road winds S along the beachfront. Leave Carmel by Hwy. 1 S. Short, easy trails at **Point Lobos SR★★** line the shore. Enjoy the wild beauty of the **Big Sur★★★** coastline en route to San Simeon, where **Hearst Castle★★★**, the magnificent estate of a former newspaper magnate, overlooks the Pacific Ocean. Continue S on Hwy. 1 to **Morro Bay**, where the tour ends.

Bixby Creek Bridge, Big Sur

Colorado Rockies★★★
499 miles/803 kilometers   Map 35
Note: Rte. 82 S of Leadville to Aspen is closed mid-Oct to Memorial Day due to snow.

From **Golden★★**, **W of Denver★★**, drive W on US-6 along Clear Creek to Rte. 119, heading N on the *Peak to Peak Highway★★* to **Nederland★**. Continue N on Rte. 72, then follow Rte. 7 N to the town of **Estes Park★★**. Take US-36 W to enter **Rocky Mountain NP★★★**. Drive **Trail Ridge Road★★★** (US-34) S to the town of **Grand Lake★**. Continue S to Granby, turn left on US-40 to I-70 at Empire. Head W on I-70 past **Georgetown★** and through **Eisenhower Tunnel**. You'll pass ski areas Arapahoe Basin, **Keystone Resort★** and **Breckenridge★★**. At Exit 195 for **Copper Mountain Resort★**, take Rte. 91 S to **Leadville★★**, Colorado's former silver capital. Then travel S on US-24 to Rte. 82 W over **Independence Pass★★** to **Aspen★★★**. Head NW to I-70, passing **Glenwood Springs★★** with its **Hot Springs Pool★★**. Drive E on I-70 along **Glenwood Canyon★★** and the Colorado River to **Vail★★**. Continue E on I-70 to the old mining town of **Idaho Springs** to return to Golden via Rte. 119.

Colorado Rockies

Lake Tahoe Loop★★
71 miles/114 kilometers   Maps 31, 32

Begin in **Tahoe City** at the intersection of Rtes. 89 and 28. Drive S on Rte. 89. **Ed Z'berg-Sugar Pine Point State Park★** encompasses a promontory topped by **Ehrman Mansion★** and other historic buildings. Farther S, **Emerald Bay State Park★★** surrounds beautiful **Emerald Bay★★**. At the bay's tip stands **Vikingsholm★★**, a mansion that resembles an ancient Nordic castle. At **Tallac Historic Site★★**, preserved summer estates recall Tahoe's turn-of-the-19C opulence. From Tahoe Valley, take Rte. 50 NE. **South Lake Tahoe**, the lake's largest town, offers lodging, dining and shopping. High-rise hotel-casinos characterize neighboring **Stateline** in Nevada. Continue N to Spooner Junction. Then follow Nevada Rte. 28 N to **Sand Harbor** (7mi), where picnic tables and a sandy beach fringe a sheltered cove. Continue through Kings Beach to end the tour at Tahoe City.

Emerald Bay, Lake Tahoe

Maui's Hana Highway★★
108 miles/174 kilometers   Maps 72, 73

Leave **Kahului** on Rte. 36 E toward **Paia**, an old sugar-plantation town. Continue E on Rte. 36, which becomes Rte. 360, the **Hana Highway★★**. The road passes **Ho'okipa Beach Park**, famous for windsurfing, and **Puohokamoa Falls**, a good picnic stop, before arriving in **Hana**, a little village on an attractive bay. If adventurous, continue S on the Pulaui Highway to **Ohe'o Gulch★★** in **Haleakala NP★★★**, where small waterfalls tumble from the SE flank of the dormant volcano Haleakala. Past the gulch the grave of aviator **Charles Lindbergh** can be found in the churchyard at Palapala Hoomau Hawaiian Church. End the tour at Kipahulu.

Haleakala volcano crater, Maui

Redwood Empire★★
182 miles/293 kilometers   Map 31

In **Leggett**, S of the junction of Hwy. 1 and US-101, go N on US-101 to pass through a massive redwood trunk at **Chandelier Drive-Thru Tree Park**. To the N, see breathtaking groves along 31mi **Avenue of the Giants★★★**. **Humboldt Redwoods SP★★** contains **Rockefeller Forest★★**, the world's largest virgin redwood forest. From US-101, detour 4mi to **Ferndale★**, a quaint Victorian village. N. along US-101, **Eureka★** preserves a logging camp cookhouse and other historic sites. The sleepy fishing town of **Trinidad★** is home to a marine research lab. **Patrick's Point SP★★** offers dense forests, agate-strewn beaches and clifftop **view★★**. At **Orick**, enter the **Redwood National and State Parks★★**, which protect a 379ft-high, 750-year-old **tree★**. The tour ends in Crescent City.

Avenue of the Giants, Redwood Empire

Santa Fe Area★★★
267 miles/430 kilometers   Maps 47, 48

From **Albuquerque★**, drive E on I-40 to Exit 175 and take Rte. 14, the **Turquoise Trail★★**, N to **Santa Fe★★★**. This 52mi back road runs along the scenic Sandia Mountains and passes dry washes, arroyos and a series of revived "ghost towns." Continue N on US-84/285, turning NE onto Rte. 76, the **High Road to Taos★★**. East of Vadito, take Rte. 518 N to Rte. 68 N into the rustic Spanish colonial town of **Taos★★**, a center for the arts. Head N on US-64 to the junction of Rte. 522. Continue W on US-64 for an 18mi round-trip detour to see the 1,200ft-long, three-span **Rio Grande Gorge Bridge** over the river. Return to Rte. 522 and take this route, part of the **Enchanted Circle★★** Scenic Byway, N to **Questa**, starting point for white-water trips on the Rio Grande. Turn onto Rte. 38, heading E to the old mining town of **Eagle Nest**. There, detour 23mi E on US-64 to **Cimarron**, a Wild West haunt. Back at Eagle Nest, travel SW on US-64, detouring on Rte. 434 S to tiny **Angel Fire**. Return to Taos on US-64 W to end the tour.

Taos Pueblo, Santa Fe Area

Sedona/Grand Canyon NP★★★
482 miles/776 kilometers   Map 46

Drive N from **Phoenix★** on I-17 to Exit 298 and take Rte. 179 N toward **Sedona★★** in the heart of **Red Rock Country★★★**. The red-rock formations are best accessed by four-wheel-drive vehicle via 12mi **Schnebly Hill Road★** (off Rte. 179, across Oak Creek bridge from US-89A "Y" junction), which offers splendid **views★★★**. Then head N on Rte. 89A through Sedona to begin 14mi drive of **Oak Creek Canyon★★**. Continue N on Rte. 89A

Grand Canyon NP

and I-17 to **Flagstaff★**, commercial hub for the region. Take US-180 NW to Rte. 64, which leads N to the **South Rim★★★** of **Grand Canyon NP★★★**. Take the shuttle (or drive, if permitted) along **West Rim Drive★★** to **Hermits Rest★**. Then travel **East Rim Drive★★★** (Rte. 64 E) to **Desert View Watchtower★** for **views★★★** of the canyon. Continue to the junction with US-89 at Cameron. Return S to Flagstaff, then S to Phoenix via I-17.

NORTHEAST

The Berkshires Loop★★★
57 miles/92 kilometers Map 29
From **Great Barrington**, take US-23 E to Monterey, turning left onto Tyringham Rd., which becomes Monterey Rd., to experience scenic **Tyringham Valley★**. Continue N on Main Rd. to Tyringham Rd., which leads to **Lee**, famous for its marble. Then go NW on US-20 to **Lenox★**, with its inviting inns and restaurants. Detour on Rte. 183 W to **Tanglewood★**, site of a popular summer music festival. Return to Lenox and drive N on US-7 to **Pittsfield**, the commercial capital of the region. Head W on US-20 to enjoy **Hancock Shaker Village★★★**, a museum village that relates the history of a Shaker community established here in 1790. Rte. 41 S passes West Stockbridge, then opt for Rte. 102 SE to **Stockbridge★★** and its picturesque **Main Street★**. Follow US-7 S to the junction with Rte. 23, passing **Monument Mountain★** en route. Return to Great Barrington.

Cape Cod★★★
164 miles/264 kilometers Map 29
At US-6 and Rte. 3, cross **Cape Cod Canal** via Sagamore Bridge and turn onto Rte. 6A to tour the Cape's **North Shore★★**. Bear right onto Rte. 130 to reach **Sandwich★**, famous for glass manufacturing. Continue on Rte. 6A E to Orleans. Take US-6 N along **Cape Cod National Seashore★★★**, with its wooded and marshland trails, to reach **Provincetown★★**, a seaside town and longtime LGBTQ retreat offering **dune tours★★** and summer theater. Return to Orleans and take Rte. 28 S through **Chatham★**, then W to Hyannis, where ferries depart for **Nantucket★★★**. Continue to quaint **Falmouth★**. Take Surf Dr., which becomes Oyster Pond Rd. to nearby **Woods Hole**, a world center for marine research and departure point for ferries to **Martha's Vineyard★★**. Take Woods Hole Rd., N to Rte. 28. Cross the canal via Bourne Bridge and head E on US-6 to end the tour at Rte. 3.

Brant Point Light, Nantucket, Cape Cod

Maine Coast★★
238 miles/383 kilometers Maps 29, 30
From **Kittery**, drive N on US-1 to **York★**, then along US-1A to see the 18C buildings of **Colonial York★★**. Continue N on coastal US-1A to **Ogunquit★**. Rejoin US-1 and head N to Rte. 9, turn right, and drive to **Kennebunkport**, with its colorful shops. Take Rte. 9A/35 to **Kennebunk**. Then travel N on US-1 to **Portland★★**, Maine's largest city, where the **Old Port★★** brims with galleries and boutiques. Take US-1 N through the outlet town of **Freeport**, then on to

Brunswick, home of **Bowdoin College**. Turn NE through **Bath★**, **Wiscasset**, **Rockland**, **Camden★★**, **Searsport** and **Bucksport**. At Ellsworth, take Rte. 3 S to enter **Acadia NP★★★** on **Mount Desert Island★★★**, where **Park Loop Road★★★** (closed in winter) parallels open coast. From the top of **Cadillac Mountain★★★**, the **views★★★** are breathtaking. The tour ends at **Bar Harbor★**, a popular charming town just outside Acadia NP.

Acadia NP, Maine Coast

Mohawk Valley★
114 miles/184 kilometers Maps 28, 29
From the state capital of **Albany★**, take I-90 NW to Exit 25 for I-890 into **Schenectady**, founded by Dutch settlers in 1661. Follow Rte. 5 W along the Mohawk River. In Fort Hunter, **Schoharie Crossing SHS★** stretches along a canal towpath. Near Little Falls, **Herkimer Home SHS** (Rte. 169 at Thruway Exit 29A) interprets colonial farm life. Rte. 5 continues W along the Erie Canal to Utica. From Utica, drive W on Rte. 49 to Rome, where the river turns N and peters out. The tour ends in Rome, site of **Fort Stanwix NM★**.

South Shore Lake Superior★
530 miles/853 kilometers Maps 15, 16
From **Duluth★**, drive SE on I-535/US-53 to the junction of Rte. 13 at Parkland. Follow Rte. 13 E to quaint Bayfield, gateway to **Apostle Islands NL★★**, accessible by boat. Head S to the junction of US-2, and E through Ashland, Ironwood and Wakefield. There, turn left onto Rte. 28, heading NE to Bergland, and turning left onto Rte. 64. Drive N to Silver City and take Rte. M-107 W into **Porcupine Mountains Wilderness SP★**. Return to Rte. 64 and go E to Ontonagon. Take Rte. 38 SE to Greenland, then follow Rte. 26 NE to Houghton. Cross to Hancock on US-41 and continue NE to Phoenix. Turn left onto Rte. 26 to Eagle River and on to Copper Harbor via **Brockway Mountain Drive★★**. Return S to Houghton via US-41, then travel S and E past Marquette, turning left onto Rte. 28. Head E to Munising, then take County Road H-58 E and N through **Pictured Rocks NL★**. End the tour at Grand Marais.

Villages of Southern Vermont★★
118 miles/190 kilometers Map 29
Head N from the resort town of **Manchester★** by Rte. 7A. At Manchester Center, take Rte. 11 E past **Bromley Mountain**, a popular ski area, to Peru. Turn left on the backroad to **Weston★**, a favorite tourist stop along Rte. 100. Continue to **Chester**, turning right onto Rte. 35 S to reach **Grafton★**, with its **Old Tavern**. Farther S, Rte. 30 S from Townshend leads to **Newfane** and its lovely **village green★**. Return to Townshend, then travel W, following Rte. 30 through West Townshend, passing **Stratton Mountain** en route to Manchester. S of Manchester by Rte. 7A, the crest of Mt. Equinox is accessible via **Equinox Skyline Drive** (fee). Then continue S on Rte. 7A to end the tour at **Arlington**, known for its trout fishing.

The White Mountains Loop★★★
127 miles/204 kilometers Map 29
From the all-season resort of Conway, drive N on Rte. 16 to **North Conway★**, abundant with tourist facilities. Continue N on US-302/Rte. 16 through **Glen**, passing **Glen Ellis Falls★** and **Pinkham Notch★★** en route to Glen House. There, drive the Auto Road to the top of **Mount Washington★★** (or take guided van tour). Head N on Rte. 16 to Gorham, near the Androscoggin River, then W on US-2 to Jefferson Highlands. Travel SW on Rte. 115 to Carroll, then S on US-3 to Twin Mountain. Go SW on US-3 to join I-93. Head S on I-93/Rte.3, passing scenic **Franconia Notch★★★** and **Profile Lake★★**. Bear E on

White Mountain National Forest

Rte. 3 where it separates from the interstate to visit **The Flume★★**, a natural gorge 90ft deep. Rejoin I-93 S to the intersection with Rte. 112. Head E on Rte. 112 through Lincoln on the **Kancamagus Highway★★★** until it joins Rte. 16 back to Conway.

SOUTHEAST

Blue Ridge Parkway★★
574 miles/924 kilometers Map 42
From **Front Royal**, take US-340 S to begin **Skyline Drive★★**, the best-known feature of **Shenandoah NP★★**. The drive follows former Indian trails along the **Blue Ridge Parkway★★**. **Marys Rock Tunnel to Rockfish Entrance Station★★** passes the oldest rock in the park and **Big Meadows★**. The Drive ends at **Rockfish Gap** at I-64, but continue S on the Parkway. From Terrapin Hill Overlook, detour 16mi W on Rte. 130 to see **Natural Bridge★★**. Enter NC at **Cumberland Knob**, then pass **Blowing Rock★**, **Grandfather Mountain★★** and **Linville Falls★★**. Detour 4.8mi to **Mount Mitchell SP★** to drive to the top of the tallest mountain (6,684ft) E of the Mississippi. At mile 382, the **Folk Art Center** stocks high-quality regional crafts. Popular **Biltmore Estate★★** in **Asheville★** (North Exit of US-25, then 4mi N) includes formal **gardens★★**. The rugged stretch from **French Broad River to Cherokee** courses 17 tunnels within two national forests. **Looking Glass Rock★★** is breathtaking. The Parkway ends at **Cherokee**, gateway to **Great Smoky Mountains NP★★★** and home of Cherokee tribe members.

Skyline Drive, Shenandoah NP, Blue Ridge Parkway

Central Kentucky★★
379 miles/610 kilometers Maps 40, 41
From **Louisville★★**, home of the **Kentucky Derby★★★**, take I-64 E to **Frankfort**, the state capital. Continue E to **Lexington★★**, heart of **Bluegrass Country★★** with its rolling meadows and white-fenced horse farms. Stop at the **Kentucky Horse Park★★★** (4089 Iron Works Pkwy.) for the daily **Parade of Breeds**. Then head S on I-75 through Richmond to the craft center/college town of **Berea**. Return to Lexington and follow the Blue Grass Parkway SW to Exit 25. There, US-150 W leads to Bardstown, site of **My Old Kentucky Home SP★**, immortalized by Stephen Foster in what is now the state song. Drive S from Bardstown on US-31E past **Abraham Lincoln Birthplace NHS★**. Turn right onto Rte. 70 to Cave City, then take US-31W to Park City, gateway to **Mammoth Cave NP★★★**, which features the world's longest cave system. Return to Louisville via I-65 to end the tour.

Florida's Northeast Coast★★
174 miles/280 kilometers Map 67
From **Jacksonville★**, drive E on Rte. 10 to **Atlantic Beach**, the most affluent of Jacksonville's beach towns. Head S on Rte. A1A through residential **Neptune Beach**, **Jacksonville Beach** and upscale **Ponte Vedra Beach** to reach **St. Augustine★★★**, the oldest city in the US and former capital of Spanish Florida. Farther S, car-racing mecca **Daytona Beach** is known for its **international**

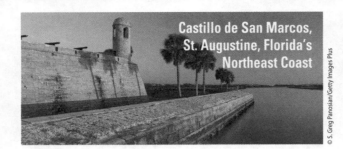
Castillo de San Marcos, St. Augustine, Florida's Northeast Coast

speedway. Take US-92 across the Intracoastal Waterway to US-1, heading S to **Titusville**. Take Rte. 402 across the Indian River to **Merritt Island NWR**★★ to begin **Black Point Wildlife Drive**★. Return to **Titusville** and follow Rte. 405 to **Kennedy Space Center**★★★, one of Florida's top attractions, to end the tour.

Florida Keys★★
168 miles/270 kilometers   Map 67
Note: Green **mile-marker** *(MM) posts, sometimes difficult to see, line US-1 (Overseas Hwy.), showing distances from Key West (MM 0). Much of the route is two-lane, and traffic can be heavy from December to April and on weekends. Allow 3hrs for the drive. Crossing 43 bridges and causeways (only one over land), the highway offers fine views of the Atlantic Ocean (E) and Florida Bay (W).*
Drive S from **Miami**★★★ on US-1. Near **Key Largo**★, **John Pennekamp Coral Reef SP**★★ habors tropical fish, coral and fine snorkeling waters. To the SW, **Islamorada** is known for **charter fishing**. At **Marathon** (MM 50), **Sombrero Beach** is a good swimming spot, but **Bahia Honda SP**★★ (MM 36.8) is considered the best **beach**★★ in the Keys. Pass **National Key Deer Refuge**★ (MM 30.5), haven to the 2ft-tall deer unique to the lower Keys. End at **Key West**★★★, joining others at **Mallory Square Dock** to view the **sunset**★★.

Bahia Honda SP, Florida Keys

The Ozarks★
343 miles/552 kilometers   Map 51
From the state capital of **Little Rock**, take I-30 SW to Exit 111, then US-70 W to Hot Springs. Drive N on Rte. 7/Central Ave. to **Hot Springs NP**★★ to enjoy the therapeutic waters. Travel N on Rte. 7 across the Arkansas River to Russellville. Continue on **Scenic Highway 7**★ N through **Ozark National Forest** and across the **Buffalo National River** to Harrison. Take US-62/65 NW to Bear Creek Springs, continuing W on US-62 through **Eureka Springs**★, with its historic district, to **Pea Ridge NMP**★, a Civil War site. Return E on US-62 to the junction of Rte. 21 at Berryville. Travel N on Rte. 21 to Blue Eye, taking Rte. 86 E to US-65, which leads N to the entertainment hub of **Branson**, Missouri, to end the tour.

River Road Plantations★★
200 miles/323 kilometers   Maps 63, 64
From **New Orleans**★★★, take US-90 W to Rte. 48 along the Mississippi River to Destrehan. **Destrehan**★★ is considered the oldest plantation house in the Mississippi Valley. Continue NW on Rte. 48 to US-61 to Laplace to connect to Rte. 44. Head N past **San Francisco Plantation**★, built in 1856. At Burnside, take Rte. 75 N to St. Gabriel. En route, watch for **Houmas House**★ (40136 Hwy. 942). Take Rte. 30 to **Baton Rouge**★, the state capital. Then drive S along the **West Bank**★★ on Rte. 1 to White Castle, site of **Nottoway**★, the largest plantation home in the South. Continue to Donaldsonville, then turn onto Rte. 18. Travel E to Gretna, passing **Oak Alley**★★ (no. 3645) and **Laura Plantation**★★ (no. 2247) along the way. From Gretna, take US-90 to New Orleans, where the tour ends.

CANADA

Gaspésie, Québec★★★
933 kilometers/578 miles (loop)   Map 87
Leave **Sainte-Flavie** via Rte. 132 NE, stopping to visit **Reford Gardens**★★★ en route to **Matane**. After Cap-Chat, take Rte. 299 S to **Gaspésie Park**★ for expansive **views**★★. Back on Rte. 132, follow the **Scenic Route from La Martre to Rivière-au-Renard**★★. Continue to **Cap-des-Rosiers**, entrance to majestic **Forillon NP**★★. Follow Rte. 132 along the coast through **Gaspé**★, the administrative center of the peninsula, to **Percé**★★★, a coastal village known for **Percé Rock**★★, a mammoth offshore rock wall. Drive SW on Rt. 132 through **Paspébiac** to **Carleton**, which offers a **panorama**★★ from the summit of **Mont Saint-Joseph**. Farther SW, detour 6km/4mi S to see an array of fossils at **Parc de Miguasha**★. Back on Rte. 132, travel W to **Matapédia**, then follow Rte. 132 N, passing **Causapscal**—a departure point for salmon fishing expeditions—to end the tour at Sainte-Flavie.

Percé Rock, Québec

North Shore Lake Superior★★
275 kilometers/171 miles   Map 16
From the port city of **Thunder Bay**★★—and nearby **Old Fort William**★★—drive the Trans-Canada Hwy. (Rte. 11/17) E to Rte. 587. Detour to **Sleeping Giant PP**★, which offers fine **views**★ of the lake. Back along the Trans-Canada Hwy., **Amethyst Mine** (take E. Loon Rd.) is a rock hound's delight (fee). Farther NE, located 12km/8mi off the highway, **Ouimet Canyon**★★ is a startling environment for the area. Just after the highway's Red Rock turnoff, watch for **Red Rock Cuesta**, a natural formation 210m/690ft high. Cross the Nipigon River and continue along **Nipigon Bay**★★, enjoying **views**★★ of the rocky, conifer-covered islands. The **view**★★ of **Kama Bay** through **Kama Rock Cut** is striking. Continue to **Schreiber** to end the tour.

Nova Scotia's Cabot Trail★★
338 kilometers/210 miles   Map 89
From **Baddeck**★, follow Hwy. 105 S to the junction with **Cabot Trail** to **North East Margaree**★ in salmon-fishing country. Take this road NW to Margaree Harbour, then N to **Chéticamp**, an enclave of Acadian culture. Heading inland, the route enters **Cape Breton Highlands NP**★★, combining seashore and mountains. At Cape North, detour N around Aspy Bay to **Bay St. Lawrence**★★. Then head W to tiny **Capstick** for shoreline **views**★. Return S to Cape North, then drive E to South Harbour. Take the coast road, traveling S through the fishing villages of **New Haven** and **Neils Harbour**★. Rejoin Cabot Trail S, passing the resort area of the **Ingonishs**. Take the right fork after Indian Brook to reach St. Ann's, home of **Gaelic College**★, specializing in bagpipe and Highland dance classes. Rejoin Hwy. 105 to return to Baddeck.

Cabot Trail, Cape Breton Highlands NP

Moraine Lake, Banff NP, Canadian Rockies

Canadian Rockies★★★
467 kilometers/290 miles   Map 79
Note: Some roads in Yoho NP are closed to cars mid-Oct to June due to snow, but are open for skiing.
Leave **Banff**★★ by Hwy. 1, traveling W. After 5.5km/3.5mi, take **Bow Valley Parkway**★ (Hwy. 1A) NW within **Banff NP**★★★. At Lake Louise Village, detour W to find **Lake Louise**★★★. Back on Hwy. 1, head N to the junction of Hwy. 93, turn W and follow Hwy. 1 past Kicking Horse Pass into **Yoho NP**★★. Continue through Field, and turn right onto the road N to **Emerald Lake**★★★. Return to the junction of Rte. 93 and Hwy. 1, heading N on Rte. 93 along the Icefields **Parkway**★★★. Pass **Crowfoot Glacier**★★ and **Bow Lake**★★ on the left. **Peyto Lake**★★★ is reached by spur road. After **Parker Ridge**★★, massive **Athabasca Glacier**★★★ looms on the left. Continue to **Jasper**★ and **Jasper NP**★★★. From Jasper, turn left onto Hwy. 16 and head into **Mount Robson PP**★★, home to **Mount Robson**★★★ (3,954m/12,972ft.). End the tour at Tête Jaune Cache.

Vancouver Island★★★
337 kilometers/209 miles   Map 78
To enjoy a scenic drive that begins 11mi N of **Victoria**★★★, take Douglas St. N from Victoria to the Trans-Canada Highway (Hwy. 1) and follow **Malahat Drive**★ (between Goldstream PP and Mill Bay Rd.) for 12mi. Continue N on Hwy. 1 past Duncan, **Chemainus**★—known for its murals—and Nanaimo to Parksville. Take winding Rte. 4 W (Pacific Rim Hwy.) passing **Englishman River Falls PP**★ and **Cameron Lake**. Just beyond the lake, **Cathedral Grove**★★ holds 800-year-old Douglas firs. The road descends to **Port Alberni**, departure point for cruises on Barkley Sound, and follows Sproat Lake before climbing Klitsa Mountain. The route leads to the Pacific along the Kennedy River. At the coast, turn left and drive SE to Ucluelet. Then head N to enter **Pacific Rim NPR**★★★. Continue to road's end at **Tofino**★ to end the tour.

Kluane NPR, Yukon Circuit

Yukon Circuit★★
1,485 kilometers/921 miles   Map 75
Note: Top of the World Highway is closed mid-Oct to mid-May due to snow.
From **Whitehorse**★, capital of Yukon Territory, drive N on the **Klondike Hwy.** (Rte. 2), crossing the Yukon River at **Carmacks**. After 196km/122mi, small islands divide the river into fast-flowing channels at **Five Finger Rapids**★. From Stewart Crossing, continue NW on Rte. 2 to **Dawson**★★, a historic frontier town. Ferry across the river and drive the **Top of the World Hwy.**★★ (Rte. 9), with its **views**★★★, to the Alaska border. Rte. 9 joins Rte. 5, passing tiny **Chicken**, Alaska. At Tetlin Junction, head SE on Rte. 2, paralleling **Tetlin NWR**. Enter Canada and follow the **Alaska Highway**★★ (Rte. 1) SE along **Kluane Lake**★★ to **Haines Junction**, gateway to **Kluane NPR**★★, home of **Mount Logan**, Canada's highest peak (5,959m/19,550ft). Continue E to Rte. 2 to return to Whitehorse.

Atlas 2025
LARGE FORMAT
USA • CANADA • MEXICO

ROAD MAPS are organized geographically. *United States, Canada, and Mexico road maps are organized in a grid layout, starting in the northwest of each country. To find your way, use either the **Key to Map Pages** inside the front cover, the **Listing of State and City Maps** on page 3, or the **index** in the back of the atlas.*

COUNTRY COLORS
Colors represent countries throughout the atlas.
Red → Canada
Green → Mexico
Blue → United States
Purple → United States (Northeast Corridor)

MAP SCALES
Scale bars use consistent increments throughout the atlas for quick and easy scale comparison between regions.

DRIVING DISTANCES
Use this chart to check driving distances between major cities within each map. Refer to distance and driving time information at the back of the atlas for travel over greater distances.

LOCATOR MAPS
A quick glance at this miniature map lets you check which states and/or provinces are shown on each page.

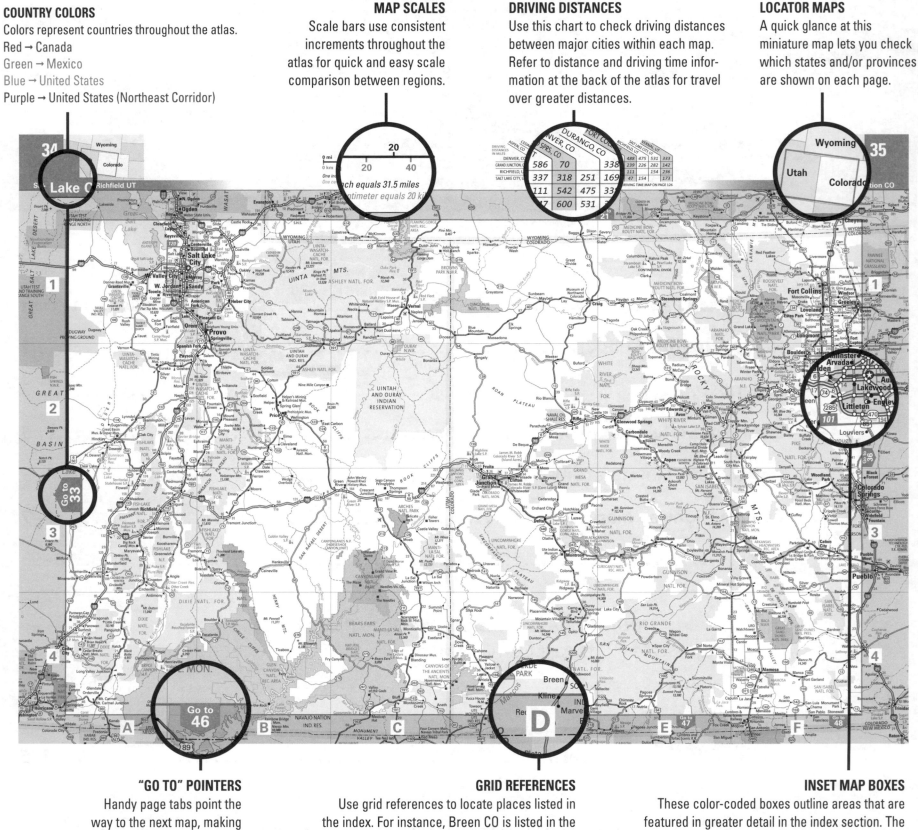

"GO TO" POINTERS
Handy page tabs point the way to the next map, making navigation a breeze.

GRID REFERENCES
Use grid references to locate places listed in the index. For instance, Breen CO is listed in the index with "35" and "D4", indicating that the town may be found on page 35 in grid square D4.

INSET MAP BOXES
These color-coded boxes outline areas that are featured in greater detail in the index section. The tab with "101" (above) indicates that a detailed map of Denver may be found on page 101 (below).

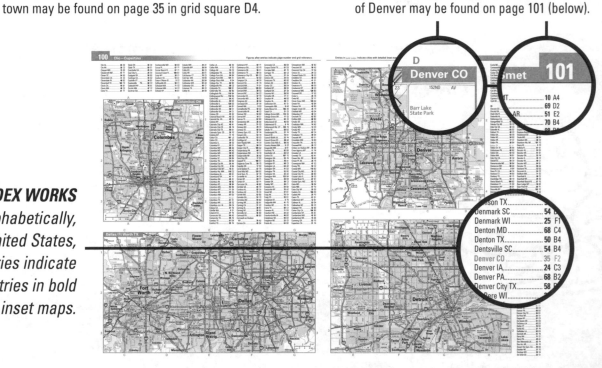

HOW THE INDEX WORKS
Cities and towns are listed alphabetically, with separate indexes for the United States, Canada, and Mexico. Figures after entries indicate page number and grid reference. Entries in bold color indicate cities with detailed inset maps.

TRANSPORTATION

HIGHWAYS

Freeway

Tollway; Toll Booth
City maps only

Under Construction

Interchange and Exit Number

Rest Area; Service Area
City maps only; Yellow with facilities

Primary; Secondary Highway

Multilane Divided Highway
Primary and secondary highways only

Other Paved Road; Unpaved Road
Check conditions locally

HIGHWAY MARKERS

Interstate Route

U.S. Route; State or Provincial Route

County or Other Route

Business Route

Trans-Canada Highway; Yellowhead Route

Canadian Provincial Autoroute

Mexican Federal Route

OTHER SYMBOLS

Distances along Major Highways
Miles in U.S.; kilometers in Canada and Mexico

Tunnel; Pass

Airport

Auto Ferry; Passenger Ferry

FEATURES OF INTEREST

National Park

National Forest; National Grassland

Other Large Park or Recreation Area

Small State Park with and without Camping

Public Campsite
City maps only

Trail

Point of Interest

Visitor Information Center
City maps only

Public Golf Course; Private Golf Course
City maps only; Selected professional tournament location

Hospital
City maps only

Ski Area

CITIES AND TOWNS

National Capital; State or Provincial Capital

Cities, Towns, and Populated Places
Type size indicates relative importance

Urban Area
State and province maps only

Large Incorporated Cities
City maps only

OTHER MAP FEATURES

Inset Map Boxes and Page Tabs
Tab indicates page where detailed inset map may be found

"Go to" Pointers
Page tabs to direct you to adjacent maps

International; State or Province Boundary

Time Zone Boundary

Mountain Peak; Elevation
Feet in U.S.; meters in Canada and Mexico
Mt. Olympus 7,965

Perennial; Intermittent River

Perennial; Intermittent or Dry Water Body

Dam; Swamp

0 mi · 125 · 250 · 375
0 km · 125 · 250 · 375 · 500

One inch equals 150.4 miles
One centimeter equals 95.3 kilometers

CANADA

BRITISH COLUMBIA · ALBERTA · SASKATCHEWAN · MANITOBA

Vancouver · Victoria · Nanaimo · Vancouver Island · Cape Flattery · Merritt · Kelowna · Kamloops · Hope · Osoyoos · High River · Calgary · Brooks · Medicine Hat · Lethbridge · Macleod · Cranbrook · Kalispell · Saskatoon · Moose Jaw · Swift Current · Regina · Weyburn · Estevan · Brandon · Winnipeg · Yorkton · Dauphin · Swan River · Emerson · Grand Forks

Bellingham · Everett · Seattle · Tacoma · Olympia · Aberdeen · Astoria · Spokane · Wenatchee · Yakima · Kennewick · Lewiston · Coeur d'Alene · Missoula · Great Falls · Havre · Glasgow · Williston · Minot · Dickinson · Bismarck · Jamestown · Fargo · Aberdeen · Watertown

WASHINGTON · **OREGON** · **IDAHO** · **MONTANA** · **NORTH DAKOTA** · **SOUTH DAKOTA**

Portland · Salem · Corvallis · Eugene · Coos Bay · Medford · Klamath Falls · Bend · Burns · Ontario · Boise · Nampa · Twin Falls · Idaho Falls · Pocatello · Helena · Butte · Bozeman · Billings · Miles City · Sheridan · Gillette · Rapid City · Pierre · Cody

WYOMING · **NEBRASKA**

Casper · Douglas · Chadron · Cheyenne · Laramie · Rawlins · Rock Springs · Green River · Ogallala · North Platte · Grand Island · Kearney · Columbus · Lincoln

Eureka · Redding · Susanville · Reno · Carson City · Winnemucca · Elko · Salt Lake City · Ogden · Logan · Provo · Vernal · Fort Collins · Denver · Boulder

NEVADA · **UTAH** · **COLORADO** · **KANSAS**

Santa Rosa · Sacramento · Stockton · San Francisco · Oakland · San Jose · Salinas · Monterey · Fresno · Bakersfield · Tonopah · Ely · Bishop · Cedar City · St. George · Richfield · Green River · Grand Junction · Montrose · Durango · Colorado Springs · Pueblo · Trinidad · Lamar · Dodge City · Garden City · Liberal · Hutchinson · Wichita

CALIFORNIA

San Luis Obispo · Santa Barbara · Los Angeles · Long Beach · San Bernardino · Riverside · San Diego · Las Vegas · Henderson · Barstow · Kingman · Flagstaff · Winslow · Holbrook · Gallup · Albuquerque · Santa Fe · Las Vegas · Amarillo · Oklahoma City · Lawton

ARIZONA · **NEW MEXICO** · **OKLAHOMA**

Tijuana · Mexicali · Yuma · Phoenix · Globe · Casa Grande · Tucson · Nogales · Socorro · Roswell · Clovis · Plainview · Lubbock · Wichita Falls · Fort Worth · Abilene

TEXAS

El Paso · Ciudad Juárez · Las Cruces · Alamogordo · Carlsbad · Midland · Odessa · San Angelo · Van Horn · Fort Stockton · Del Rio · San Antonio · Austin · Waco · Dallas

MEXICO · BAJA CALIFORNIA · SONORA · CHIHUAHUA · COAHUILA · NUEVO LEÓN · TAMAULIPAS

Ensenada · San Felipe · Puerto Peñasco · Caborca · Santa Ana · Cananea · Agua Prieta · Villa Ahumada · Chihuahua · Piedras Negras · Nuevo Laredo · Laredo · Monclova · Saltillo · Monterrey · Reynosa · Matamoros · Brownsville · McAllen · Corpus Christi · Victoria

PACIFIC OCEAN

Alaska inset

ALASKA · RUSSIA · CANADA · YUKON · NORTHWEST TERRITORIES · BRITISH COLUMBIA

ARCTIC OCEAN · Chukchi Sea · Beaufort Sea · Bering Strait · Norton Sound · Bristol Bay · Gulf of Alaska · PACIFIC OCEAN

Utqiagvik (Barrow) · Pt. Barrow · Prudhoe Bay · Inuvik · Kotzebue · Nome · Bethel · Anchorage · Fairbanks · Palmer · Valdez · Cordova · Kenai · Homer · Seward · Kodiak · Juneau · Sitka · Ketchikan · Whitehorse · Dawson

BROOKS RANGE · ALASKA RANGE · Denali (Mt. McKinley)

0 · 150 · 300 mi
0 · 150 · 300 km

Hawai'i inset

HAWAI'I

Ni'ihau · Kaua'i · O'ahu · Moloka'i · Lāna'i · Maui · Kaho'olawe · Hawai'i

Honolulu · Waipahu · Waialua · Lā'ie · Kāne'ohe · Kaunakakai · Lahaina · Wailuku · Kihei · Hāna · Lāna'i City · Kailua-Kona · Kalaoa · Waimea · Honoka'a · Hilo · Pāhoa · Nā'ālehu

Mauna Kea · HAWAI'I VOLCANOES N.P. · HALEAKALĀ N.P.

PACIFIC OCEAN

0 · 50 · 100 mi
0 · 50 · 100 km

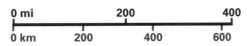

One inch equals 173.3 miles/Un pouce équivaut à 173.3 milles
One cm equals 109.9 km/Un cm équivaut à 109.9 km

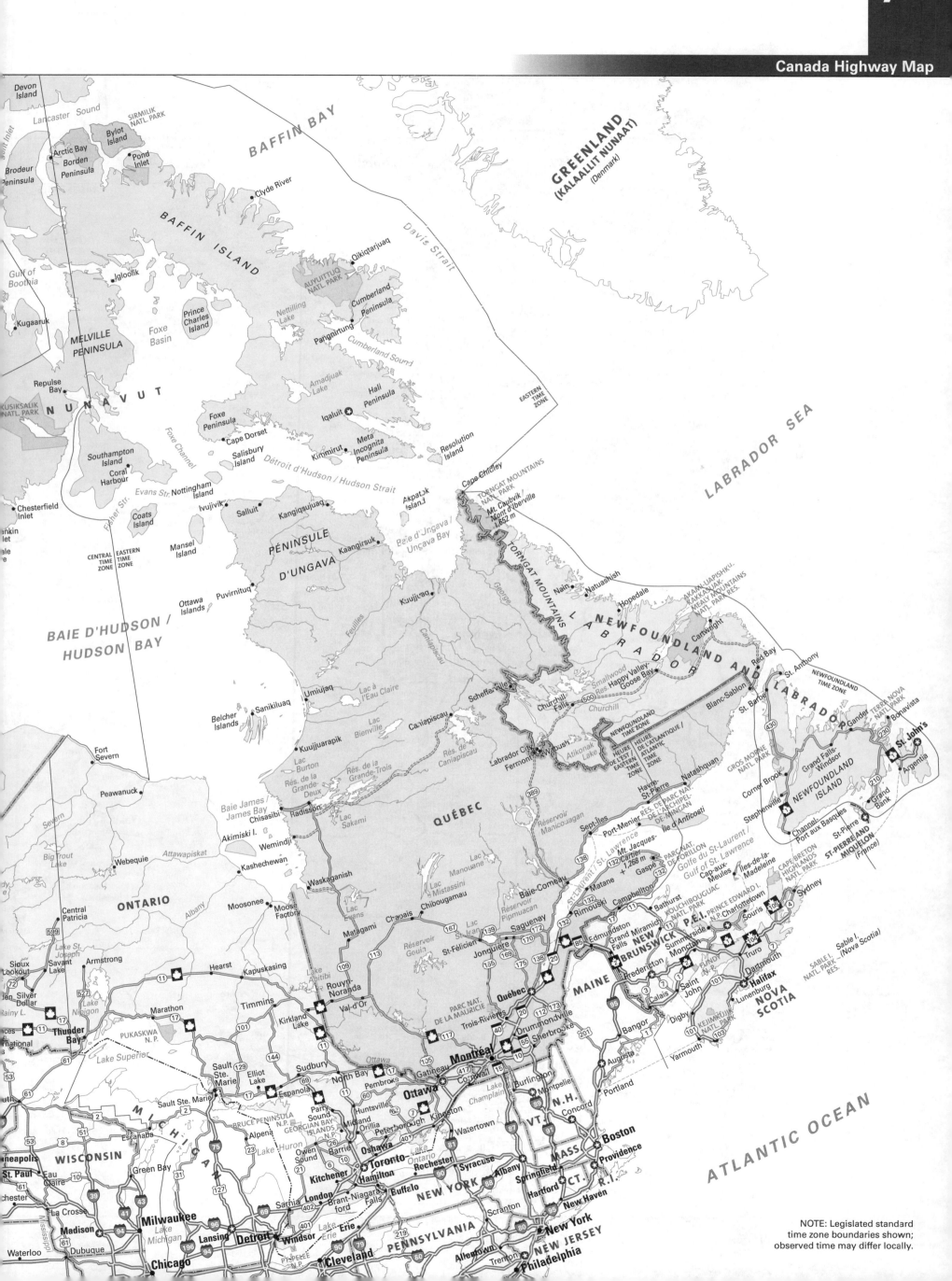

B.C.

Washington

Montana

Oregon   Idaho

0 mi   20   40   60
0 km   20   40   60   80

One inch equals 23.2 miles
One centimeter equals 14.7 kilometers

Go to 79

Go to 10

Go to 18

Go to 19

DRIVING DISTANCES IN MILES	ABERDEEN, WA	BELLINGHAM, WA	COEUR D'ALENE, ID	KENNEWICK, WA	LEWISTON, ID	OLYMPIA, WA	PORTLAND, OR	SEATTLE, WA	SPOKANE, WA	VANCOUVER, BC	WENATCHEE, WA	YAKIMA WA
KENNEWICK, WA	324	307	171		131	275	212	226	139	359	133	86
PORTLAND, OR	143	261	383	212	343	114		170	351	313	311	187
SEATTLE, WA	105	88	310	226	338	56	170		278	140	148	140
SPOKANE, WA	376	360	33	139	103	327	351	278		412	171	203

SEE ALSO DISTANCE AND DRIVING TIME MAP ON PAGE 126

B.C.

Washington

Montana

Oregon

Idaho

12

Saskatchewan Manitoba
Montana North Dakota Minn.
South Dakota

Williston ND / Miles City MT

0 mi 20 40 60
0 km 20 40 60 80
One inch equals 23.2 miles
One centimeter equals 14.7 kilometers

Row 1

Mountain • Lisieux • Fife Lake • 705 • 705 • 6 • 361 • Lampman • Alida
Saskatchewan • Rockglen • 36 • Fife Lake • 34 • Big Muddy Lake • 28 • Tribune • Macoun • 39 • Hitchcock • Steelman • Alameda • Frobisher • Oxbow • Glen Ewen • 318 • Carn

GRASSLANDS NATL. PARK • Killdeer • 2 • 18 • Coronach • 18 • Big Beaver • Minton • 6 18 • Gladmar • Lake Alma • Beaubier • Bromhead • Torquay • 605 • 18 • Estevan • Roche Percee • Bienfait • 9 • Northgate

SASKATCHEWAN MONTANA • CENTRAL TIME ZONE • MOUNTAIN TIME ZONE • Regway • CANADA UNITED STATES • 85 • Boundary Dam Res. • 47 • North Portal • Portal • Northgate

Opheim • 2 • Glentana • 248 • 13 • 511 • Whitetail • Outlook • 374 • Raymond • Westby • Alkabo • 85 • Fortuna • 5 • Crosby • 51 • Columbus • 52 • Flaxton • 8 • DES LACS N.W.R.
Richland • 438 • Four Buttes • Madoc • Flaxville • 16 • Redstone • 5 • Noonan • 40 • Larson • Lignite • 30 • Bowbells • 52 • Tolley
Peerless • Scobey • Plentywood • Writing Rock St. Hist. Site • 85 • 42 • Larson • 5 • Coteau • Kenmare

Row 2 (1)

St. Marie • Larslan • 251 • Antelope • 517 • Coalridge • Grenora • Zahl • Wildrose • McGregor • Battleview • Powers Lake • 50 • Niobe • UPPER SOURIS N.W.R.
Lustre • 13 • Reserve • 258 • Dagmar • 50 • Appam • 40 • Lostwood • Donnybrook • 43 52 • Carpio
FORT PECK IND. RES. • Medicine Lake • Homestead • Medicine Lake N.W.R. • Lake Zahl N.W.R. • Ray • 100 • White Earth • Tioga • Palermo • Blaisdell • Tagus
236 • Froid • 16 • McCabe • 2 • Epping • Wheelock • Ross • Stanley • 2 • Berthold
Glasgow • Nashua • 2 • 43 • Wolf Point • Brockton • Poplar • Culbertson • 2 • Williston • 1804 • Belden • Shell Lake N.W.R.
Fort Peck • 117 • Frazer • Oswego • 25 • Missouri • 54 • Bainville • 327 • Trenton • Lewis and Clark S.P. • Lake Sakakawea • 1804
Fort Peck Dam • 13 • 201 • 201 • Fort Union Trading Post N.H.S. • Ft. Buford S.H.S. • 58 • 85 • 1806 • Keene • New Town • 8
Hell Creek S.P. • 24 • 341 • Vida • 480 • Fairview • Cartwright • 200 • Alexander • 41 • Arnegard • Watford City • 73 • LITTLE MISSOURI NATL. GRASSLAND • Three Affiliated Tribes Museum • Parshall • Makoti • 23 • Plaza

Row 3 (2)

CHARLES M. RUSSELL NATIONAL WILDLIFE REFUGE • Richey • 200 • Enid • Lambert • Sidney • 23 • 68 • THEODORE ROOSEVELT NATL. PARK (NORTH UNIT) • 37 1804 • McLean N.W.R. • Roseglen • 37 • Raub • White Shield
Circle • Bloomfield • 254 • Savage • 261 • 16 • LITTLE MISSOURI • Flat Rock Butte 2,775 • 67 • Killdeer Mtn. Battlefield St. Hist. Site • Little Missouri S.P. • Twin Buttes • 8 • Lake Sakakawea • 1804
43 • Jordan • 200 • 36 • 31 • Brockway • 47 • Lindsay • 16 • Intake • NATL. GRASSLAND • Trotters • Grassy Butte • 85 • CENTRAL TIME ZONE MOUNTAIN TIME ZONE • Killdeer • Dunn Center • Halliday • Dodge • 200 • Zap
Cohagen • Little Dry Cr. • 253 • 200 • 200S • Frontier Gateway Museum • 215 • 261 • THEODORE ROOSEVELT NATL. PARK (Elkhorn Ranch Unit) • Knife • LAKE ILO N.W.R. • 200 • Golden Valley • Beulah
59 • 462 • 211 • Glendive • 29 • Makoshika S.P. • 236 • 241 • 242 • Fairfield • 22 • Manning • Marshall • Knife • 49
Rock Springs • 185 • Fallon • 70 • 335 • Hodges • Wibaux • 248 • 10 • 50 • New Hradec • 8
Angela • 253 • Terry • 340 • Mildred • Beach • Sentinel Butte • 24 • Medora • Fryburg • Belfield • 42 94 51 19 56 61 • Dickinson Mus. Ctr. & Badlands Dinosaur Museum • Taylor • Richardton • Hebron • 102

Row 4 (3)

59 • Kinsey • 489 • 148 • St. Phillip • Sentinel Butte 3,430 • Chateau de Mores St. Hist. Site • Sully Creek S.R.A. • Golva • 85 • S. Heart • Patterson Lake Rec. Area • Dickinson • Gladstone • 84 • 90 • 49
Miles City • Range Riders Mus. • 141 • 138 • 320 • Ismay • Carlyle • Bullion Butte 3,366 • LITTLE MISSOURI • New England • 21 • Lefor • MOUNTAIN TIME ZONE CENTRAL TIME ZONE • Glen Ullin
87 • Rosebud • Hathaway • 94 • 12 • 135 • 75 • Plevna • 12 • NATL. GRASSLAND • 59 • White Lake N.W.R. • 21 22 • Regent • North Star Butte 2,818 • New Leipzig • Elgin
93 • 103 • 106 • Horton • 126 • 45 • 117 • Mizpah • Willard • 322 • Baker • Marmarth • Pretty Butte 3,182 • Fort Dilts St. Hist. Site • Black Butte 3,465 • White Butte Highest Pt. in N. Dak. 3,506 • Stewart Lake N.W.R. • Amidon • 21 • Mott • Burt
447 • 332 • Garlanc • 7 • Mizpah • 46 • Rhame • 67 • Bowman • 12 • Scranton • 22 • Bucyrus • 8 21 • 49

Row 5 (4)

39 • Colstrip • 59 • Volborg • Powderville • Medicine Rocks S.P. • 322 • 85 • Pioneer Trails Reg. Mus. • Gascoyne • Reeder • Hettinger • Haley • 22 • Haynes • Lemmon • 12 • Morristo
Badger Pk. 4,422 • 212 • 447 • Ashland • Epsie • Broadus • Ekalaka • 323 • CUSTER-GALLATIN NATL. FOR. • Ludlow • 46 • Ralph • Lodgepole • GRAND RIVER NATL. GRASSLAND • 73
Lame Deer • NORTHERN CHEYENNE IND. RES. • 484 • CUSTER-GALLATIN NATL. FOR. • 328 • Camp Crook • 20 • Capitol • NORTH DAKOTA SOUTH DAKOTA • Ladner • CUSTER-GALLATIN NATL. FOR. • Buffalo • 79 • S. Fork Grand • Llewellyn Johns Rec. Area • White Butte • Shadehill • Shadehill Res. • Shadehill Rec. Area
Birney • 556 • Sonnette • Olive • Harding • 70 • Reva • 20 79 • Prairie City • Meadow • 73 • GRAND RIVER NATIONAL GRASSLAND
Tongue River Ind. Res. • Otter • Quietus • Biddle • Hammond • 64 • Boyes • 59 • Redig • Reva Gap • Sorum • Bison • 20 73 • Thunder Butte 2,755 • Usta • Thunder Bu
Moorhead • Ridge • Alzada • 212 • Lightning Flat • Colony • Castle Rock Buttes 3,741 • Geographic Center of the U.S. • 79 • Hoover • Zeona • Mud Butte • Iron Lightning
MONTANA WYOMING • Rockypoint • 212 • Little Missouri • 323 • Castle Rock • 85 • 212 • Maui • Faith • Sulphur • Re • Elk

Go to 80 • Go to 11 • Go to 21 • Go to 22

A • B • C

14

Manitoba   Ontario
North
Dakota   Minnesota   Michigan
South
Dakota   Wisconsin

Fargo ND / St Cloud MN

0 mi   20   40   60
0 km   20   40   60   80
One inch equals 23.2 miles
One centimeter equals 14.7 kilometers

Go to 81

Go to 13

Go to 23

Go to 24

A   B   C

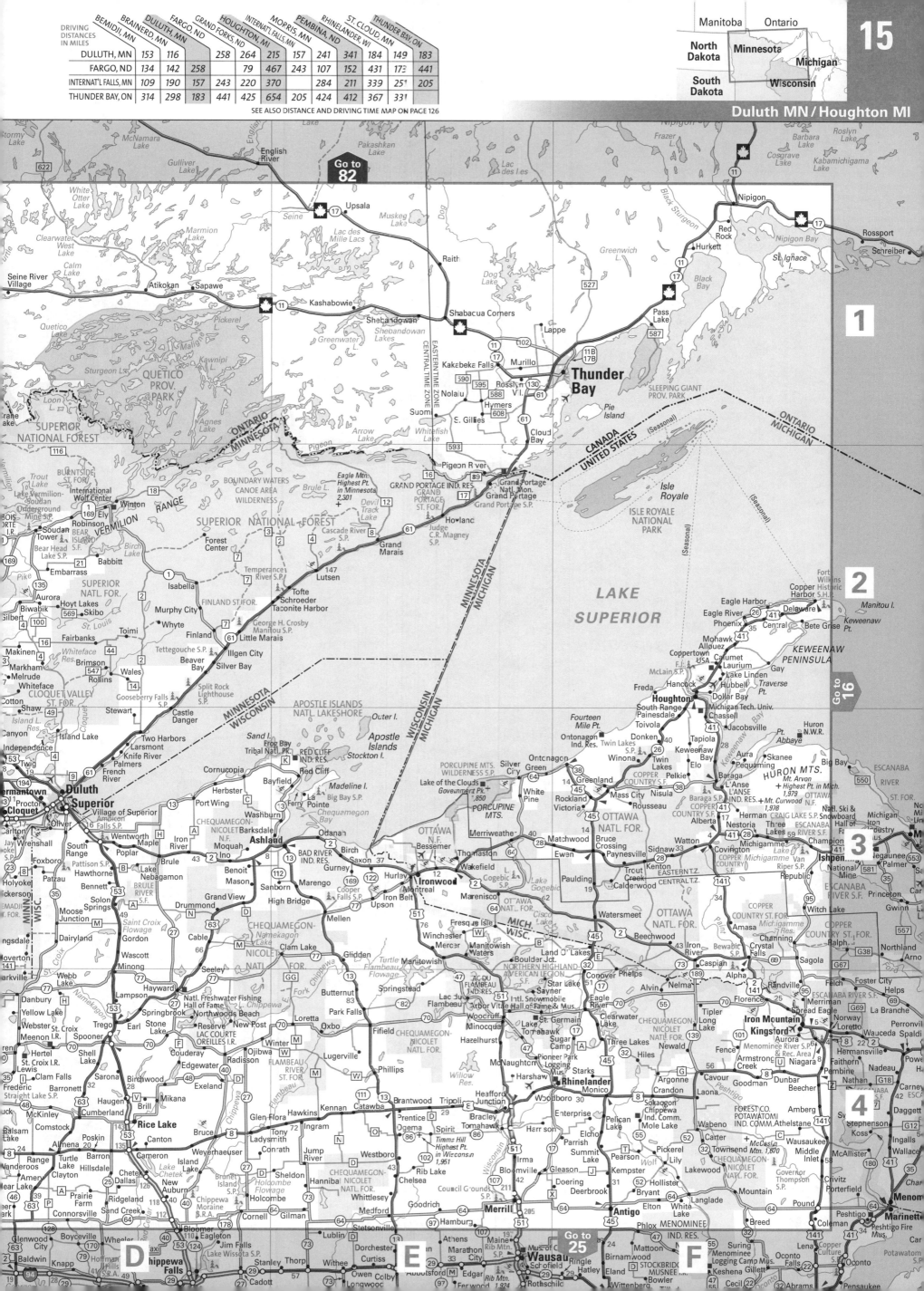

Manitoba Ontario
North Dakota Minnesota
Michigan
South Dakota Wisconsin

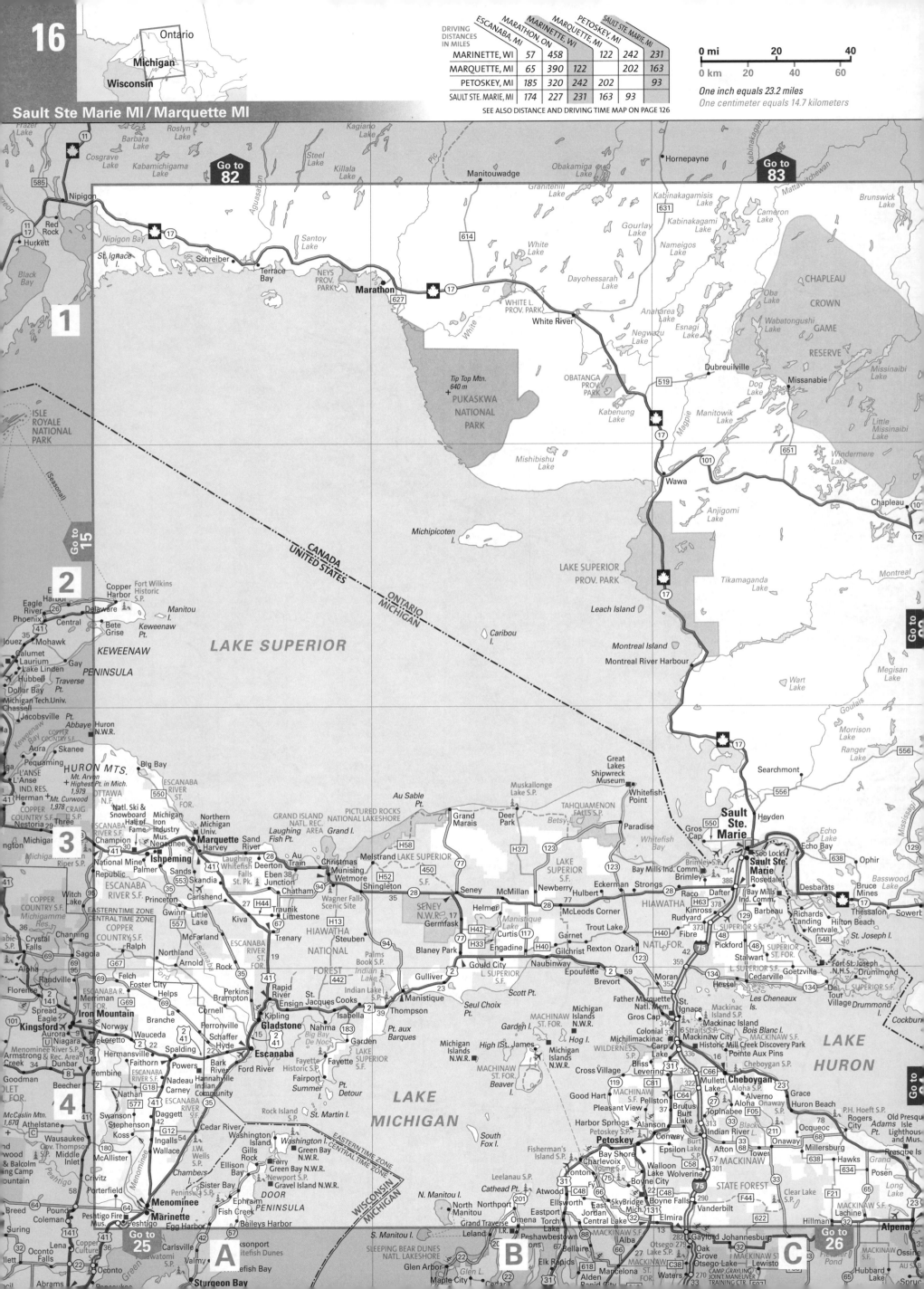

Ontario
Michigan
Wisconsin

Go to 82
Go to 83
Go to 15
Go to 25
Go to 26

DRIVING DISTANCES IN MILES	ESCANABA, MI	MARATHON, ON	MARINETTE, WI	MARQUETTE, MI	PETOSKEY, MI	SAULT STE. MARIE, MI
MARINETTE, WI	57	458		122	242	231
MARQUETTE, MI	65	390	122		202	163
PETOSKEY, MI	185	320	242	202		93
SAULT STE. MARIE, MI	174	227	231	163	93	

SEE ALSO DISTANCE AND DRIVING TIME MAP ON PAGE 126

0 mi   20   40
0 km   20   40   60

One inch equals 23.2 miles
One centimeter equals 14.7 kilometers

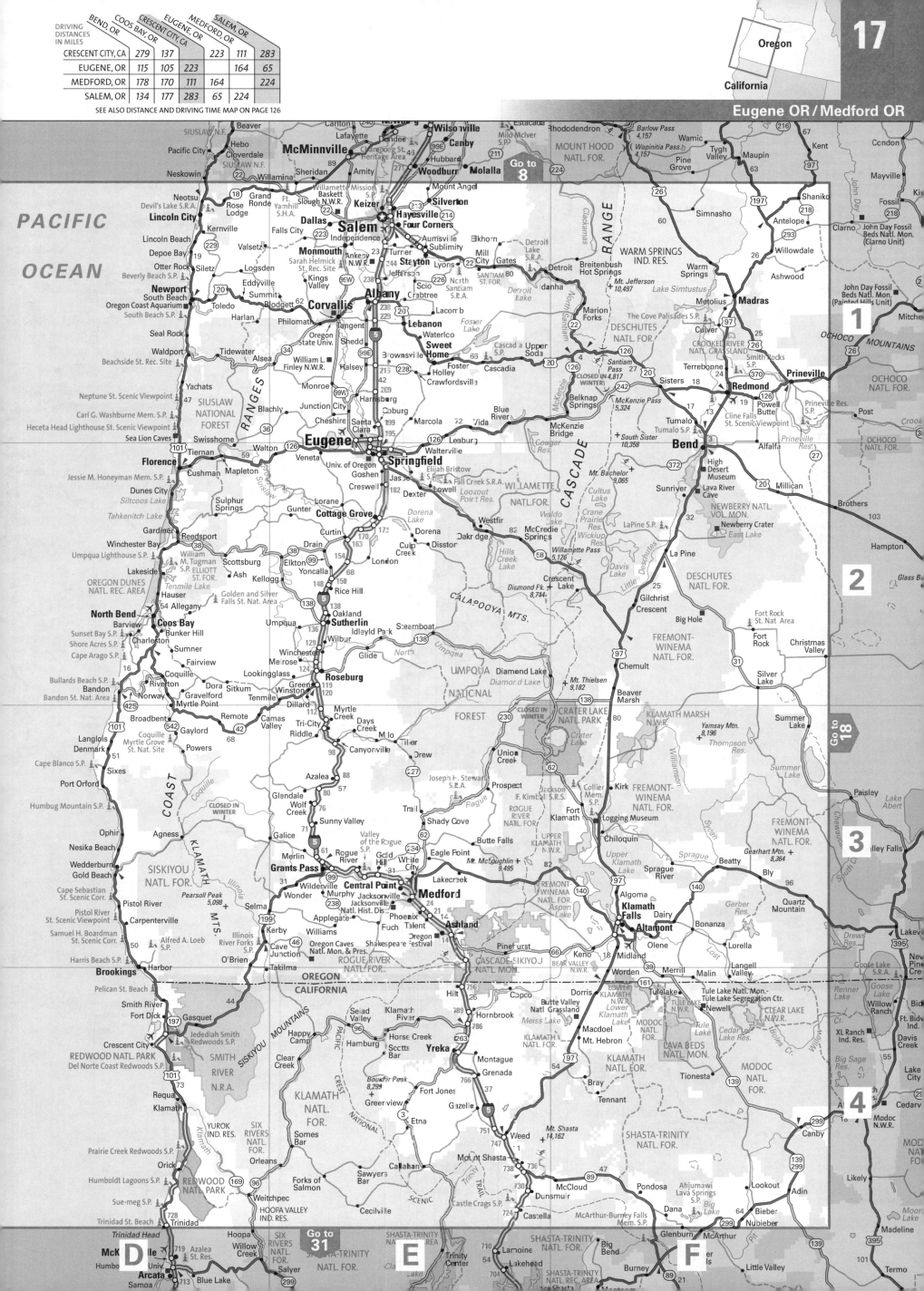

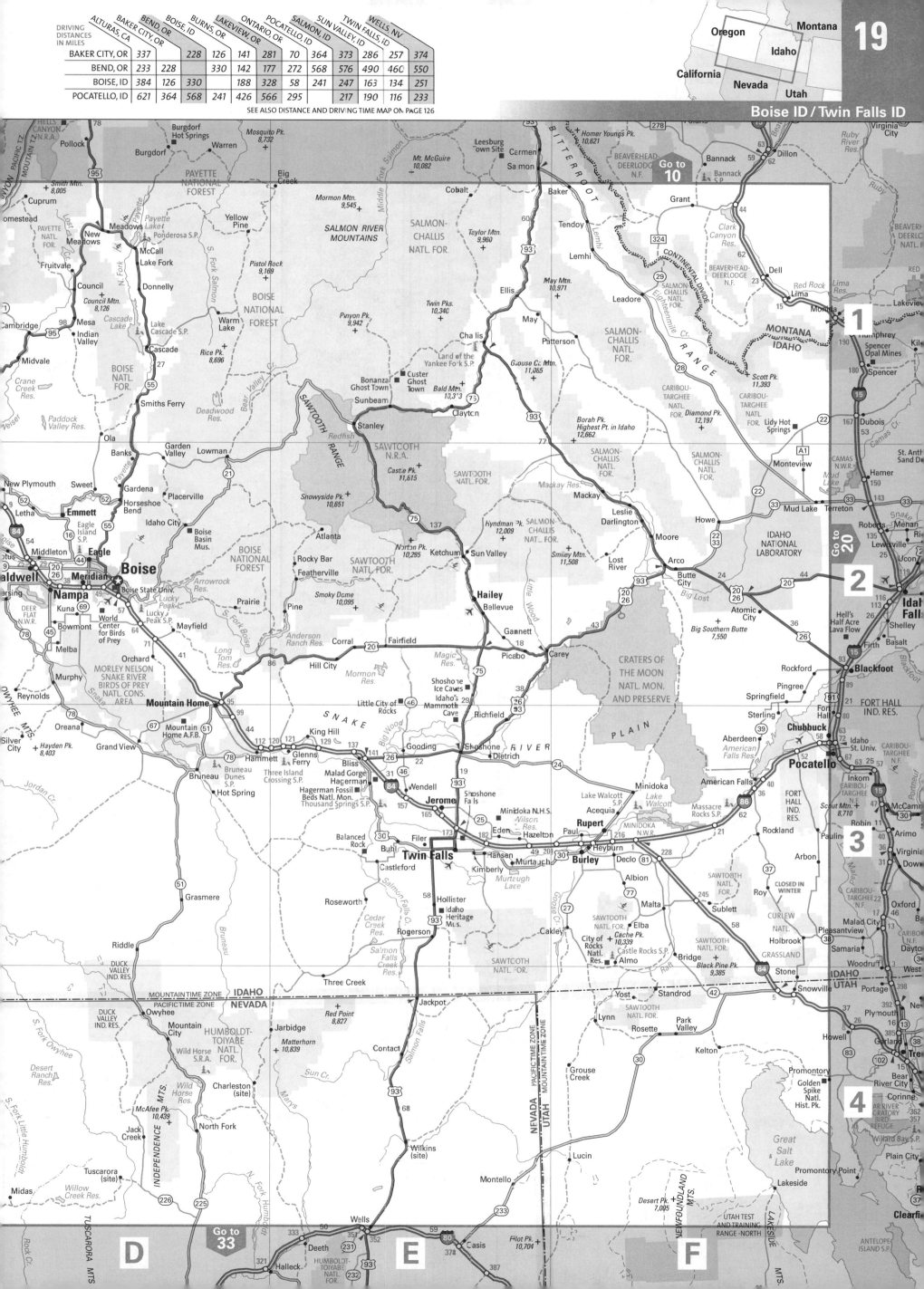

Go to 10

Go to 20

Go to 33

DRIVING DISTANCES IN MILES	ALTURAS, CA	BAKER CITY, OR	BEND, OR	BOISE, ID	BURNS, OR	LAKEVIEW, OR	ONTARIO, OR	POCATELLO, ID	SALMON, ID	SUN VALLEY, ID	TWIN FALLS, ID	WELLS, NV
BAKER CITY, OR	337		228	126	141	281	70	364	373	286	257	374
BEND, OR	233	228		330	142	177	272	568	576	490	460	550
BOISE, ID	384	126	330		188	328	58	241	247	163	134	251
POCATELLO, ID	621	364	568	241		426	566	295	217	190	116	233

SEE ALSO DISTANCE AND DRIVING TIME MAP ON PAGE 126

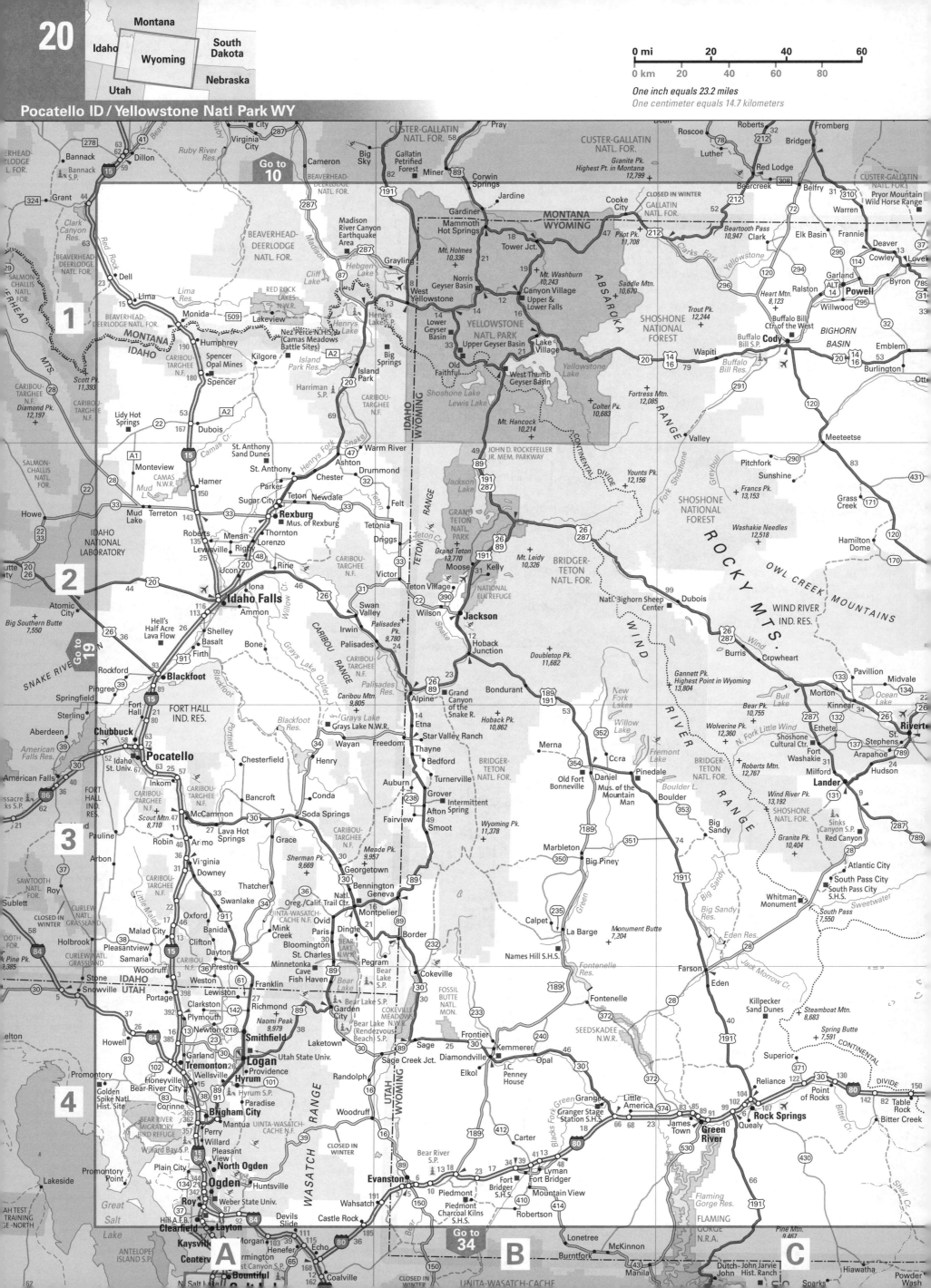

20

Montana
Idaho
Wyoming
South Dakota
Nebraska
Utah

Pocatello ID / Yellowstone Natl Park WY

0 mi   20   40   60
0 km   20   40   60   80
One inch equals 23.2 miles
One centimeter equals 14.7 kilometers

DRIVING DISTANCES IN MILES	CASPER, WY	CHEYENNE, WY	IDAHO FALLS, ID	JACKSON, WY	LANDER, WY	LOGAN, UT	OGDEN, UT	POCATELLO, ID	ROCK SPRINGS WY	SHERIDAN, WY	SPEARFISH, SD	W. YELLOWSTONE, MT
CASPER, WY		175	374	282	144	428	380	426	214	149	227	345
LOGAN, UT	428	474	154	184	245		46	104	217	577	655	261
SPEARFISH, SD	227	297	673	512	374	655	607	724	441	202		564
W. YELLOWSTONE, MT	345	561	109	128	227	261	284	160	304	363	564	

SEE ALSO DISTANCE AND DRIVING TIME MAP ON PAGE 126

0 mi   20   40   60
0 km   20   40   60   80

One inch equals 23.2 miles
One centimeter equals 14.7 kilometers

MONTANA / SOUTH DAKOTA

Thunder Butte 2,755

Go to 12

Go to 13

CHEYENNE RIVER IND. RES.

Lake Oahe

Redig
Zeona
Hoover
Castle Rock Buttes 3,741
Geographic Center of the U.S.
Castle Rock
Mud Butte
Maurine
Usta
Iron Lightning
Faith
Red Elm
Dupree
Parade
Ridgeview
Eagle Butte
Lantry
Whitehorse
La Plant
Akaska
Lowry
Swan L.
Cathedral on the Prairie
Lebanon
Gettysburg
Agar
Onida

Colony
Alzada
Albion
MONT. WYO.
Alva
Hulett
Devils Tower
Beulah
Sundance
Aladdin
Belle Fourche
Fruitdale
Nisland
Newell
St. Onge
Whitewood
Spearfish
Sturgis
Deadwood
Lead
Tilford
Piedmont
Nemo
Summerset
Blackhawk
Rapid City
Ellsworth A.F.B.
Box Elder
New Underwood
Wasta
Wall Drug Store
Wall
Quinn
Philip
Midland
Nowlin
Capa
Van Metre
Pierre
Fort Pierre
South Dakota Cultural Heritage Center
Blunt
Harrold
Canning

Fairpoint
Stoneville
Red Owl
Marcus
Howes
White Owl
Union Center
Enning
Plainview
Bridger
Cherry Creek
Red Scaffold
Mission Ridge
Cedar Butte 2,053

BLACK HILLS NATL. FOR.
Rockford
Silver City
Hill City
Keystone
Mt. Rushmore Natl. Mem.
Crazy Horse Mem.
Custer
Jewel Cave Natl. Mon.
Pringle
Wind Cave Natl. Park
Hot Springs
Buffalo Gap
Oral
Parker Pk. 4848

Hereford
Elm Springs
Pedro
Milesville
Creighton
Ottumwa
Hayes
Wendte

BADLANDS NATL. PARK
Scenic
Imlay
Interior
Kadoka
Belvidere
Minuteman Missile N.H.S.
Cottonwood
Prairie Homestead Hist. Site
Stamford
Okaton
Murdo
Draper
Vivian
Presho
Kennebec
Lyman

PINE RIDGE IND. RES.
Wanblee
Potato Creek
Kyle
Eagle Nest Butte 3,410
Hisle
Allen
Longvalley
Norris
Cedar Butte
White River
Wood
Mosher
Witten
Okreek
Carter
Winner
Colome

CENTRAL TIME ZONE
MOUNTAIN TIME ZONE

Manderson
Porcupine
Patricia
Vetal
Parmelee
Mission
Antelope
Hidden Timber
Clearfield
Keyapaha
Millboro
Wewela

Oglala
Wounded Knee
Swett
Martin
Harrington
Rosebud
St. Francis
Olsonville
ROSEBUD IND. RES.

Pine Ridge
Denby
Batesland
Tuthill
Lacreek N.W.R.
Buechel Mem. Lakota Mus.
Ardmore

SOUTH DAKOTA / NEBRASKA

Go to 21

Whitney
Chadron
Museum of the Fur Trade
Crawford
Fort Robinson
Harrison
Van Tassell
Marsland
Agate Fossil Beds Natl. Mon.
Hemingford
Berea
Carhenge
Alliance
Antioch
Lakeside
Bingham
Ellsworth
Ashby
Whitman
Mullen
Seneca
Thedford
Halsey
Brewster

Whiteclay
Gordon
Clinton
Rushville
Hay Springs
Merriman
Cody
Kilgore
Crookston
Valentine
Nenzel
Sparks
Norden
Springview

SAND HILLS
SURVEY VALLEY

Stagecoach Mus.
Node
Jay Em
Lingle
Torrington
Henry
Morrill
Mitchell
Scottsbluff
Gering
Minatare
McGrew
Bayard
Bridgeport
Northport
Broadwater
Chimney Rock N.H.S.
Courthouse Rock and Jail Rock
Harrisburg
Redington
Lisco
Dalton
Gurley
Oshkosh
Lewellen
Lemoyne
Keystone
Sarben
Sutherland
Hershey
North Platte
Bailey RR Yard & Golden Spike Tower

Fort Niobrara N.W.R.
Niobrara Valley Preserve
Wood Lake
Keller Park St. Rec. Area
Johnstown
Ainsworth
Long Pine
Springview

Samuel R. McKelvie Natl. For.
Merritt Res. St. Rec. Area
Valentine N.W.R.
Brownlee
Purdum
Elsmere
Dunning
Milburn
Victoria Springs St. Rec. Area
Anselmo

Arthur
Tryon
Ringgold
Stapleton
Arnold
Callaway

WYO. COLO.
Pine Bluffs
Bushnell
Kimball
Dix
Potter
Brownson
Sidney
Sunol
Lodgepole
Colton
Chappell
Big Springs
Brule
Ogallala
Roscoe
Paxton
Maxwell

Highest Point in Nebraska 5,424

Fort Sidney Mus. and Post Commander's Home
Ash Hollow St. Hist. Park
Lake C. West McConaughy
Lake McConaughy St. Rec. Area
Lake Ogallala S.R.A.
Buffalo Bill Ranch S.R.A. and Golf

NEBRASKA / COLORADO
Go to 36

Julesburg
Sedgwick
Ovid
Crook

A   **B**   **C**

DRIVING DISTANCES IN MILES

	CHADRON, NE	MARSHALL, MN	NORTH PLATTE, NE	OMAHA, NE	O'NEILL NE	PIERRE, SD	RAPID CITY, SD	SCOTTSBLUFF, NE	SIOUX CITY, IA	SIOUX FALLS, SD	SPEARFISH, SD	VALENTINE, NE
OMAHA, NE	508	273	278		188	405	525	452	99	183	578	298
RAPID CITY, SD	101	429	345	525	322	193		191	427	346	53	215
SCOTTSBLUFF, NE	96	566	175	452	324	329	191		548	483	228	214
SIOUX FALLS, SD	406	91	458	183	175	226	346	483	85		398	268

SEE ALSO DISTANCE AND DRIVING TIME MAP ON PAGE 126

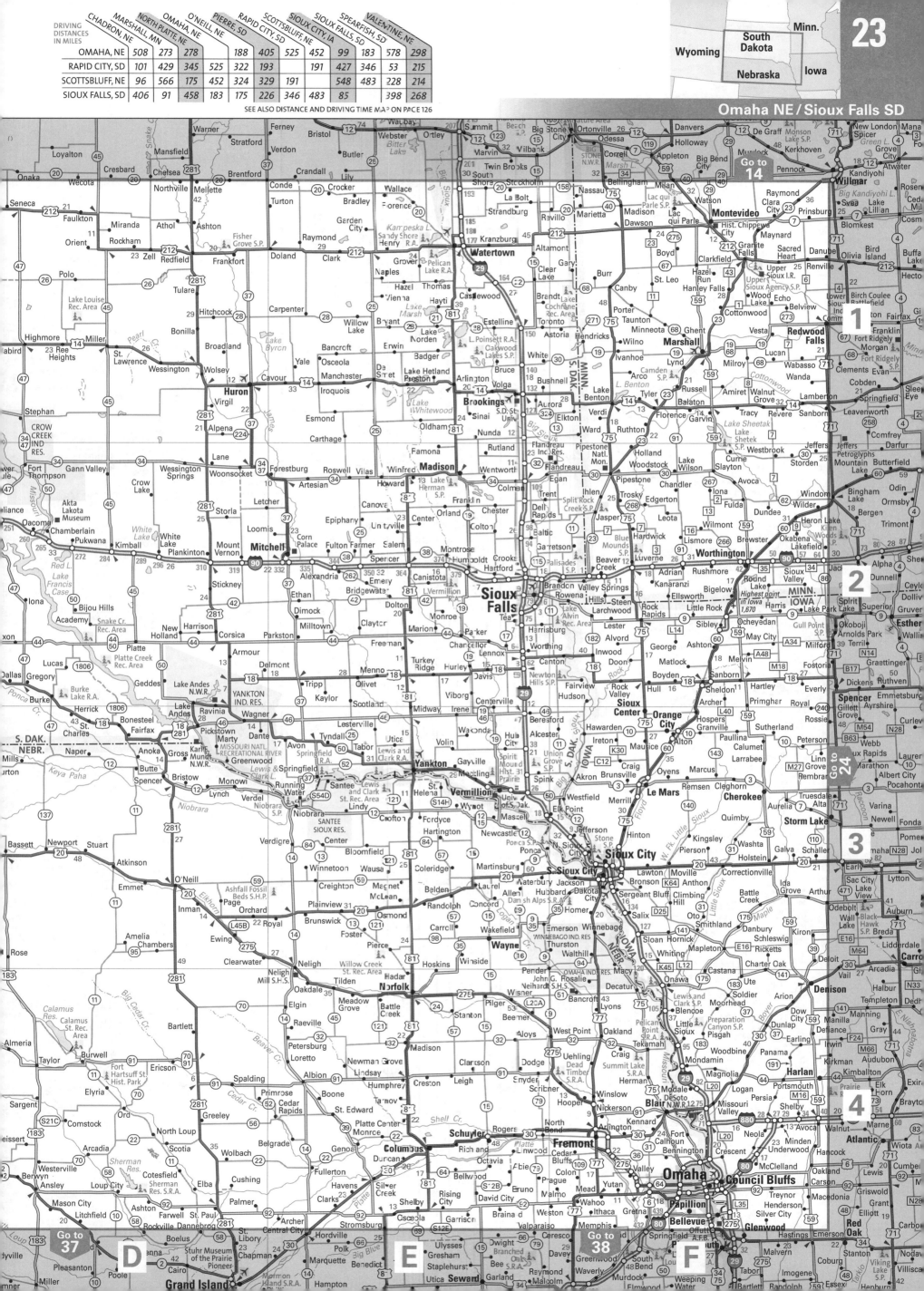

24

Minn.
Wisconsin
Michigan
Iowa
Illinois   Ind.

Minneapolis MN / Des Moines IA

0 mi   20   40   60
0 km   20   40   60   80

One inch equals 23.2 miles
One centimeter equals 14.7 kilometers

Go to 14

Minneapolis
St. Paul
Bloomington
Apple Valley
Hastings
Red Wing
Northfield
Faribault
Rochester
Winona
La Crosse
Eau Claire
Altoona
Menomonie
Chippewa Falls

Willmar
Montevideo
Hutchinson
Glencoe
Redwood Falls
New Ulm
Mankato
N. Mankato
St. Peter
Marshall
Owatonna
Austin
Albert Lea
Fairmont
Worthington
Decorah

MINNESOTA
IOWA

Mason City
Clear Lake
Charles City
Waverly
Cedar Falls
Waterloo
Independence
Manchester
Cedar Rapids
Marion
Iowa City
Coralville

Spencer
Storm Lake
Algona
Fort Dodge
Webster City
Iowa Falls
Carroll
Denison
Ames
Boone
Nevada
Marshalltown
Vinton
Anamosa

Des Moines
W. Des Moines
Ankeny
Urbandale
Altoona
Newton
Grinnell
Perry
Indianola
Knoxville
Oskaloosa
Pella
Washington

Council Bluffs
Atlantic
Creston

Go to 23
Go to 38

Fairfield
Mount Pleasant

A   B   C
1   2   3   4

Go to 15
Go to 16
Go to 26
Go to 39
Go to 40

DRIVING DISTANCES IN MILES	CEDAR RAPIDS, IA	CHICAGO, IL	DES MOINES, IA	FORT DODGE, IA	GREEN BAY, WI	LA CROSSE, WI	MADISON, WI	MASON CITY, IA	MILWAUKEE, WI	MINNEAPOLIS, MN	ROCKFORD, IL	WAUSAU, WI
CHICAGO, IL	252		337	420	204	283	149	381	89	409	86	283
DES MOINES, IA	129	337		94	493	274	289	378	246	292	415
MADISON, WI	160	149	289	294	135	141		223	78	267	78	141
MINNEAPOLIS, MN	277	409	246	217	278	157	267	137	337		337	184

SEE ALSO DISTANCE AND DRIVING TIME MAP ON PAGE 126

DRIVING DISTANCES IN MILES

	ALPENA, MI	BUFFALO, NY	CLEVELAND, OH	DETROIT, MI	ERIE, PA	GRAND RAPIDS, MI	LANSING, MI	SAGINAW, MI	SOUTH BEND, IN	TOLEDO, OH	TORONTO, ON	TRAVERSE CITY, MI
BUFFALO, NY	471		197	277	96	403	345	327	456	318	106	487
CLEVELAND, OH	405	197		171	106	303	237	261	257	119	303	421
DETROIT, MI	242	277	171		278	153	86	98	213	60	233	258
GRAND RAPIDS, MI	254	403	303	153	411		67	144	117	181	359	141

SEE ALSO DISTANCE AND DRIVING TIME MAP ON PAGE 126

0 mi   20   40   60
0 km   20   40   60   80

One inch equals 23.2 miles
One centimeter equals 14.7 kilometers

DRIVING DISTANCES IN MILES

	ALBANY, NY	BOSTON, MA	BURLINGTON, VT	CORNWALL, ON	HARTFORD, CT	MANCHESTER NH	PORTLAND, ME	PROVIDENCE, RI	ROCHESTER, NY	SCRANTON, PA	SYRACUSE, NY	WATERTOWN, NY
ALBANY, NY		172	147	227	111	145	270	170	228	180	146	179
BOSTON, MA	172		214	370	102	54	107	52	398	296	316	349
ROCHESTER, NY	228	398	311	264	337	364	496	396		220	38	146
SCRANTON, PA	180	296	328	316	194	326	394	272	220		135	198

SEE ALSO DISTANCE AND DRIVING TIME MAP ON PAGE 126

DRIVING DISTANCES IN MILES

	AUGUSTA, ME	BANGOR, ME	BAR HARBOR, ME	HOULTON, ME	PORTLAND, ME	QUEBEC, QC
BANGOR, ME	77		45	122	131	223
BAR HARBOR, ME	120	45		166	175	266
HOULTON, ME	196	122	166		251	286
PORTLAND, ME	58	131	175	251		264

SEE ALSO DISTANCE AND DRIVING TIME MAP ON PAGE 126

0 mi 20 40
0 km 20 40 60
One inch equals 23.2 miles
One centimeter equals 14.7 kilometers

DRIVING DISTANCES IN MILES	EUREKA, CA	MONTEREY, CA	REDDING, CA	SACRAMENTO, CA	SAN FRANCISCO, CA	SAN JOSE, CA
EUREKA, CA		380	133	278	263	306
MONTEREY, CA	380		323	188	114	74
SACRAMENTO, CA	278	188		166	87	115
SAN FRANCISCO, CA	263	114	222	87		43

SEE ALSO DISTANCE AND DRIVING TIME MAP ON PAGE 126

California

Go to 17

Go to 32

PACIFIC OCEAN

PACIFIC OCEAN

FOR CONTINUATION SEE INSET AT LEFT

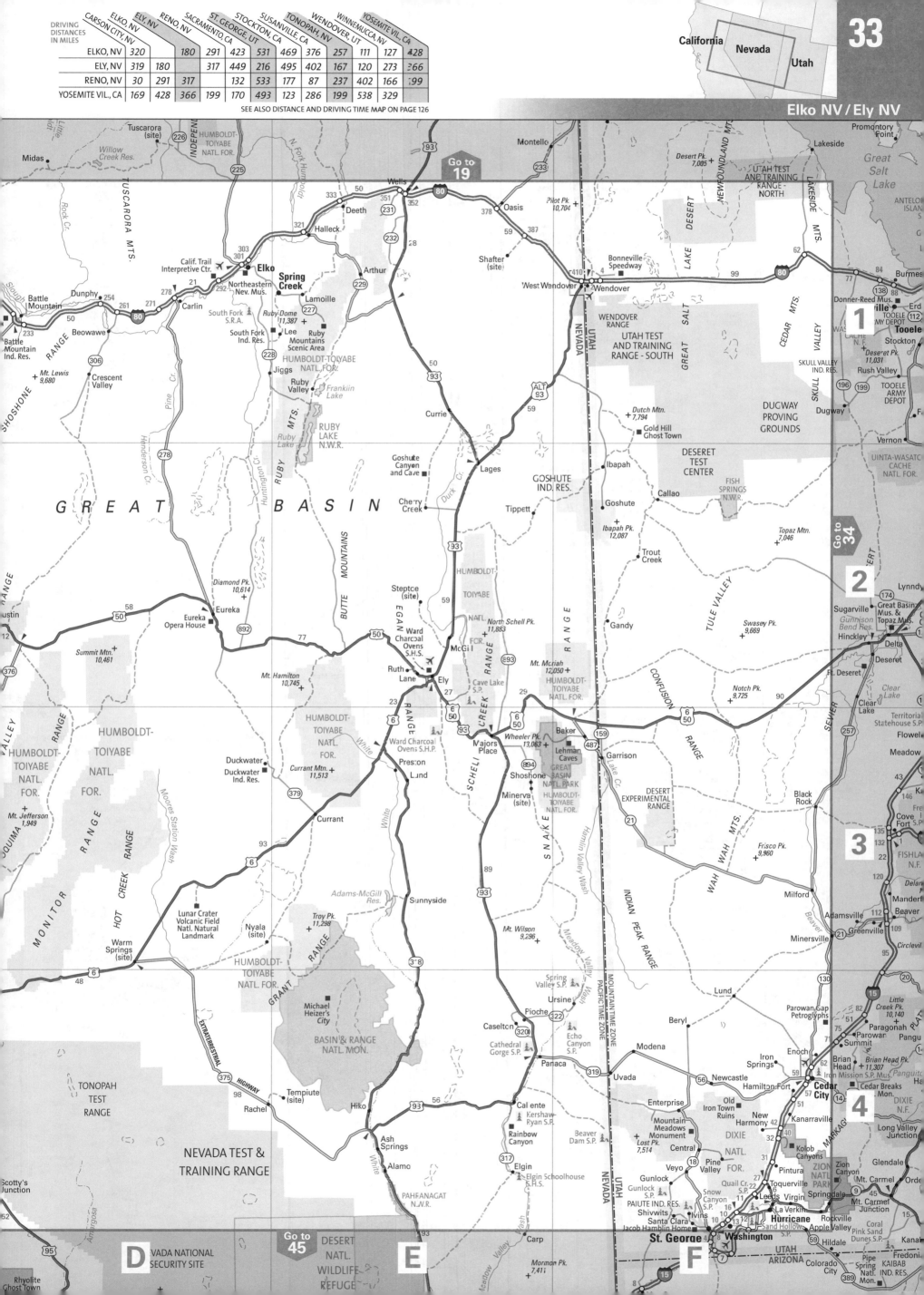

DRIVING DISTANCES IN MILES	CARSON CITY, NV	ELKO, NV	ELY, NV	RENO, NV	SACRAMENTO, CA	ST. GEORGE, UT	STOCKTON, CA	SUSANVILLE, CA	TONOPAH, NV	WENDOVER, UT	WINNEMUCCA, NV	YOSEMITE VIL., CA
ELKO, NV	320		180	291	423	531	469	376	257	111	127	428
ELY, NV	319	180		317	449	216	495	402	167	120	273	366
RENO, NV	30	291	317		132	533	177	87	237	402	166	199
YOSEMITE VIL., CA	169	428	366	199	170	493	123	286	199	538	329	

SEE ALSO DISTANCE AND DRIVING TIME MAP ON PAGE 126

Wyoming
Utah
Colorado

0 mi	20	40	60
0 km	20	40	60	80

One inch equals 23.2 miles
One centimeter equals 14.7 kilometers

Go to 20

Go to 33

Go to 46

A B C

1 2 3 4

DRIVING DISTANCES IN MILES	ASPEN, CO	CEDAR CITY, UT	COLORADO SPRS, CO	DENVER, CO	DURANGO, CO	FORT COLLINS, CO	GRAND JUNCTION, CO	MOAB, UT	PROVO, UT	RICHFIELD, UT	SALT LAKE CITY, UT	VERNAL, UT
DENVER, CO	164	586	70		338	64	251	337	488	475	531	333
GRAND JUNCTION, CO	135	337	318	251	169	311		88	239	226	282	*42
RICHFIELD, UT	359	111	542	475	338	536	226	179	111		154	236
SALT LAKE CITY, UT	415	247	600	531	394	448	282	235	47	154		*73

SEE ALSO DISTANCE AND DRIVING TIME MAP ON PAGE 126

Denver CO / Grand Junction CO

Wyoming
Nebraska
Colorado
Kansas

0 mi   20   40   60
0 km   20   40   60   80
One inch equals 23.2 miles
One centimeter equals 14.7 kilometers

MEDICINE BOW ROUTE NAT'L FOR.
Curt Gowdy S.P.
Federal
Warren A.F.B.
Cheyenne
Buford
Harriman
Virginia Dale
Buffalo Creek
Poudre Park
Masonville
Drake
Loveland
Berthoud
Lyons
Longmont
Boulder
Lafayette
Broomfield
Westminster
Arvada
Golden
Lakewood
Denver
Aurora
Englewood
Parker
The Pinery
Franktown
Elizabeth
Kiowa
Castle Rock
Larkspur
Sedalia
Louviers
Roxborough S.P.
Palmer Lake
Monument
Black Forest
Woodland Park
Florissant
Manitou Springs
Colorado Springs
Cascade
Divide
Crystola
Falcon
Ellicott
Yoder
Rush
Punkin Center
Security
Widefield
Fountain
Pikes Peak Intl. Raceway
Schriever Space Force Base
FORT CARSON
Cañon City
Penrose
Florence
Portland
Pueblo West
Pueblo
Avondale
Boone
Devine
Pueblo Chemical Depot
TRANSPORTATION TECHNOLOGY CTR.-FED. F.R. ADMIN.
Wetmore
Greenwood
Beulah
Rye
Colorado City
Cedarwood
Gardner
Farisita
Walsenburg
La Veta
Cuchara
Pryor
Aguilar
Ludlow
Hoehne
El Moro
Trinidad
A.R. Mitchell Mus. of Western Art
Jansen
Segundo
Weston
Raton
Branson
Trinchera

Cheyenne
Carpenter
Hereford
Grover
Carr
Livermore
Wellington
Nunn
Pierce
Purcell
Ault
Eaton
Galeton
Windsor
Greeley
Evans
La Salle
Gilcrest
Platteville
Fort Lupton
Hudson
Keenesburg
Roggen
Wiggins
Fort Morgan
Brush
Akron
Woodrow
Last Chance
Deer Trail
Agate
Matheson
Simla
Ramah
Calhan
Peyton
Kutch
Karval
Boyero
Aroya
Wild Horse
Kit Carson
Firstview
Cheyenne Wells
Arapahoe
Weskan
Sharon Springs
Wallace
Galatea
Haswell
Eads
Chivington
Brandon
Sheridan Lake
Towner
Horace
Selkirk
Marienthal
Modoc
Arlington
Olney Springs
Ordway
Sugar City
Crowley
Fowler
Manzanola
Rocky Ford
Swink
Hawley
Cheraw
Las Animas
Hasty
Caddoa
McClave
Wiley
Lamar
Granada
Holly
Coolidge
Syracuse
Kendall
Deerfield
Holcomb
Garden City
Lakin
Timpas
Toonerville
La Junta
Bent's Old Fort Natl. Hist. Site
John Martin Res. S.P.
Amache N.H.S.
Hartman
Carlton
Kornman
May Valley
Bristol
Two Buttes
Lycan
Manter
Johnson City
Big Bow
Ulysses
Plymell
Hickok
Delhi
Thatcher
Model
Ninaview
Villegren
Kim
Pritchett
Utleyville
Vilas
Walsh
Springfield
Bartlett
Saunders
Campo
Elkhart
Richfield
Stonington
Rolla
Woods
Moscow
Hugoton
Satanta
Sublette

COMANCHE NATL. GRASSLAND
FORT CARSON
Muddy Creek Res.
SAND CREEK MASSACRE NAT'L. HIST. SITE
PAWNEE NATIONAL GRASSLAND
ROCKY MTN. ARSENAL N.W.R.
BONNY LAKE S.P.
U.S. AIR FORCE ACADEMY

Federal
Pine Bluffs
Bushnell
Kimball
Dix
Potter
Gurley
Sidney
Sunol
Lodgepole
Chappell
Big Springs
Brule
Ogallala
Roscoe
Paxton
Sutherland
North Platte
Hershey
L. MCCONAUGHY ST. REC. AREA
Lake C. West
Lewellen
Ash Hollow S.H.P.
Lemoyne
Kingsley Dam
Keystone
Sarben
Lake Maloney S.R.A.
Buffalo Bill Ranch S.H.S.
Fort Sidney Mus. and Post Commander's Home
Brownson
Lorenzo
Colton
Julesburg
Sedgwick
Ovid
Crook
Peetz
Padroni
Proctor
Iliff
St. Petersburg
Fleming
Dailey
Haxtun
Paoli
Holyoke
Amherst
Venango
Grant
Madrid
Elsie
Wallace
Dickens
Wellfleet
Brandon
Grainton
Lamar
Imperial
Champion
Enders
Wauneta
Hayes Center
Hamlet
Palisade
Culbertson
Max
Stratton
Trenton
Haigler
Benkelman
Parks
Laird
Wray
Vernon
Beecher Island
Eckley
Yuma
Otis
Platner
Hyde
Idalia
Joes
Kirk
Bethune
Vona
Stratton
Burlington
Kanorado
Goodland
Ruleton
Edson
Brewster
Levant
Colby
Halford
Mingo
Page City
Winona
Monument
Oakley
Russell Springs
Logan St. Fishing Lake
Sherman St. Fishing Lake
High Plains Mus.
Prairie Mus. of Art & History
Bird City
McDonald
Beardsley
St. Francis
Wheeler
Atwood
Ludell
Herndon
Blakeman
Scott S.P.
El Cuartelejo
Scott City
Shallow Water
Friend
Lydia
Leoti
Tribune
Mt. Sunflower Highest Pt. in Kansas 4,039

Highest Point in Nebraska 5,424

Black Mesa Highest Pt. in Oklahoma 4,973

Pikes Pk. 14,115

Go to 21
Go to 22
Go to 35
Go to 48

COLORADO / NEW MEXICO
COLORADO / OKLAHOMA
WYOMING / COLORADO
NEBRASKA / COLORADO
NEBRASKA / KANSAS
COLORADO / NEBRASKA
COLORADO / KANSAS
MOUNTAIN TIME ZONE / CENTRAL TIME ZONE

1   2   3   4
A   B   C

DRIVING DISTANCES IN MILES	BURLINGTON, CO	CHEYENNE, WY	COLORADO SPRS., CO	DENVER, CO	DODGE CITY, KS	GRAND ISLAND, NE	HAYS, KS	LINCOLN, NE	NORTH PLATTE, NE	PUEBLO, CO	SALINA, KS	WICHITA, KS
COLORADO SPRS., CO	152	169		70	312	471	324	550	328	43	416	505
DENVER, CO	168	100	70		389	406	340	486	263	111	432	521
LINCOLN, NE	362	442	550	486	344	95	265		223	592	187	276
WICHITA, KS	354	613	505	521	153	278	181	276	389	544	92	

SEE ALSO DISTANCE AND DRIVING TIME MAP ON PAGE 126

0 mi | 20 | 40 | 60
0 km | 20 | 40 | 60 | 80

One inch equals 23.2 miles
One centimeter equals 14.7 kilometers

Go to 23
Go to 24
Go to 37
Go to 50

1
2
3
4

A
B
C

Nebraska | Iowa
Illinois
Kansas | Missouri
Ky.

DRIVING DISTANCES IN MILES	CARBONDALE, IL	COLUMBIA, MO	JEFFERSON CITY, MO	KANSAS CITY, MO	LINCOLN, NE	OMAHA, NE	PEORIA, IL	QUINCY, IL	SPRINGFIELD, IL	ST. LOUIS, MO	TOPEKA, KS
KANSAS CITY, MO	352	129	161		197	188	418	251	343	169	252	63
SPRINGFIELD, IL	182	214	224	343	537	480	75	110		314	97	406
SPRINGFIELD, MO	296	163	131	169	367	358	389	262	314		209	228
ST. LOUIS, MO	105	123	132	252	449	440	172	131	97	209		315

SEE ALSO DISTANCE AND DRIVING TIME MAP ON PAGE 126

Illinois Ind. Ohio Pa.
W. Va.
Kentucky Va.

0 mi   20   40   60
0 km 20   40   60   80

One inch equals 23.2 miles
One centimeter equals 14.7 kilometers

Go to 26
Go to 27
Go to 42
Go to 54

DRIVING DISTANCES IN MILES	AKRON, OH	BECKLEY, WV	CHAMPAIGN, IL	CHARLESTON, WV	CINCINNATI, OH	COLUMBUS OH	EVANSVILLE, IN	FORT WAYNE, IN	INDIANAPOLIS, IN	LEXINGTON, KY	LOUISVILLE, KY	WHEELING, W V
AKRON, OH		274	435	214	243	129	452	237	304	326	341	116
COLUMBUS, OH	129	228	307	168	109		319	186	176	193	207	130
INDIANAPOLIS, IN	304	380	123	320	116	176	166	128		191	112	310
LOUISVILLE, KY	341	311	237	251	100	207	114	236	112	80		333

SEE ALSO DISTANCE AND DRIVING TIME MAP ON PAGE 126

DRIVING DISTANCES IN MILES

	ALLENTOWN, PA	BALTIMORE, MD	HARRISBURG, PA	HARRISONBURG, VA	MORGANTOWN, WV	NEW YORK, NY	PHILADELPHIA, PA	PITTSBURGH, PA	RICHMOND, VA	ROANOKE, VA	WASHINGTON, DC	WILLIAMSBURG, VA
NEW YORK, NY	84	192	165	358	375		91	367	342	472	228	387
PHILADELPHIA, PA	63	104	109	270	313	91		306	254	384	140	299
PITTSBURGH, PA	284	246	205	258	78	367	306		341	316	240	386
WASHINGTON, DC	193	38	124	131	205	228	140	240	108	245		153

SEE ALSO DISTANCE AND DRIVING TIME MAP ON PAGE 126

Nevada Utah
California
Arizona

0 mi 20 40 60
0 km 20 40 60 80
One inch equals 23.2 miles
One centimeter equals 14.7 kilometers

PACIFIC OCEAN

Gulf of Santa Catalina

A B C

1 2 3 4

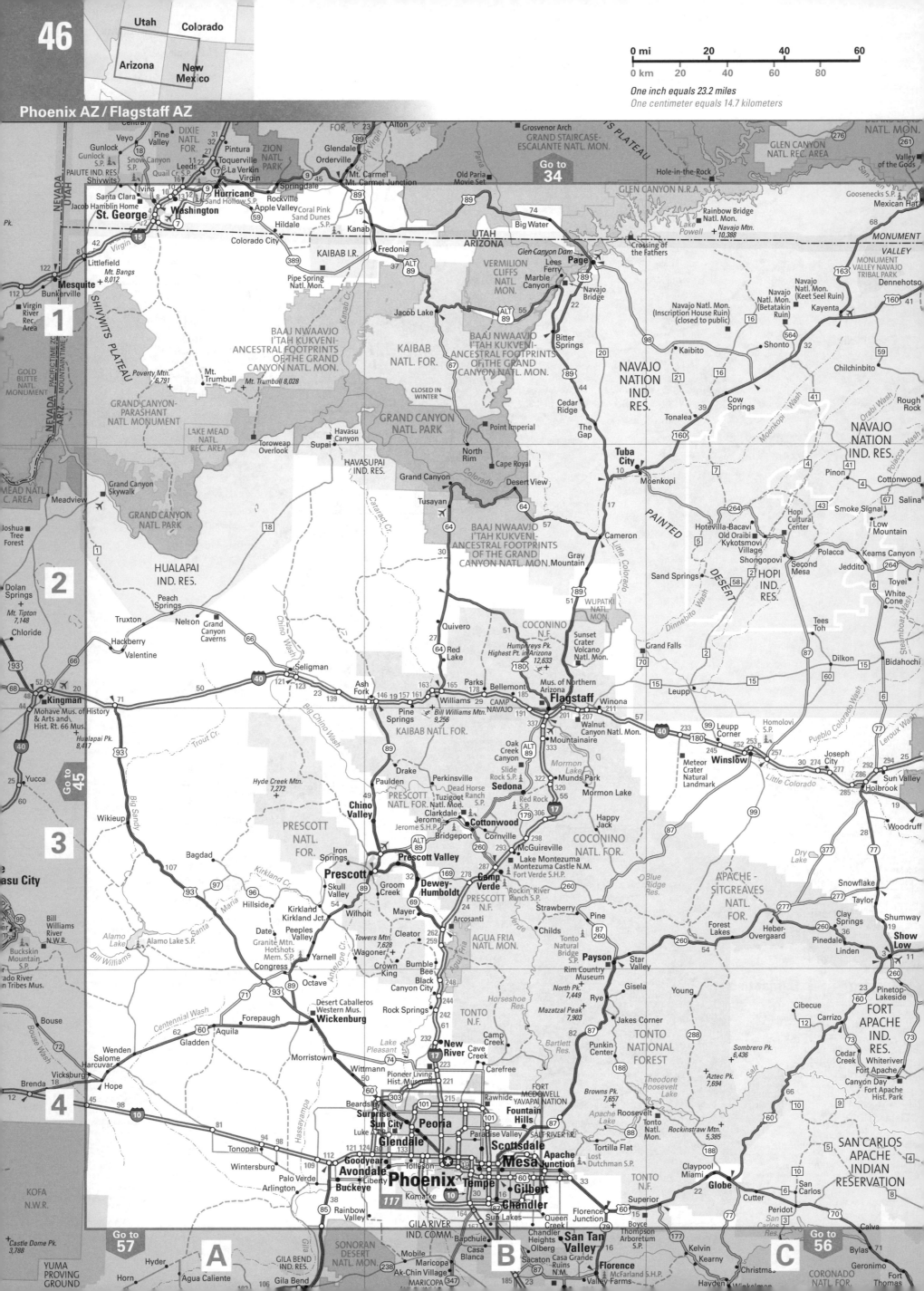

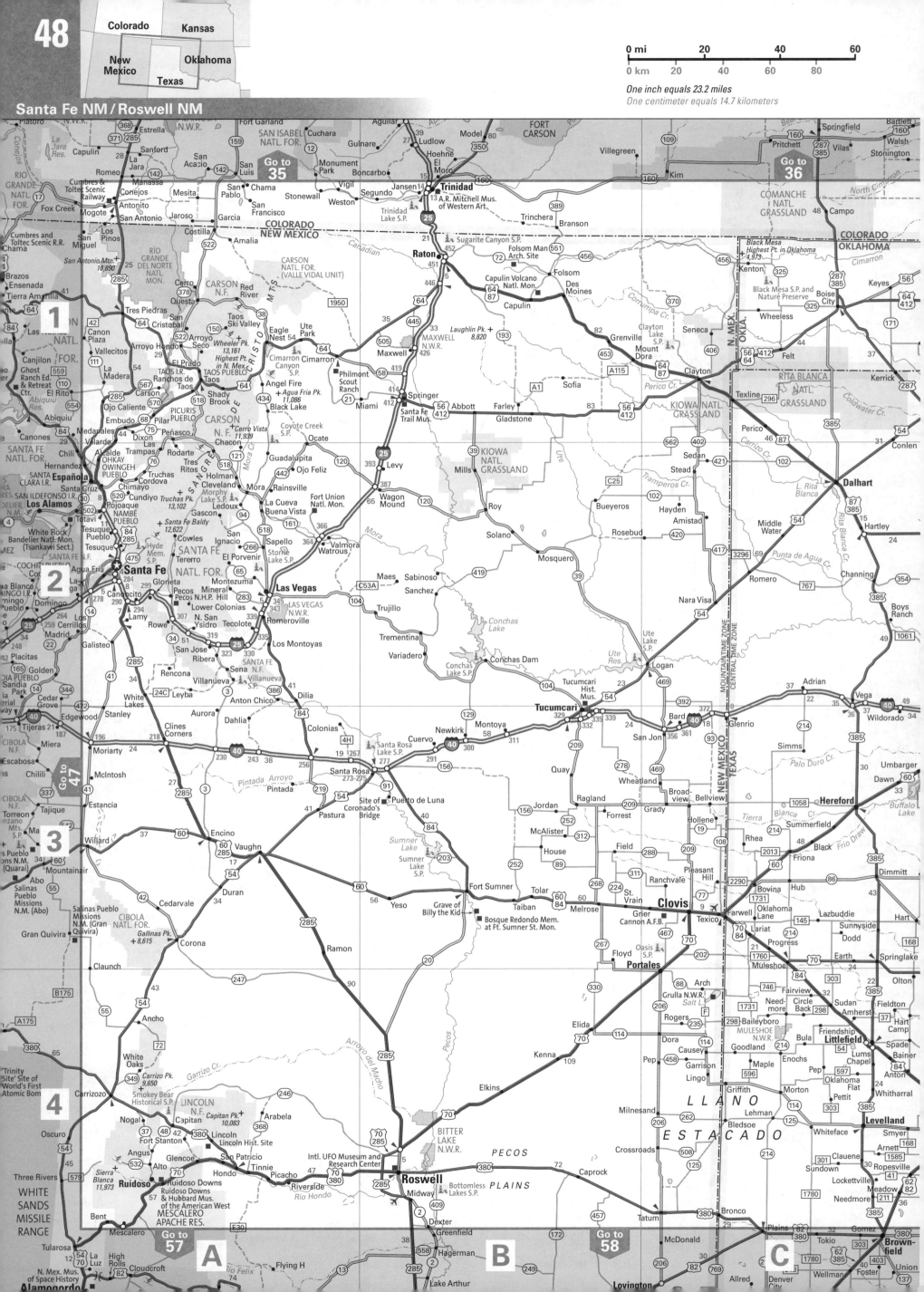

DRIVING DISTANCES IN MILES	AMARILLO, TX	CLAYTON, NM	CLINTON, OK	CLOVIS, NM	ENID, OK	LAWTON, OK	LIBERAL, KS	LUBBOCK, TX	ROSWELL, NM	SANTA FE, NM	TUCUMCARI, NM	WICHITA FALLS, TX
AMARILLO, TX		134	177	109	298	240	165	124	219	279	114	228
ROSWELL, NM	219	272	394	110	514	410	367	174		191	161	383
SANTA FE, NM	279	216	454	213	574	516	364	316	191		167	504
WICHITA FALLS, TX	228	362	153	299	197	55	308	207	383	504	339	

SEE ALSO DISTANCE AND DRIVING TIME MAP ON PAGE 126.

0 mi   20   40   60
0 km   20   40   60   80

One inch equals 23.2 miles
One centimeter equals 14.7 kilometers

KANSAS
OKLAHOMA

Major cities: Oklahoma City, Tulsa, Broken Arrow, Norman, Edmond, Midwest City, Lawton, Stillwater, Enid, Muskogee, Shawnee, Ponca City, Bartlesville, Claremore, Sapulpa, Ardmore, Duncan, McAlester, Durant, Wichita Falls, Denton, Sherman, Paris.

DRIVING DISTANCES IN MILES	ENID, OK	FAYETTEVILLE, AR	FORT SMITH, AR	JONESBORO, AR	LITTLE ROCK, AR	OKLAHOMA CITY, OK	PINE BLUFF, AR	SHERMAN, TX	SPRINGFIELD, MO	TEXARKANA AR/TX	TULSA, OK	WICHITA FALLS, TX
FAYETTEVILLE, AR	229		64	287	186	220	231	260	121	244	113	361
LITTLE ROCK, AR	405	186	165	135		355	45	332	213	153	288	489
OKLAHOMA CITY, OK	84	220	191	456	355		400	170	290	318	109	141
WICHITA FALLS, TX	197	361	325	590	489	141	475	115	437	314	250	

SEE ALSO DISTANCE AND DRIVING TIME MAP ON PAGE 126

52

Missouri Ill. Kentucky Va.
N.C.
Tennessee
Arkansas S.C.
Miss. Ala. Georgia

Memphis TN / Paducah KY

0 mi 20 40 60
0 km 20 40 60 80

One inch equals 23.2 miles
One centimeter equals 14.7 kilometers

Go to 39

Go to 51

Go to 63 Go to 64

A B C

1

2

3

4

DRIVING
DISTANCES
IN MILES

	ATLANTA, GA	BIRMINGHAM, AL	BOWLING GREEN, KY	CHATTANOOGA, TN	GREENVILLE, MS	HUNTSVILLE, AL	JONESBORO, AR	KNOXVILLE, TN	MEMPHIS, TN	NASHVILLE, TN	PADUCAH, KY	TUPELO, MS
ATLANTA, GA		150	312	113	431	191	459	216	389	242	374	284
MEMPHIS, TN	389	241	279	346	148	216	70	401		215	174	109
NASHVILLE, TN	242	194	68	131	363	112	285	184	215		133	195
PADUCAH, KY	374	325	135	264	325	245	178	317	174	133		222

SEE ALSO DISTANCE AND DRIVING TIME MAP ON PAGE 126

Virginia
Kentucky
Tennessee
North Carolina
South Carolina
Georgia

0 mi   20   40   60
0 km   20   40   60   80

One inch equals 23.2 miles
One centimeter equals 14.7 kilometers

Go to 41

Go to 53

Go to 66

Go to 97

1

2

3

4

A

B

C

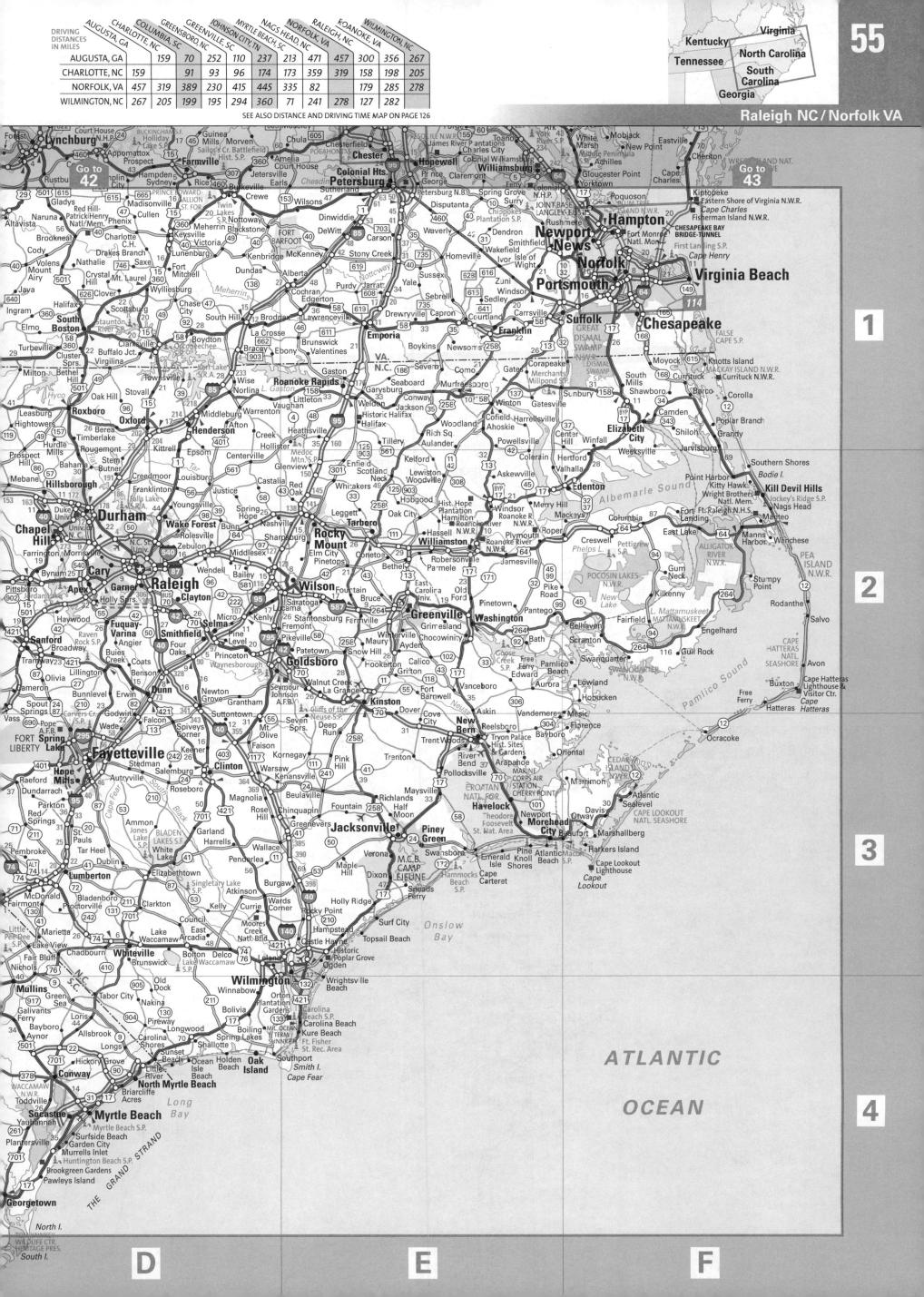

0 mi 20 40 60
0 km 20 40 60 80
One inch equals 23.2 miles
One centimeter equals 14.7 kilometers

1

Buckeye Avondale Tolleson
Arlington Palo Verde Liberty **Phoenix** Tempe
Rainbow Valley Komatke Gilbert Chandler
Sun Lakes Chandler Heights Queen Creek
Superior Globe Miami Claypool
San Carlos Cutter Peridot Calva
Go to 46

SONORAN DESERT
TOHONO O'ODHAM (GILA BEND) IND. RES.
Gila Bend
Paloma
BARRY M. GOLDWATER AIR FORCE RANGE
Ajo
Why
Go to 57

San Tan Valley
Florence
McFarland S.H.P.
Coolidge
Casa Grande
Arizola Eloy Picacho
Picacho Peak S.P.
Red Rock
Marana
Oro Valley
Tucson
Univ. of Arizona
South Tucson
Davis-Monthan A.F.B.
San Xavier
Sahuarita
Green Valley
Continental

SAGUARO NATL. PARK
Mt. Lemmon 9,157
CORONADO NATL. FOR.

Safford
Thatcher
Pima Central
CORONADO N.F.
Mt. Graham 10,720
Willcox
Bowie San Simon
NEW MEXICO ARIZONA

CHIRICAHUA NATL. MON.
Chiricahua Pk. 9,798
CORONADO NATL. FOR.
Portal Rodeo

2

UNITED STATES / MEXICO
ARIZONA SONORA

BUENOS AIRES N.W.R.
Arivaca
Tubac
Tumacacori
Sierra Vista
FORT HUACHUCA
Patagonia
Bisbee
Tombstone
Nogales **Nogales**
Go to 92
Agua Prieta **Douglas**

3

Torrance **Anaheim** Orange
Long Beach Santa Ana Irvine
Huntington Beach
Newport Beach
Laguna Beach
San Juan Capistrano
Dana Point
San Clemente

Perris San Jacinto **Palm Springs**
Lake Elsinore Hemet
Menifee
Wildomar
Mission Viejo Murrieta
Temecula
Cathedral City Indi
Rancho Mirage Palm Desert
La Quinta Coachella

CLEVELAND NATL. FOR.
MARINE CORPS BASE CAMP PENDLETON

Fallbrook
Vista
Oceanside
Carlsbad
San Marcos
Escondido
Ramona
Encinitas
Solana Beach
Del Mar
Poway
Santee
San Diego
La Mesa El Cajon
Coronado Spring Valley Lemon Grove
Chula Vista
Imperial Beach

ANZA-BORREGO DESERT S.P.
Borrego Springs
Salton Sea
Salton City
Calipatria
Brawley
Westmorland

CHOCOLATE MTS.
CHOCOLATE MOUNTAIN AERIAL GUNNERY RANGE

Imperial **El Centro** Holtville
Calexico
Mexicali
San Luis Río Colorado

4

PACIFIC OCEAN

Gulf of Santa Catalina
San Clemente Island
Santa Catalina Island
Avalon

Tijuana
Rosarito
Tecate

A | B | C

Go to 92
Ensenad
Ianeadero

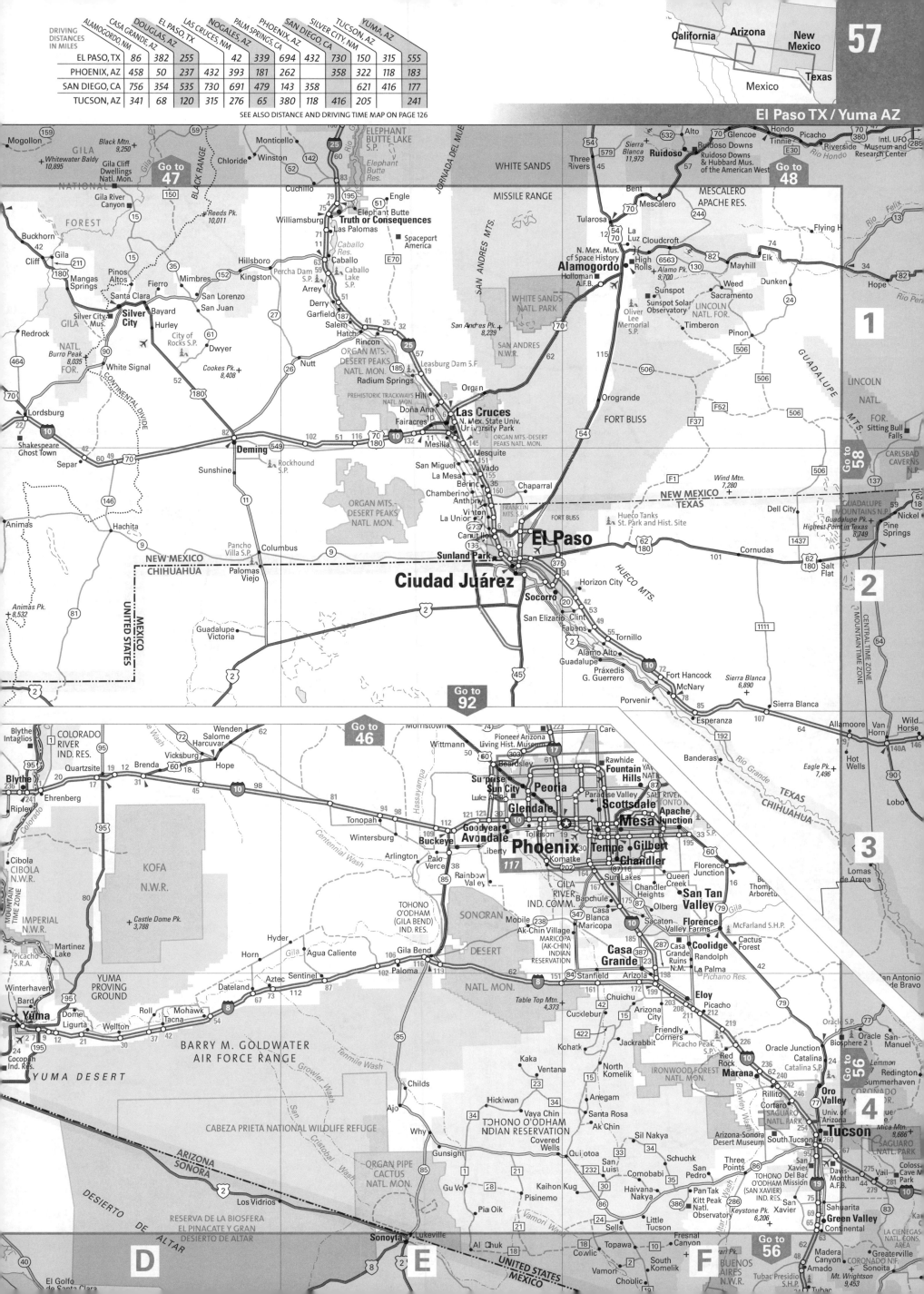

California
Arizona
New
Mexico
Texas
Mexico

DRIVING DISTANCES IN MILES

	ALAMOGORDO, NM	CASA GRANDE, AZ	DOUGLAS, AZ	EL PASO, TX	LAS CRUCES, NM	NOGALES, AZ	PALM SPRINGS, CA	PHOENIX, AZ	SAN DIEGO, CA	SILVER CITY, NM	TUCSON, AZ	YUMA, AZ
EL PASO, TX	86	382	255		42	339	694	432	730	150	315	555
PHOENIX, AZ	458	50	237	432	393	181	262		358	322	118	183
SAN DIEGO, CA	756	354	535	730	691	479	143	358		621	416	177
TUCSON, AZ	341	68	120	315	276	65	380	118	416	205		241

SEE ALSO DISTANCE AND DRIVING TIME MAP ON PAGE 126

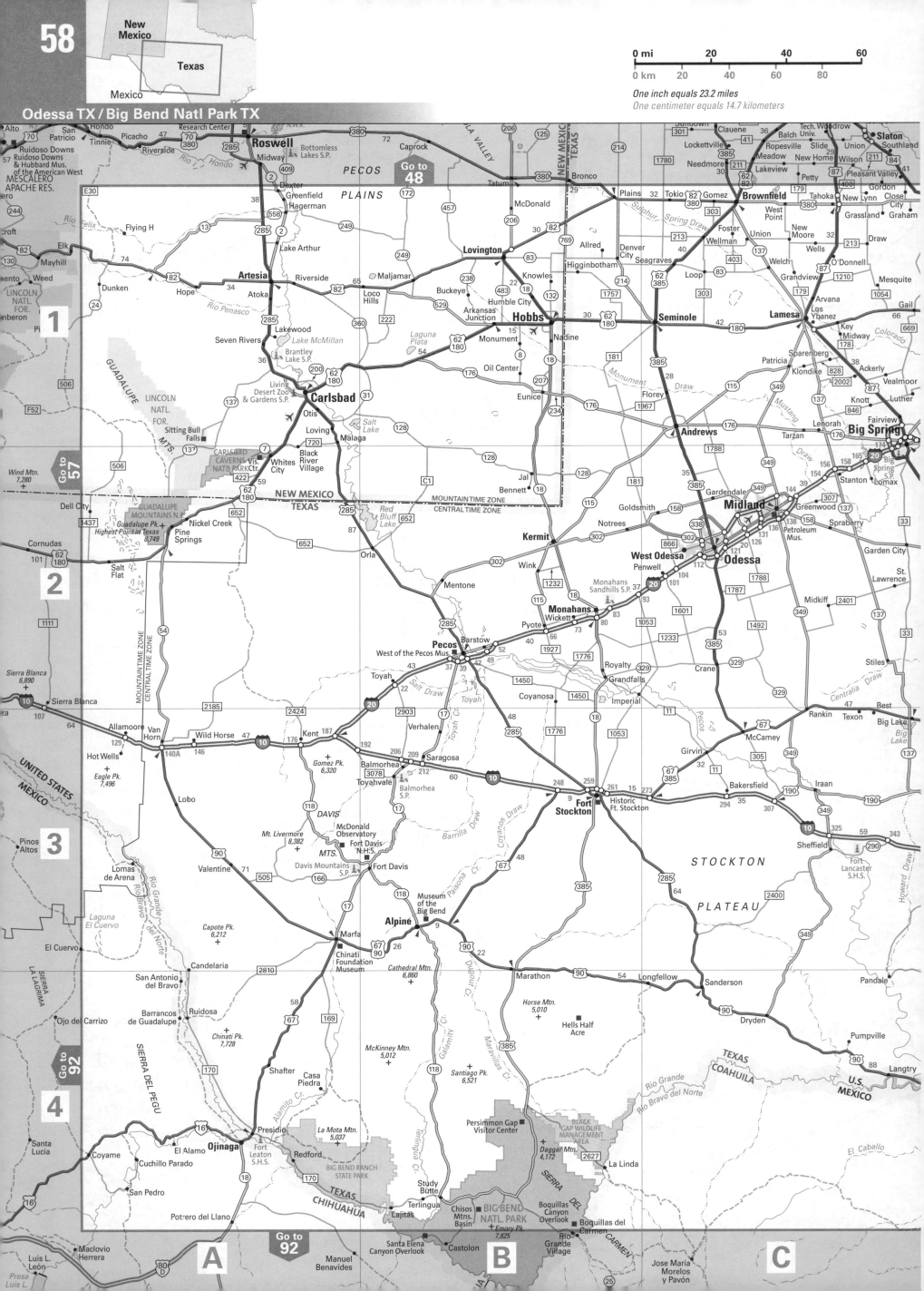

One inch equals 23.2 miles
One centimeter equals 14.7 kilometers

0 mi   20   40   60
0 km 20 40 60 80

Go to 48
Go to 57
Go to 92
Go to 92

DRIVING DISTANCES IN MILES	ABILENE, TX	AUSTIN, TX	BIG BEND NP, TX	CARLSBAD, NM	DEL RIO, TX	FORT STOCKTON, TX	FORT WORTH, TX	HOBBS, NM	ODESSA, TX	SAN ANGELO, TX	SAN ANTONIO, TX	VAN HORN, TX
ODESSA, TX	174	414	209	137	246	86	326	88		134	342	163
SAN ANGELO, TX	91	207	287	258	156	164	228	201	134		208	295
SAN ANTONIO, TX	258	78	438	457	152	315	264	431	342	208		435
VAN HORN, TX	335	507	207	116	304	119	487	198	163	295	435	

SEE ALSO DISTANCE AND DRIVING TIME MAP ON PAGE 126

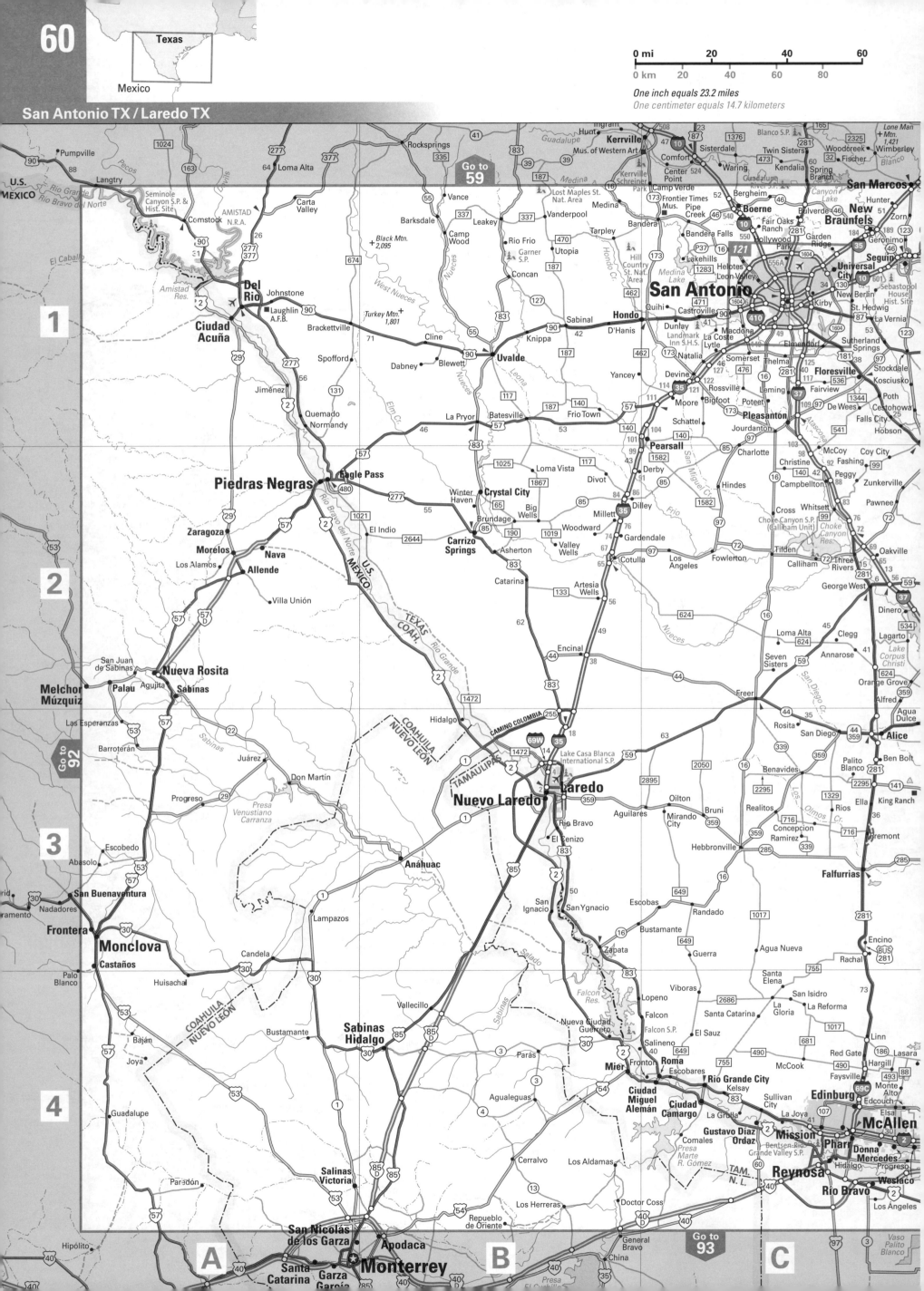

0 mi   20   40   60

0 km   20   40   60   80

One inch equals 23.2 miles
One centimeter equals 14.7 kilometers

Go to 59

Go to 92

Go to 93

1

2

3

4

A   B   C

DRIVING DISTANCES IN MILES	BROWNSVILLE, TX	CORPUS CHRISTI, TX	DEL RIO, TX	EAGLE PASS, TX	GALVESTON, TX	HOUSTON, TX	KINGSVILLE, TX	LAREDO, TX	McALLEN, TX	MONTERREY MX	SAN ANTONIO, TX	VICTORIA, TX
CORPUS CHRISTI, TX	157		272	248	223	211	38	141	152	284	147	94
HOUSTON, TX	351	211	349	343	53		233	355	346	498	200	127
LAREDO, TX	202	141	179	123	409	355	124		144	142	157	186
SAN ANTONIO, TX	279	147	152	145	253	200	161	157	243	299		118

SEE ALSO DISTANCE AND DRIVING TIME MAP ON PAGE 126

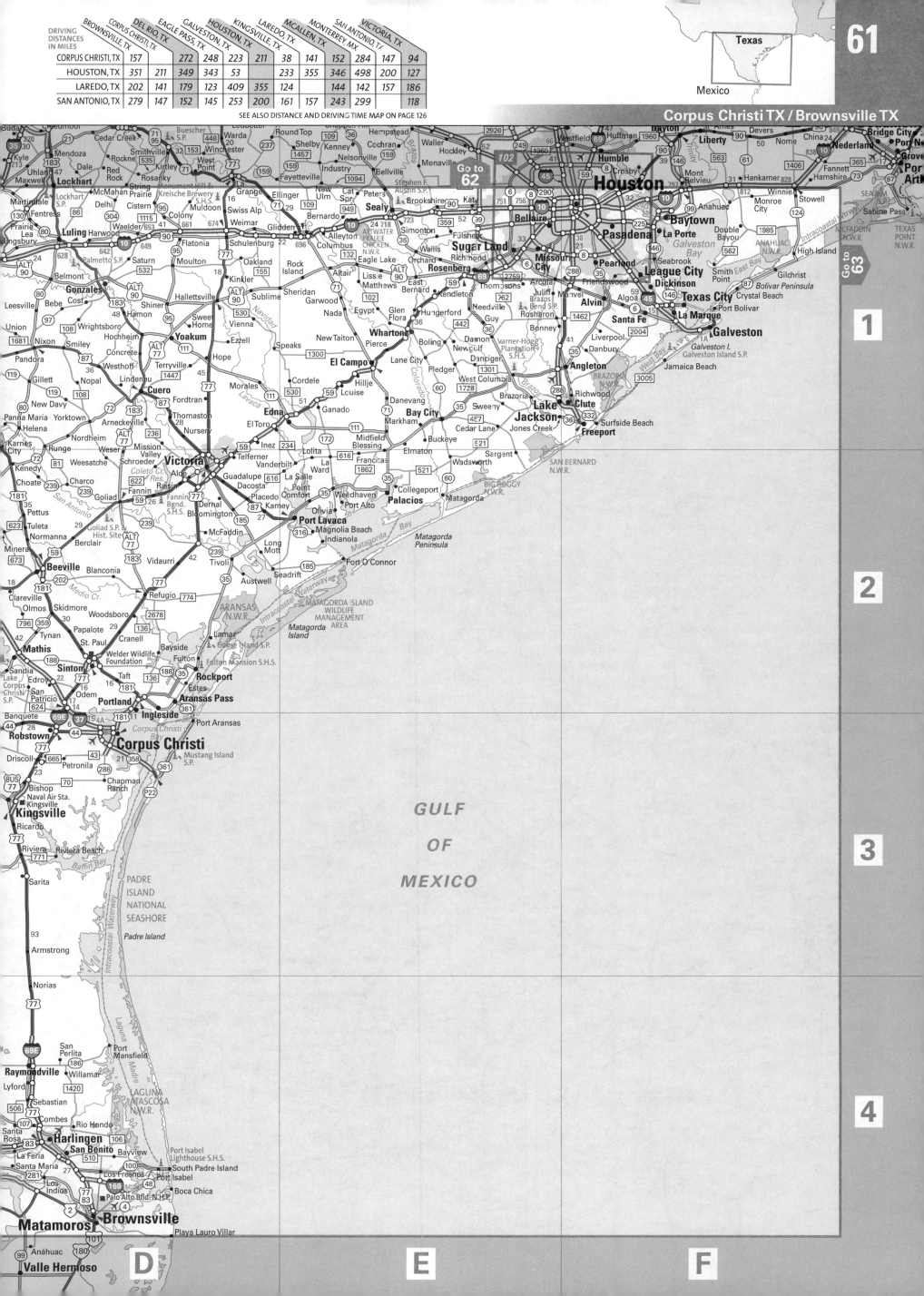

0 mi   20   40   60
0 km   20   40   60   80
One inch equals 23.2 miles
One centimeter equals 14.7 kilometers

Arkansas
Miss.
Texas
Louisiana

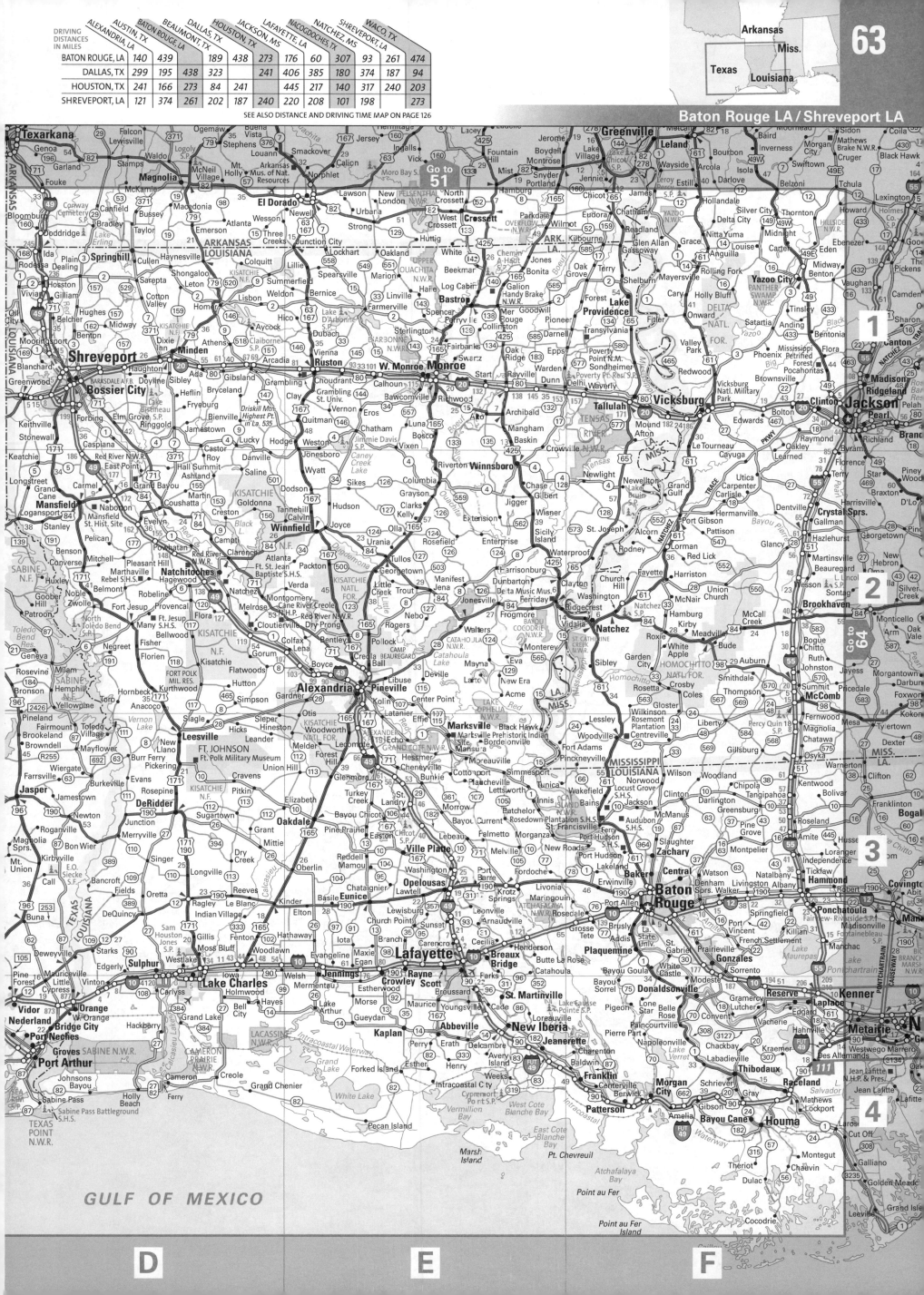

DRIVING DISTANCES IN MILES	ALEXANDRIA, LA	AUSTIN, TX	BATON ROUGE LA	BEAUMONT, TX	DALLAS, TX	HOUSTON, TX	JACKSON, MS	LAFAYETTE, LA	NACOGDOCHES,TX	NATCHEZ, MS	SHREVEPORT, LA	WACO, TX
BATON ROUGE, LA	140	439		189	438	273	176	60	307	93	261	474
DALLAS, TX	299	195	438	323		241	406	385	180	374	187	94
HOUSTON, TX	241	166	273	84	241		445	217	140	317	240	203
SHREVEPORT, LA	121	374	261	202	187	240	220	208	101	198		273

SEE ALSO DISTANCE AND DRIVING TIME MAP ON PAGE 126

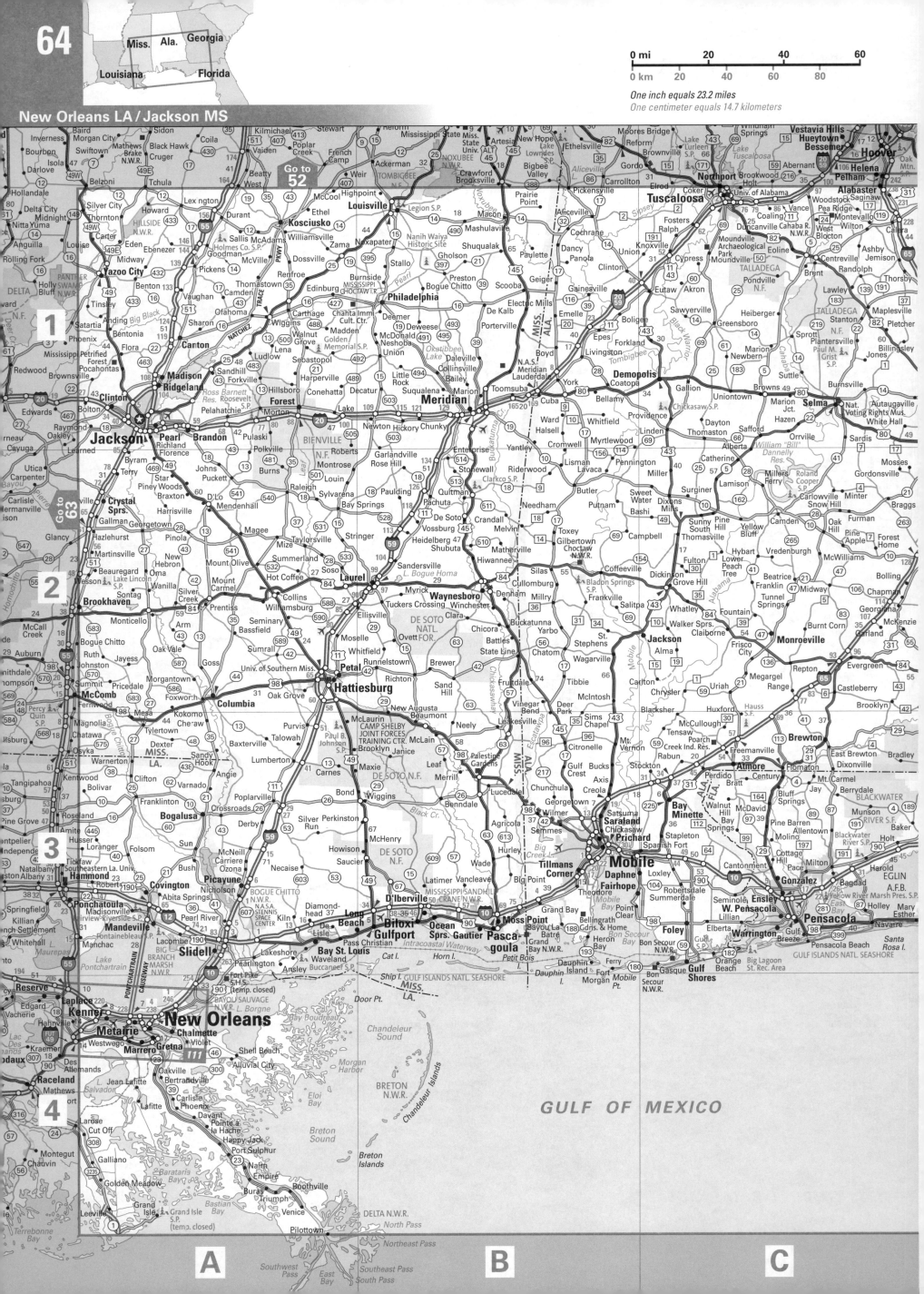

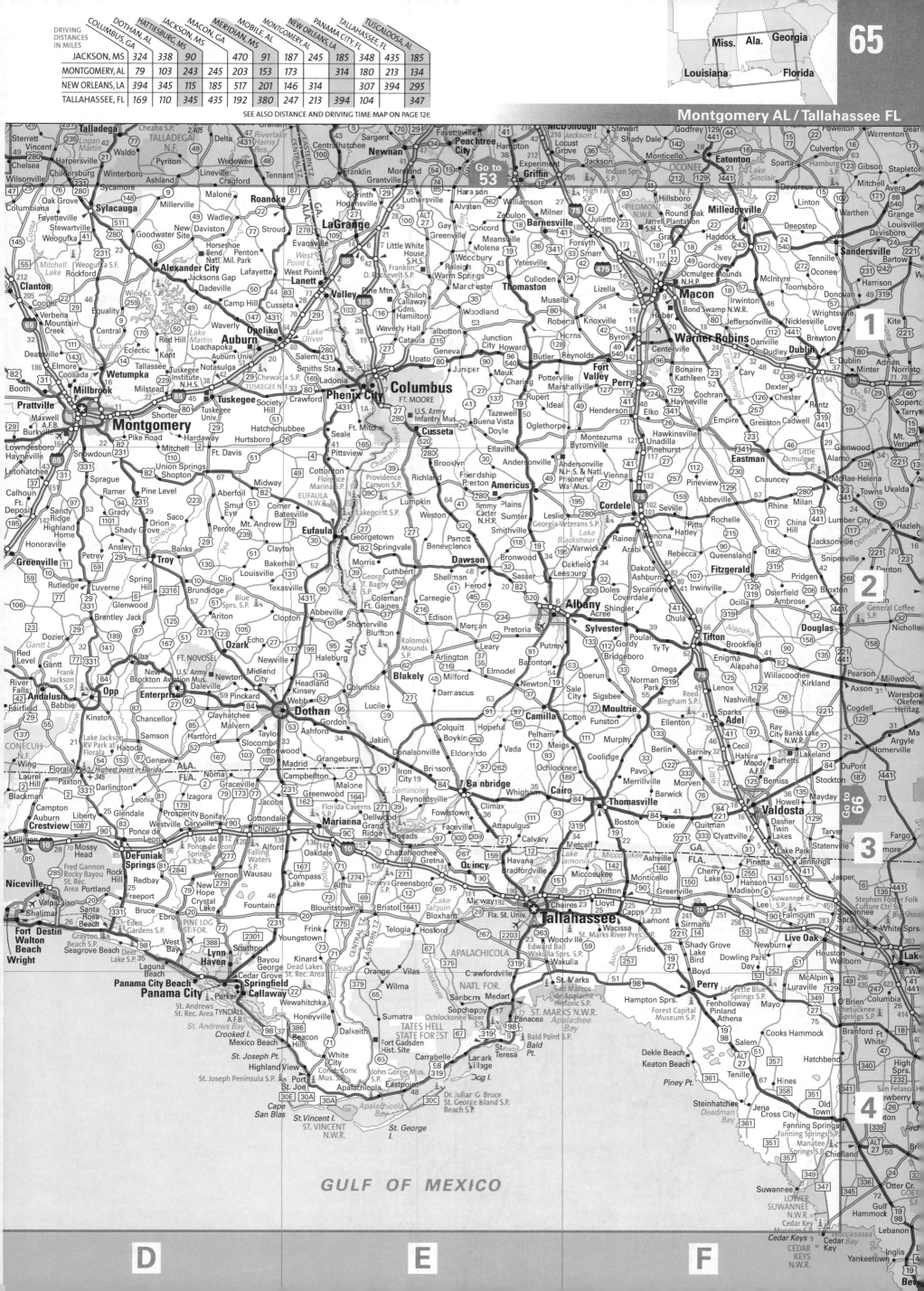

SEE ALSO DISTANCE AND DRIVING TIME MAP ON PAGE 126

DRIVING DISTANCES IN MILES	COLUMBUS, GA	DOTHAN, AL	HATTIESBURG, MS	JACKSON, MS	MACON, GA	MERIDIAN, MS	MOBILE, AL	MONTGOMERY, AL	NEW ORLEANS, LA	PANAMA CITY, FL	TALLAHASSEE, FL	TUSCALOOSA, AL
JACKSON, MS	324	338	90		470	91	187	245	185	348	435	185
MONTGOMERY, AL	79	103	243	245	203	153	173		314	180	213	134
NEW ORLEANS, LA	394	345	115	185	517	201	146	314		307	394	295
TALLAHASSEE, FL	169	110	345	435	192	380	247	213	394	104		347

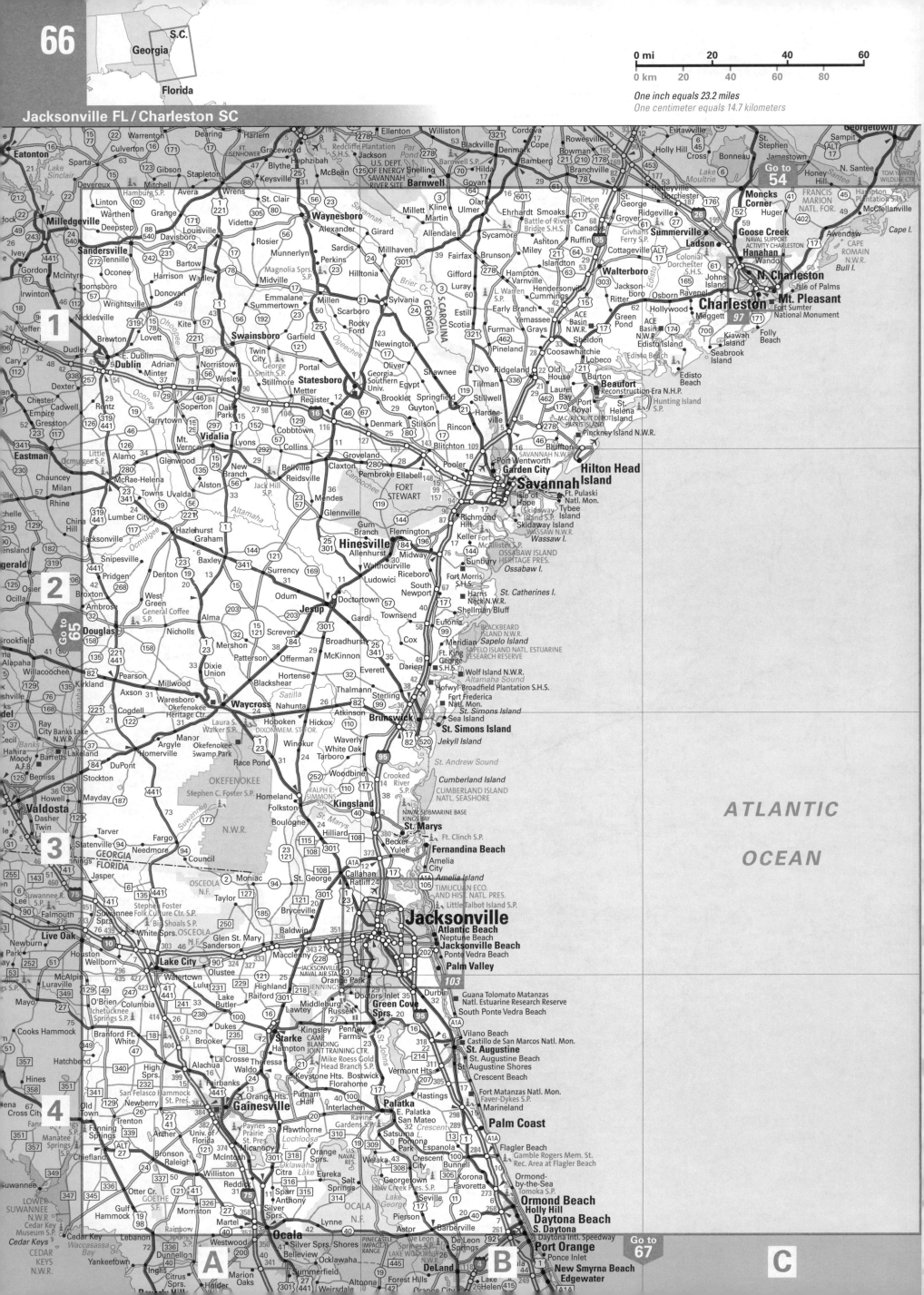

Go to 66

DRIVING DISTANCES IN MILES

	CHARLESTON, SC	DAYTONA BEACH, FL	FORT MYERS, FL	FORT PIERCE, FL	GAINESVILLE, FL	JACKSONVILLE, FL	KEY WEST, FL	MIAMI, FL	ORLANDO, FL	SARASOTA, FL	SAVANNAH, GA	TAMPA, FL
CHARLESTON, SC		329	533	461	308	238	750	583	379	487	107	434
JACKSONVILLE, FL	238	91	295	223	70		512	345	141	249	141	196
MIAMI, FL	583	260	155	122	338	345	168		232	225	486	274
TAMPA, FL	434	138	123	172	132	196	426	274	82	60		337

SEE ALSO DISTANCE AND DRIVING TIME MAP ON PAGE 126

Florida

FOR CONTINUATION SEE INSET AT LEFT

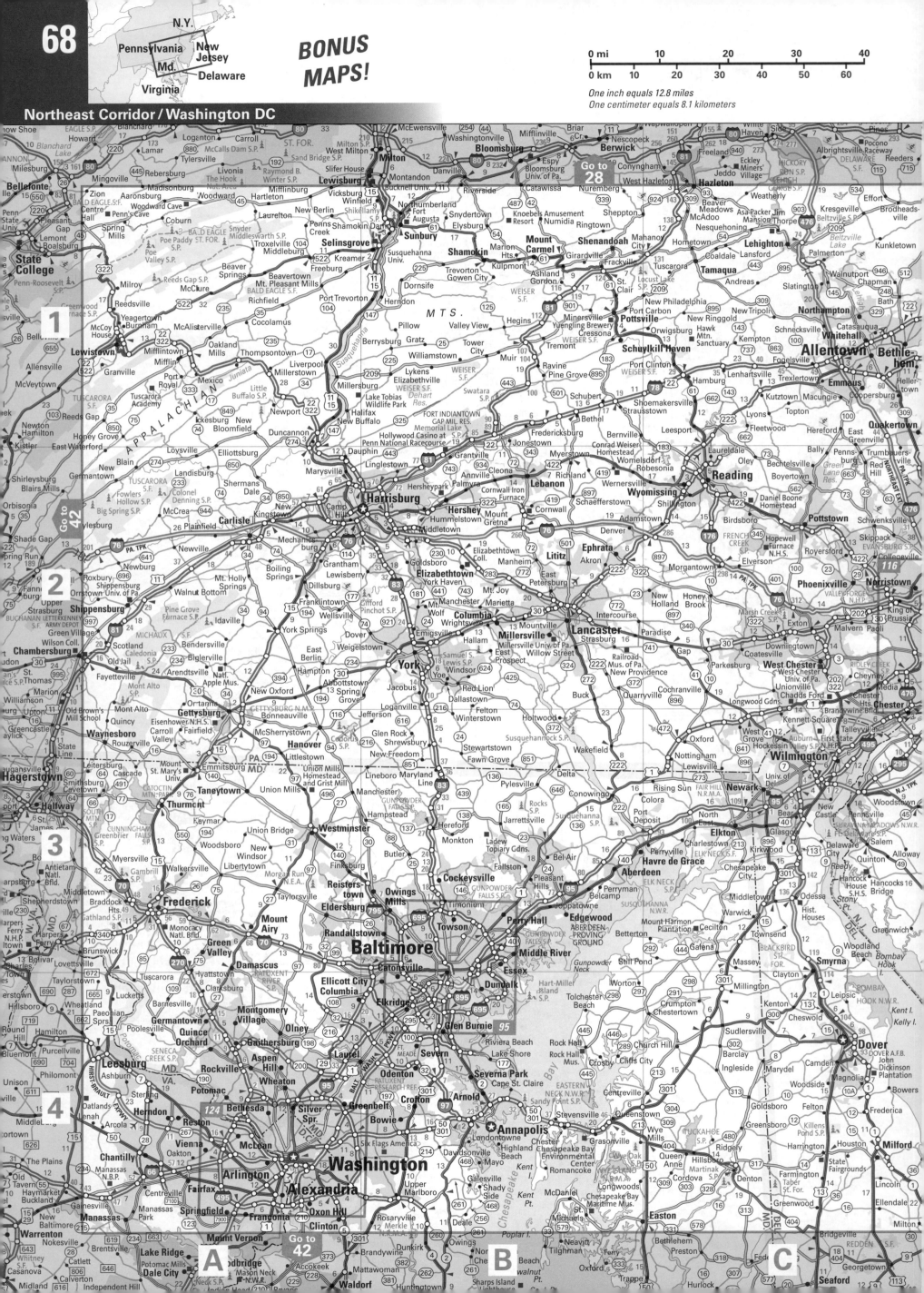

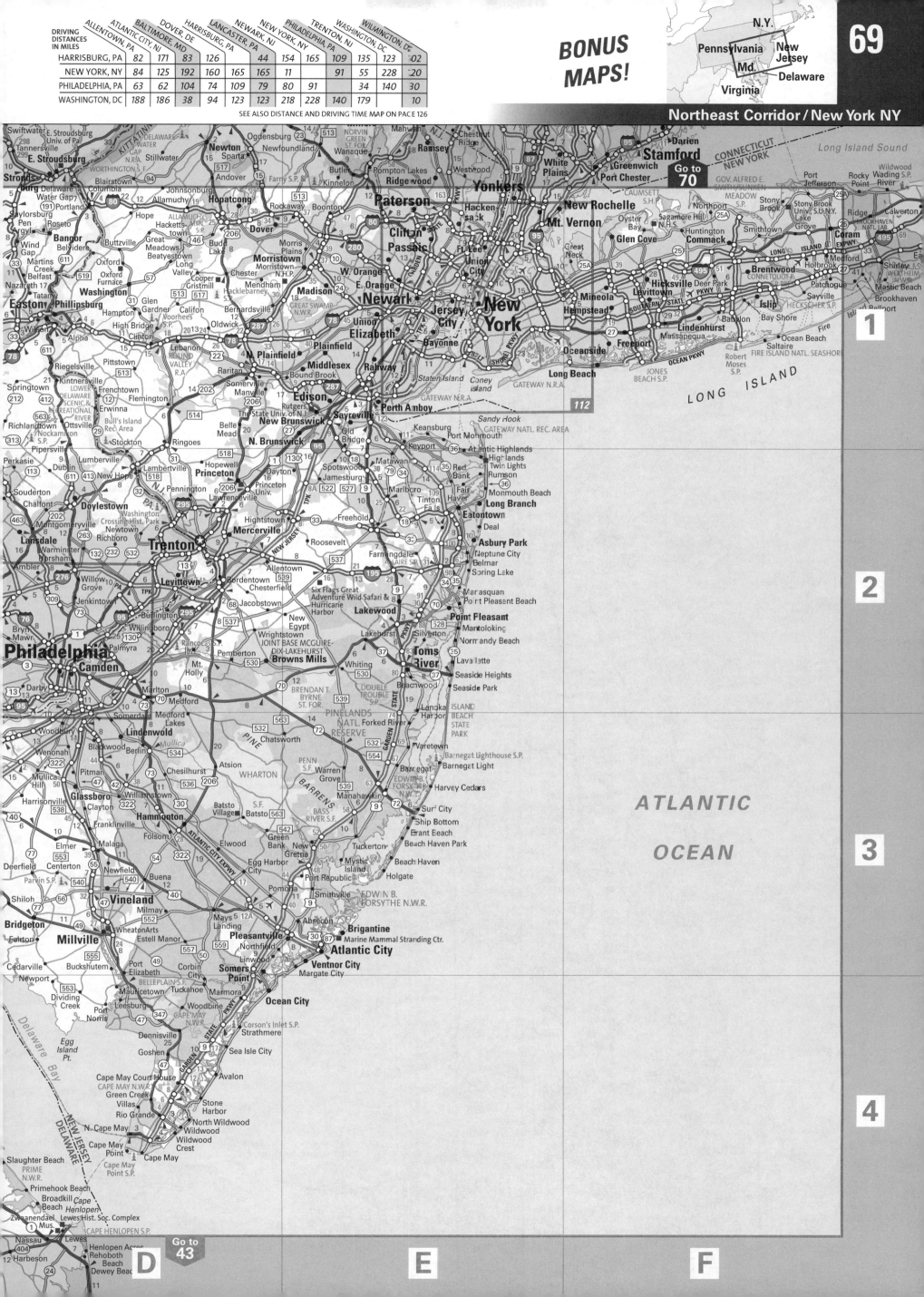

BONUS MAPS!

N.Y.

Pennsylvania | New Jersey

Md. | Delaware

Virginia

Go to 70

Go to 43

1

2

3

4

D

E

F

Vt. N.H.
New York
Massachusetts
Rhode Island
Connecticut
N.J.

BONUS MAPS!

| 0 mi | 10 | 20 | 30 | 40 |
| 0 km | 10 | 20 | 30 | 40 | 50 | 60 |

One inch equals 12.8 miles
One centimeter equals 8.1 kilometers

Go to 29
Go to 28
Go to 69

Gloversville • Saratoga Springs • Johnstown • Amsterdam • Schenectady • Rotterdam • Cohoes • Troy • Albany • Bennington • North Adams • Brattleboro • Keene • Greenfield • Pittsfield • Athol • Northampton • Amherst • Holyoke • Chicopee • Springfield • Agawam • Westfield • Hudson • Catskill • Kingston • New Paltz • Poughkeepsie • Torrington • Hartford • E. Hartford • W. Hartford • Manchester • Storrs • Bristol • New Britain • Newington • Southington • Willimantic • Waterbury • Meriden • Middletown • Naugatuck • Hamden • New Haven • Danbury • Newburgh • Beacon • Peekskill • Middletown • Port Jervis • Monroe • Goshen • Kiryas Joel • Shelton • Trumbull • Bridgeport • Fairfield • Milford • Stratford • Norwalk • Stamford • Darien • Greenwich • Port Chester • White Plains • Ossining • Yonkers • New Rochelle • Mt. Vernon • Paterson • Hackensack • Newark • New York • Long Island Sound • Long Island • Glen Cove • Hicksville • Levittown • Hempstead • Mineola • Islip • Brentwood • Coram • Riverhead • Hampton Bays

CATSKILL PARK • THE BERKSHIRES • MASS. • CONN. • N.Y. • Long Island

CONNECTICUT / NEW YORK

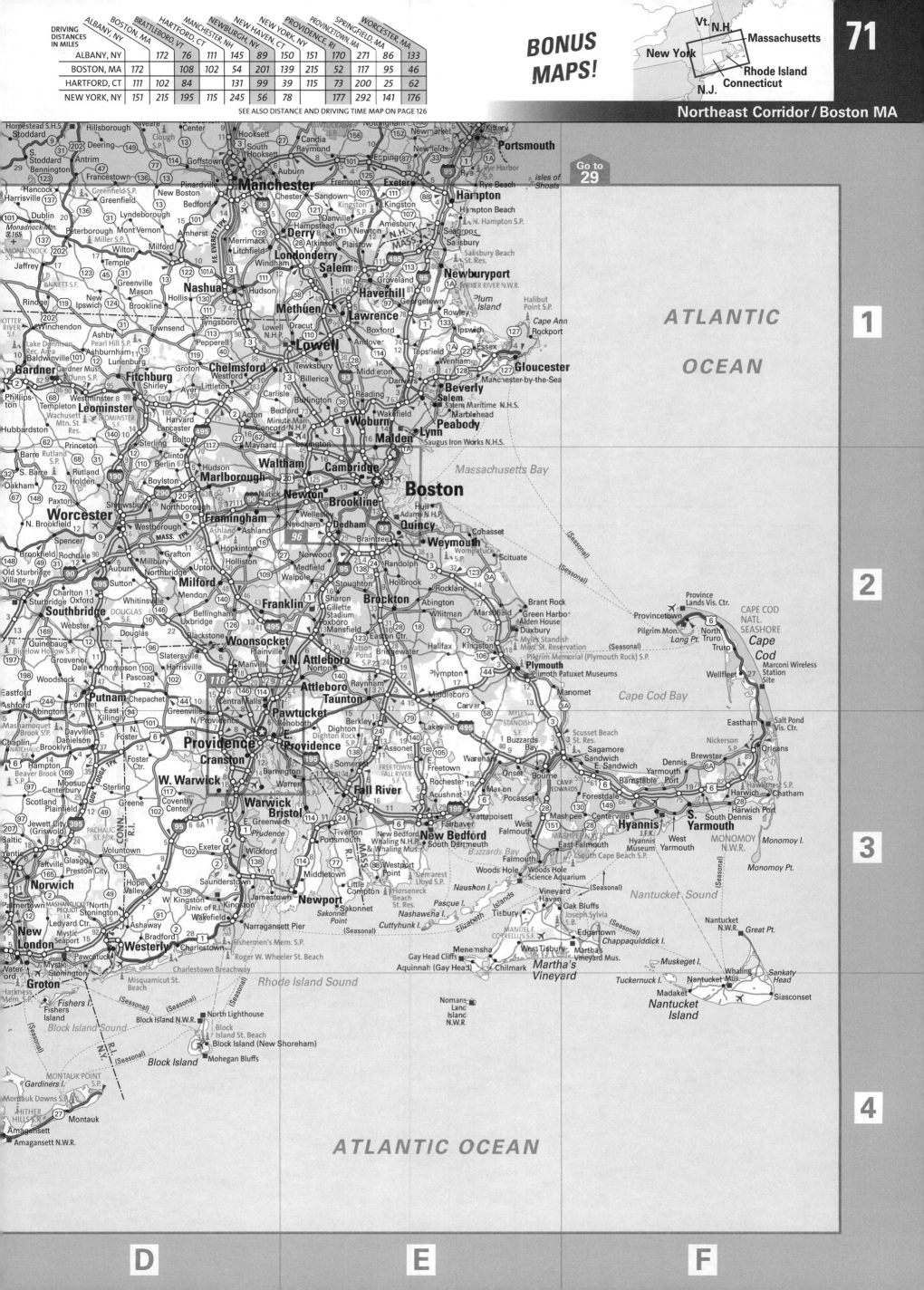

Go to 29

DRIVING DISTANCES IN MILES	ALBANY, NY	BOSTON, MA	BRATTLEBORO, VT	HARTFORD, CT	MANCHESTER, NH	NEWBURGH, NY	NEW HAVEN, CT	NEW YORK, NY	PROVIDENCE, RI	PROVINCETOWN, MA	SPRINGFIELD, MA	WORCESTER, MA
ALBANY, NY		172	76	111	145	89	150	151	170	271	86	133
BOSTON, MA	172		108	102	54	201	139	215	52	117	95	46
HARTFORD, CT	111	102	84		131	99	39	115	73	200	25	62
NEW YORK, NY	151	215	195	115	245	56	78		177	292	141	176

SEE ALSO DISTANCE AND DRIVING TIME MAP ON PAGE 126

ATLANTIC OCEAN

ATLANTIC OCEAN

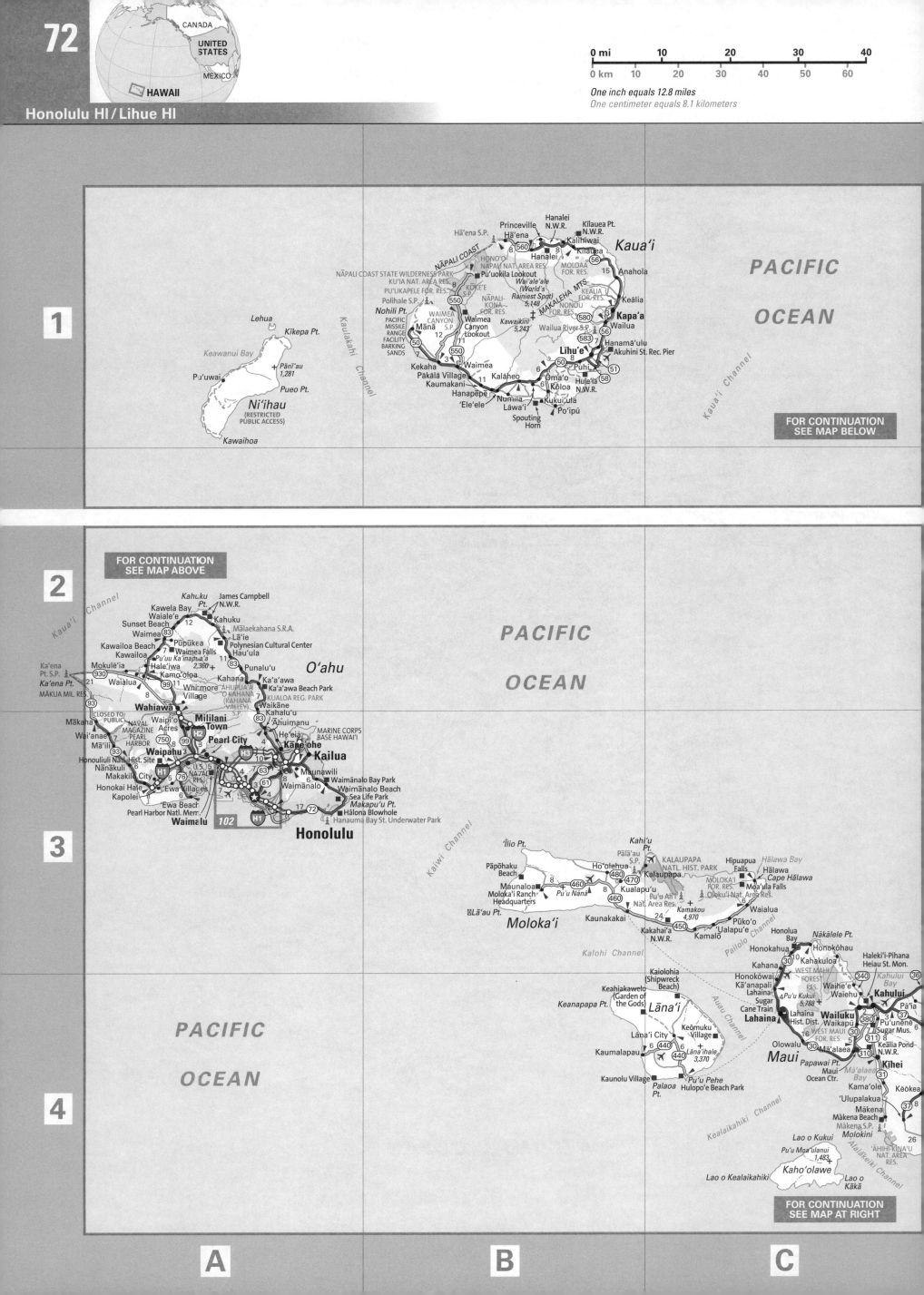

CANADA
UNITED STATES
MEXICO
HAWAII

0 mi   10   20   30   40
0 km   10   20   30   40   50   60

One inch equals 12.8 miles
One centimeter equals 8.1 kilometers

1

FOR CONTINUATION
SEE MAP BELOW

PACIFIC OCEAN

Kaua'i

Princeville · Hanalei · Kīlauea Pt. N.W.R.
Hā'ena S.P. · Hā'ena · Hanalei N.W.R. · Kalihiwai · Kīlauea
560 · 8 · 56
HONO'O NĀPALI NAT. AREA RES. · MOLOAA FOR. RES. · 15 · Anahola
NĀPALI COAST STATE WILDERNESS PARK · Pu'uokila Lookout · KEALIA FOR. RES.
KU'IA NAT. AREA RES. · Wai'ale'ale (World's Rainiest Spot) 5,148
PU'UKAPELE FOR. RES. · NĀPALI-KONA FOR. RES. · NONOU FOR. RES. · 580 · Kapa'a
Polihale S.P. · 550 · KŌKE'E S.P. · Kawaikini 5,243 · Wailua · 56
Nohili Pt. · WAIMEA CANYON S.P. · 583
PACIFIC MISSILE RANGE FACILITY BARKING SANDS · Mānā · 12 · Waimea Canyon Lookout · Wailua River S.P. · Lihu'e
50 · 550 · Hanamā'ulu
Kekaha · Waimea · Akuhini St. Rec. Pier
Pākalā Village · 3 · 50 · Puhi
Kaumakani · Kalāheo · 6 · Ōma'o · 51
Hanapēpē · 11 · Kōloa · Hule'ia N.W.R. · 58
'Ele'ele · Numila · Kukui'ula
Lāwa'i · Po'ipū
Spouting Horn

PACIFIC OCEAN

Kaua'i Channel

2

FOR CONTINUATION
SEE MAP ABOVE

Kaua'i Channel

PACIFIC OCEAN

Kahuku Pt. · James Campbell N.W.R.
Kawela Bay · Kahuku
Waiale'e · 12 · Mālaekahana S.R.A.
Sunset Beach · Lā'ie
Waimea · 83 · Polynesian Cultural Center
Kawailoa Beach · Pūpūkea · Hau'ula
Kawailoa · Waimea Falls · Punalu'u
Mokulē'ia · Pu'uu Ka'inapua'a 2,360 · 83 · *O'ahu*
Hale'iwa · Kahana · Ka'a'awa
Ka'ena Pt. S.P. · 930 · Kamo'oloa · 11 · Ka'a'awa Beach Park
Ka'ena Pt. · 21 · Waialua · 99 · AHUPUA'A O KAHANA (KAHANA VALLEY) · KUALOA REG. PARK
MĀKUA MIL. RES. · 8 · Whitmore Village · 7 · Waikāne
93 · Wahiawā · Kahalu'u
(CLOSED TO PUBLIC) · Waipi'o Acres · Āhuimanu
Mākaha · NAVAL MAGAZINE PEARL HARBOR · 750 · Mililani Town · He'eia · MARINE CORPS BASE HAWAI'I
Wai'anae · 99 · Pearl City · Kāne'ohe
Mā'ili · 93 · Waipahu · H2 · Kailua
Nānākuli · Honouliuli Nat. Hist. Site · H3 · 63 · Maunawili
Makakilo City · U.S. · NAVAL RES. · 61 · Waimānalo
Honokai Hale · H1 · 76 · Ewa Villages · Waimānalo Bay Park
Kapolei · 6 · 'Ewa Beach · Waimānalo Beach
Pearl Harbor Natl. Mem. · Sea Life Park
Waimalu · 102 · H1 · 17 · 72 · Makapu'u Pt.
Hālona Blowhole
Honolulu · Hanauma Bay St. Underwater Park

3

Kaiwi Channel

'Īlio Pt. · Kahi'u Pt. · PĀLĀ'AU S.P. · KALAUPAPA NATL. HIST. PARK
Pāpōhaku Beach · Ho'olehua · 480 · 470 · Kalaupapa · Hīpuapua Falls · Hālawa Bay
Maunaloa · 460 · Kualapu'u · MOLOKA'I FOR. RES. · Hālawa · Cape Hālawa
Moloka'i Ranch Headquarters · 8 · Pu'u Nānā · 460 · Pu'u Ali'i Nat. Area Res. · Moa'ula Falls
Lā'au Pt. · Kamakou 4,970 · 24 · 6 · Waialua
Moloka'i · Kaunakakai · 450 · Pūko'o
Kakahai'a N.W.R. · Kamalō · 'Ualapu'e · Honolua Bay · Nākālele Pt.
Kalohi Channel · Honokōhau
Honokahua · Nākālele Pt.
Kaiolohia (Shipwreck Beach) · 30 · WEST MAUI FOREST RES. · Haleki'i-Pihana Heiau St. Mon.
Keahiakawelo (Garden of the Gods) · Kahana · Kahakuloa · 340
Keanapapa Pt. · Honokōwai · 10 · Kā'anapali · Waihe'e · 36
Lāna'i · Pu'u Kukui 5,788 · Waihe'u · Kahului Bay
Lahaina Sugar Cane Train · Lahaina Hist. Dist. · WEST MAUI FOR. RES. · **Wailuku** · Kahului
Lāna'i City · Keōmuku Village · Lahaina · Waikapū · 380 · Pā'ia
Kaumalapau · 440 · 6 · Lāna'ihale 3,370 · 30 · 3 · Pu'unēnē Sugar Mus.
Kaunolu Village · 440 · Olowalu · Mā'alaea · 311 · Kēālia Pond N.W.R.
Palaoa Pt. · Pu'u Pehe · Hulopo'e Beach Park · *Maui* · 310 · 31 · **Kihei**
Papawai Pt. · Maui Ocean Ctr. · Mā'alaea Bay · Kama'ole · Kēōkea · 37

4

PACIFIC OCEAN

Lao o Kukui · Pu'u Moa'ulanui 1,483 · 'Ulapalakua
Lao o Kealaikahiki · *Kaho'olawe* · Lao o Kāka · Mākena · Mākena Beach · Mākena S.P.
Molokini · 26 · 'ĀHIHI-KINA'U NAT. AREA RES.

Kealaikahiki Channel · *Alalākeiki Channel*

FOR CONTINUATION
SEE MAP AT RIGHT

A   **B**   **C**

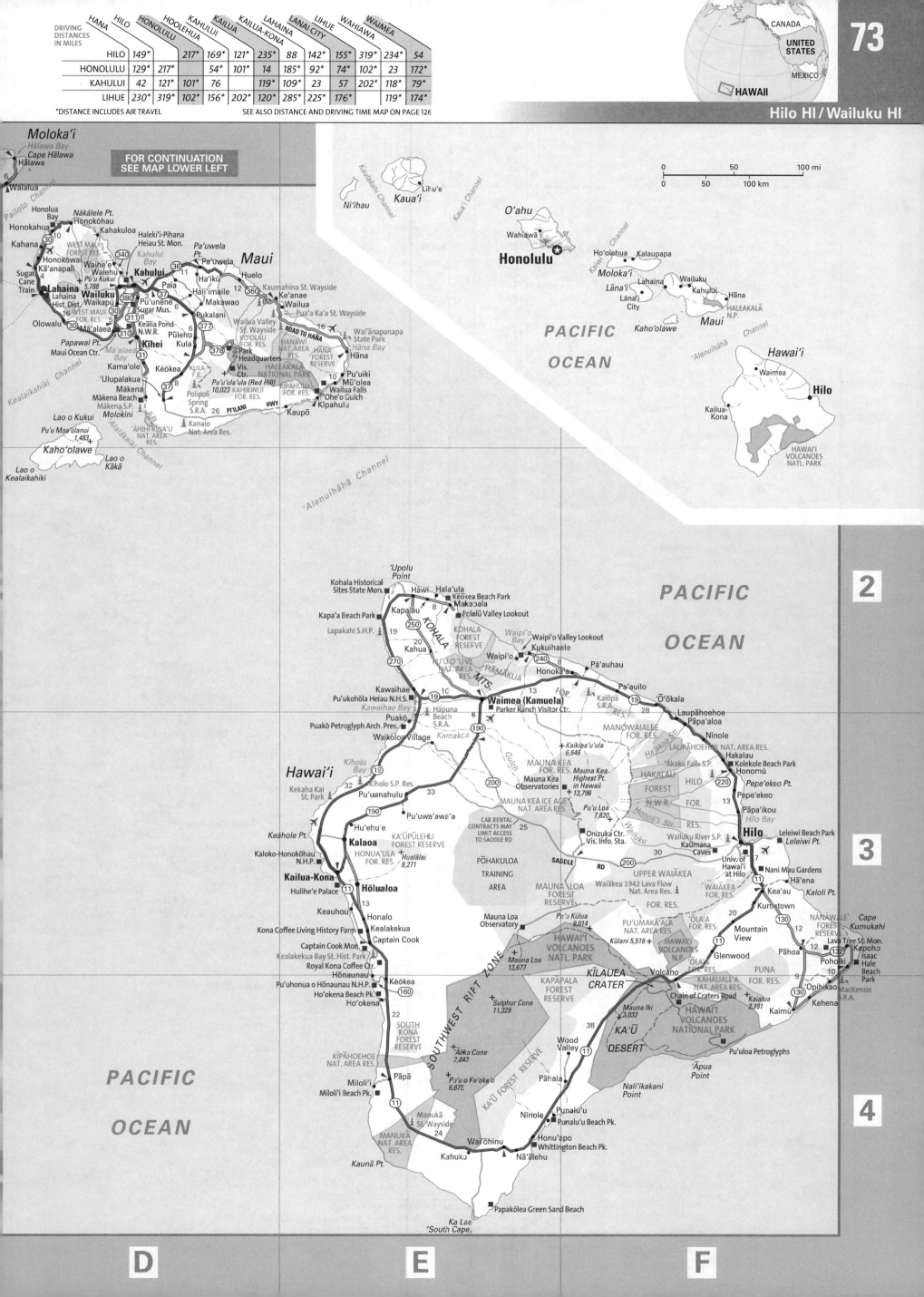

DRIVING DISTANCES IN MILES

	HILO	HONOLULU	KAHULUI	KAILUA	KAILUA-KONA	LAHAINA	LANAI CITY	LIHUE	WAHIAWA	WAIMEA	
HANA	HILO	HONOLULU	HOOLEHUA	KAHULUI	KAILUA	KAILUA-KONA	LAHAINA	LANAI CITY	LIHUE	WAHIAWA	WAIMEA
HILO	149*	217*	169*	121*	235*	88	142*	155*	319*	234*	54
HONOLULU	129*	217*	54*	101*	14	185*	92*	74*	102*	23	172*
KAHULUI	42	121*	101*	76	119*	109*	23	57	202*	118*	79*
LIHUE	230*	319*	102*	156*	202*	120*	285*	225*	176*		119*	174*

*DISTANCE INCLUDES AIR TRAVEL   SEE ALSO DISTANCE AND DRIVING TIME MAP ON PAGE 126

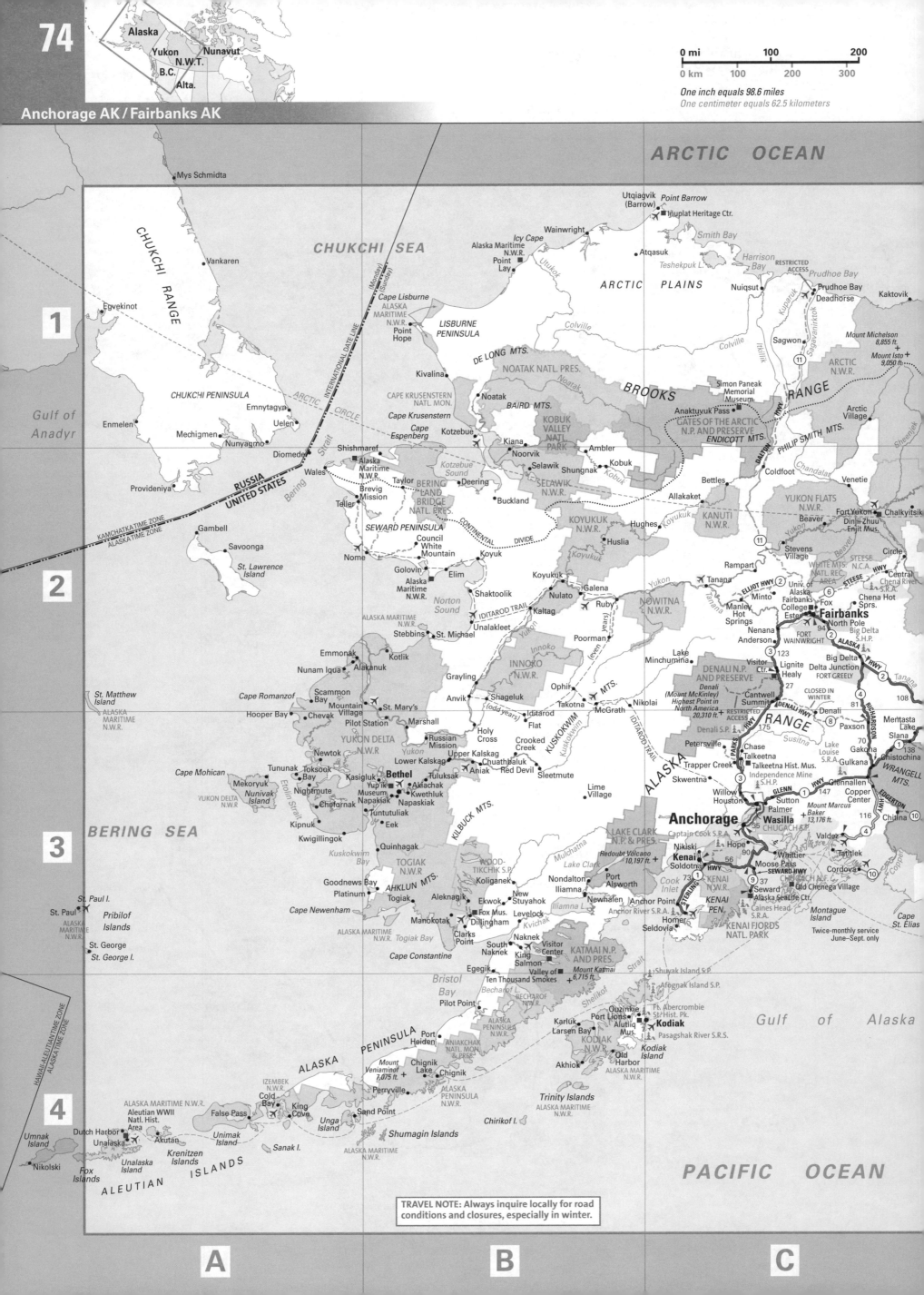

0 mi   100   200

0 km   100   200   300

One inch equals 98.6 miles
One centimeter equals 62.5 kilometers

Alaska
Yukon Nunavut
N.W.T.
B.C.
Alta.

ARCTIC OCEAN

CHUKCHI SEA

CHUKCHI RANGE

Gulf of Anadyr

CHUKCHI PENINSULA

ARCTIC PLAINS

BROOKS RANGE

ARCTIC N.W.R.

NOATAK NATL. PRES.

DE LONG MTS.

BAIRD MTS.

ENDICOTT MTS.

GATES OF THE ARCTIC N.P. AND PRESERVE

KOBUK VALLEY NATL PARK

SELAWIK N.W.R.

KANUTI N.W.R.

YUKON FLATS N.W.R.

KOYUKUK N.W.R.

NOWITNA N.W.R.

INNOKO N.W.R.

SEWARD PENINSULA

BERING LAND BRIDGE NATL. PRES.

BERING SEA

St. Matthew Island

ALASKA MARITIME N.W.R.

Pribilof Islands

YUKON DELTA N.W.R.

TOGIAK N.W.R.

AHKLUN MTS.

KILBUCK MTS.

WOOD-TIKCHIK S.P.

KUSKOKWIM MTS.

DENALI N.P. AND PRESERVE

Denali (Mount McKinley) Highest Point in North America 20,310 ft.

ALASKA RANGE

WRANGELL MTS.

CHUGACH MTS.

LAKE CLARK N.P. & PRES.

KATMAI N.P. AND PRES.

ALASKA PENINSULA

KODIAK N.W.R.

Gulf of Alaska

Bristol Bay

KENAI FJORDS NATL PARK

KENAI PEN.

ALEUTIAN ISLANDS

PACIFIC OCEAN

ARCTIC OCEAN

Utqiagvik (Barrow) Point Barrow
Inuplat Heritage Ctr.
Wainwright
Icy Cape
Atqasuk
Smith Bay
Alaska Maritime N.W.R.
Point Lay
Teshekpuk L.
Harrison Bay
RESTRICTED ACCESS
Prudhoe Bay
Nuiqsut
Prudhoe Bay
Deadhorse
Kaktovik
Cape Lisburne
Sagwon
Mount Michelson 8,855 ft.
Mount Isto 9,050 ft.
Point Hope
LISBURNE PENINSULA
Colville
Mys Schmidta
Vankaren
Egvekinot
Kivalina
Noatak
Simon Paneak Memorial Museum
Anaktuvuk Pass
Arctic Village
CAPE KRUSENSTERN NATL. MON.
Kotzebue
Kiana
Noorvik
Ambler
Kobuk
Shungnak
Bettles
Coldfoot
Venetie
Emnytagyn
Cape Krusenstern
Cape Espenberg
Selawik
Allakaket
Enmelen
Mechigmen
Uelen
Shishmaref
Kotzebue Sound
Hughes
Fort Yukon
Beaver
Dinjii Zhuu Enjit Mus.
Chalkyitsik
Nunyagmo
Diomede
Wales
Alaska Maritime N.W.R.
Taylor
Deering
Buckland
Huslia
Circle
Providéniya
Teller
Brevig Mission
SEWARD PENINSULA
Council White Mountain
Koyuk
Galena
Koyukuk
Rampart
Stevens Village
Central
Gambell
Savoonga
St. Lawrence Island
Nome
Golovin
Elim
Nulato
Ruby
Tanana
Minto
Fox
Chena Hot Sprs.
Shaktoolik
Kaltag
Poorman
College
Fairbanks
North Pole
Stebbins
St. Michael
Unalakleet
Galena
McGrath
Nenana
Anderson
Big Delta
Emmonak
Kotlik
Grayling
Anvik
Shageluk
Ophir
Nikolai
Lake Minchumina
Healy
Delta Junction
Nunam Iqua
Alakanuk
Takotna
Lignite
FORT GREELY
Scammon Bay
Mountain Village
St. Mary's
Iditarod
Flat
Cantwell
Denali
Paxson
Cape Romanzof
Hooper Bay
Chevak
Pilot Station
Marshall
Holy Cross
Crooked Creek
Petersville
Chase
Talkeetna
Mentasta Lake
Slana
Gakona
Chistochina
Russian Mission
Upper Kalskag
Chuathbaluk
Red Devil
Lime Village
Trapper Creek
Talkeetna Hist. Mus.
Gulkana
Newtok
Lower Kalskag
Aniak
Sleetmute
Skwentna
Independence Mine
Glennallen
Copper Center
Chitina
Cape Mohican
Tununak
Toksook Bay
Kasigluk
Bethel
Tuluksak
Willow
Houston
Palmer
Mount Marcus Baker 13,176 ft.
Mekoryuk
Nightmute
Napakiak
Napaskiak
Anchorage
Wasilla
Sutton
Valdez
Chefornak
Tuntutuliak
Eek
Kenai
Soldotna
Hope
Moose Pass
Whittier
Tatitlek
Kipnuk
Nikiski
Seward
Cordova
Kwigillingok
Quinhagak
Koliganek
New Stuyahok
Nondalton
Iliamna
Port Alsworth
Newhalen
Anchor Point
Homer
Seldovia
Old Chenega Village
Goodnews Bay
Platinum
Togiak
Aleknagik
Ekwok
Levelock
Manokotak
Dillingham
Clarks Point
Naknek
South Naknek
King Salmon
Egegik
Pilot Point
Mount Katmai 6,715 ft.
Valley of Ten Thousand Smokes
Shuyak Island S.P.
Afognak Island S.P.
Ouzinkie
Port Lions
Kodiak
Karluk
Larsen Bay
Old Harbor
Akhiok
Port Heiden
Mount Veniaminof 7,075 ft.
Chignik Lake
Chignik
Perryville
Sand Point
Trinity Islands
Cold Bay
King Cove
False Pass
St. Paul I.
St. Paul
St. George
St. George I.
Dutch Harbor
Unalaska
Akutan
Nikolski
Fox Islands

ARCTIC CIRCLE

CONTINENTAL DIVIDE

IDITAROD TRAIL

DALTON HWY

RICHARDSON HWY

DENALI HWY

PARKS HWY

STEESE HWY

ELLIOT HWY

GLENN HWY

SEWARD HWY

STERLING HWY

EDGERTON HWY

KAMCHATKA TIME ZONE
ALASKA TIME ZONE

HAWAII-ALEUTIAN TIME ZONE
ALASKA TIME ZONE

RUSSIA
UNITED STATES

Bering Strait

Norton Sound

Yukon

Kuskokwim

Cook Inlet

Susitna

Twice-monthly service June–Sept. only

TRAVEL NOTE: Always inquire locally for road conditions and closures, especially in winter.

A   B   C

1   2   3   4

DRIVING DISTANCES IN MILES	ANCHORAGE, AK	DAWSON CREEK, BC	DENALI NP, AK	FAIRBANKS, AK	HOMER, AK	JUNEAU, AK	PRINCE GEORGE, BC	PRINCE RUPERT, BC	SKAGWAY, AK	TOK, AK	WHITEHORSE, YT	YELLOWKNIFE, NT
ANCHORAGE, AK		1516	275	378	225	841*	1679	1514	807	323	697	1844
DAWSON CREEK, BC	1516		1503	1400	1740	963*	224	625	862	1193	819	741
FAIRBANKS, AK	378	1400	103		603	726*	1564	1398	691	207	581	1729
WHITEHORSE, YT	697	819	684	581	921	211*	982	817	110	374		1147

*DISTANCE INCLUDES FERRY TRAVEL   SEE ALSO DISTANCE AND DRIVING TIME MAP ON PAGE 126

Distances in the U.S. shown in miles.
Distances in Canada shown in kilometers.

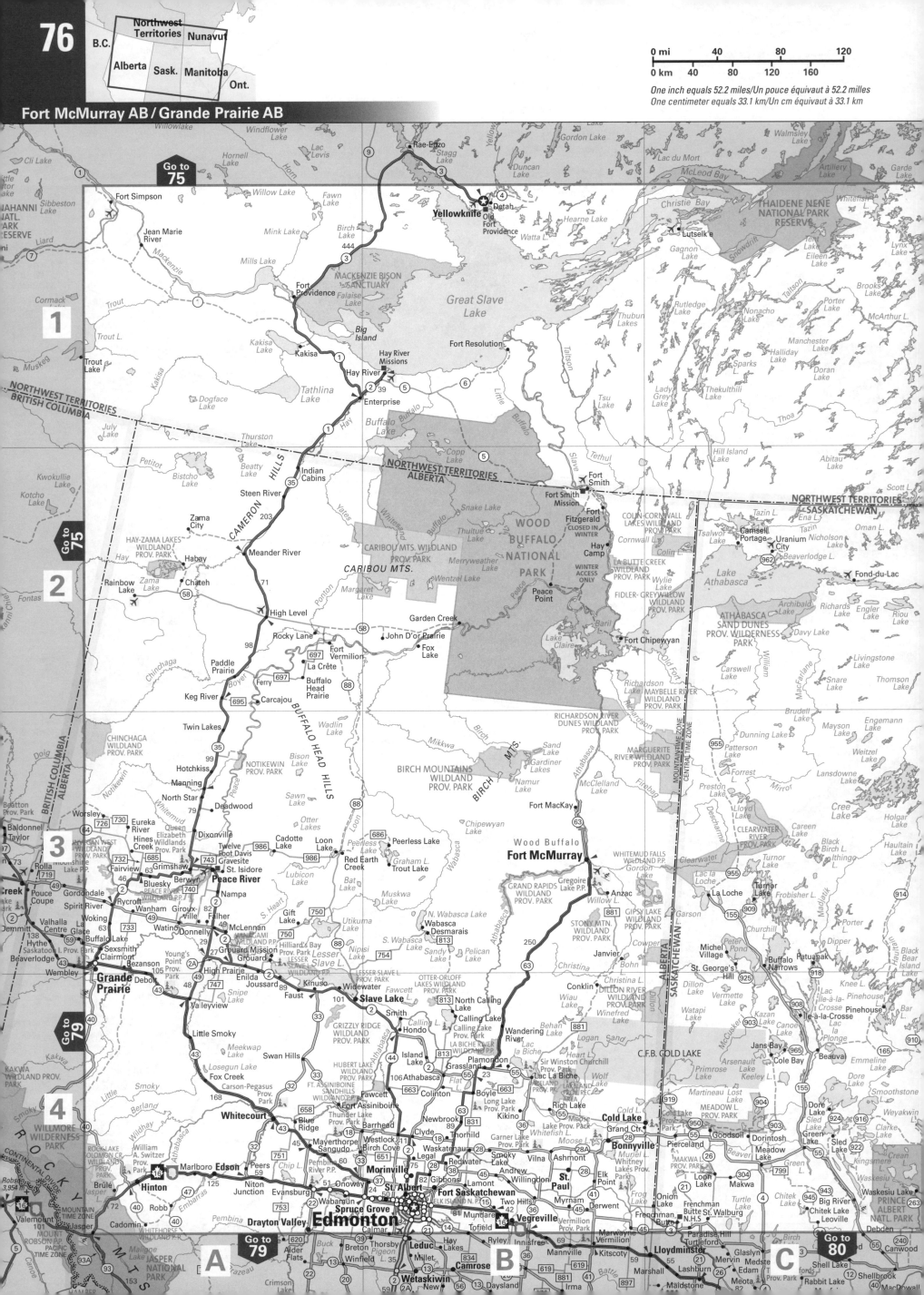

DRIVING DISTANCES IN KM /
DISTANCES ROUTIÈRES EN KM

	FLIN FLON, MB	FORT MCMURRAY, AB	GRANDE PRAIRIE, AB	GRAND RAPIDS, MB	JASPER, AB	LA RONGE, SK	PEACE RIVER, AB	PRINCE ALBERT, SK	SLAVE LAKE, AB	THOMPSON, MB	YELLOWKNIFE NT
EDMONTON, AB	955	439	462	1172	367	830	484	577	251	1302	1405
JASPER, AB	367	1312	796	397	1530	1187	578	932	464	1657	1532
PRINCE ALBERT, SK	577	375	944	1035	604	932	238	1055	822	729	2065
THOMPSON, MB	1302	380	1668	1760	328	1657	704	1779	729	1547	2790

SEE ALSO DISTANCE AND DRIVING TIME MAP ON PAGE 126 / VOIR AUSSI CARTE DES DISTANCES ET DES TEMPS DE PARCOURS PAGE 126

DISTANCES IN CANADA SHOWN IN KILOMETERS

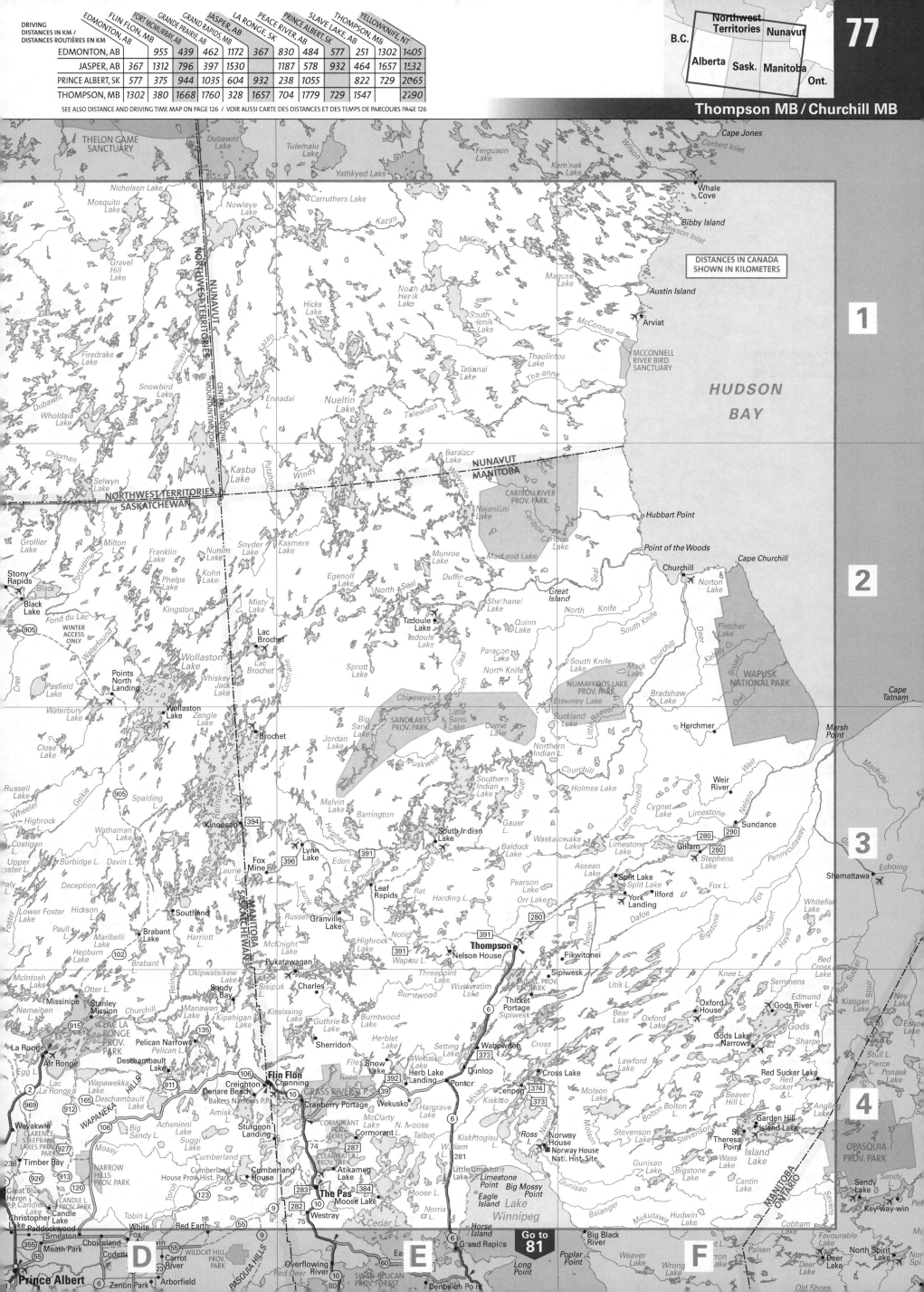

One inch equals 40.6 miles/Un pouce équivaut à 40.6 milles
One centimeter equals 25.7 km/Un cm équivaut à 25.7 km

0 mi 20   40   60   80
0 km 20 40 60 80 100

FOR CONTINUATION
SEE INSET BELOW

Go to
75

Go to
8

DISTANCES IN CANADA
SHOWN IN KILOMETERS

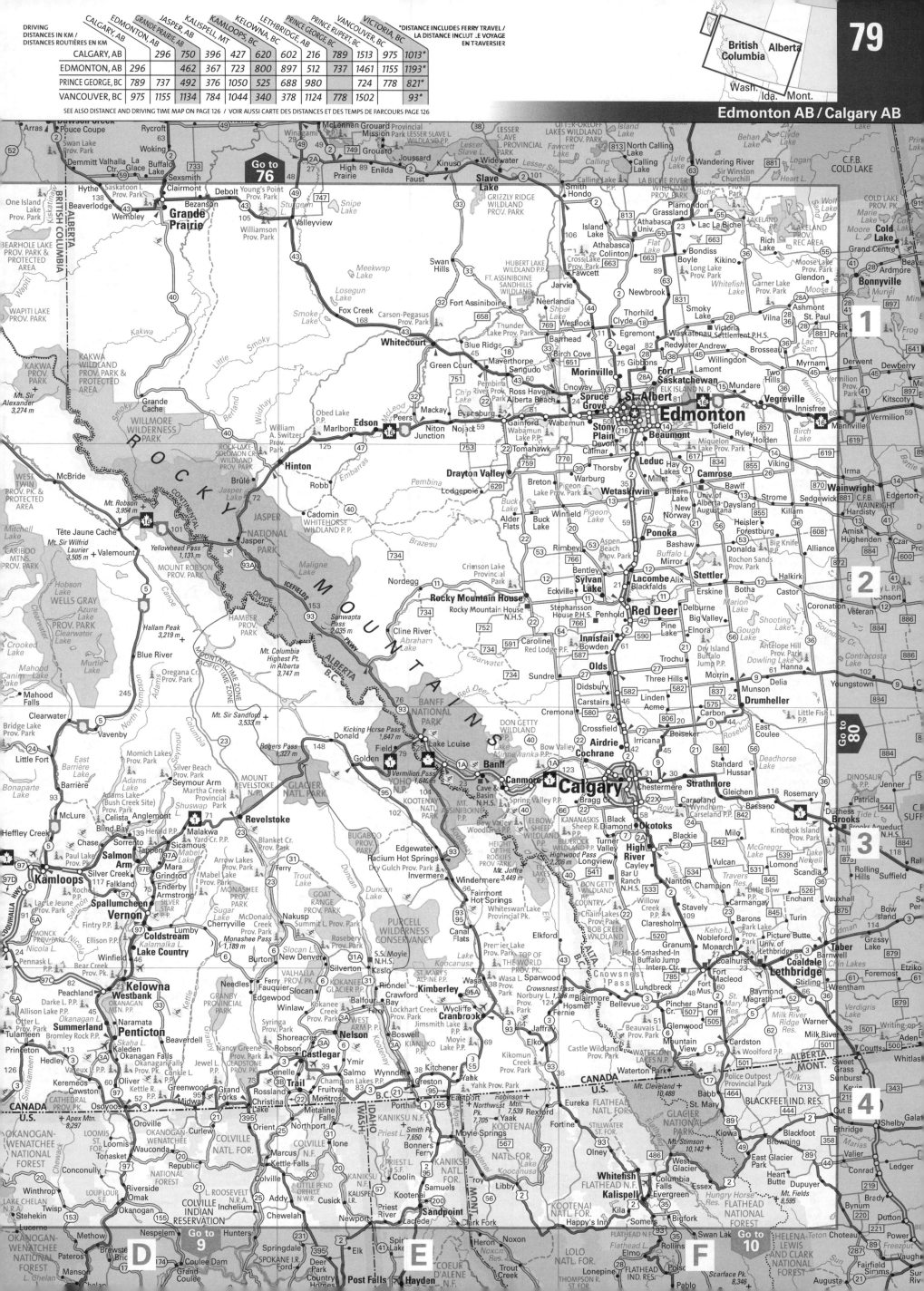

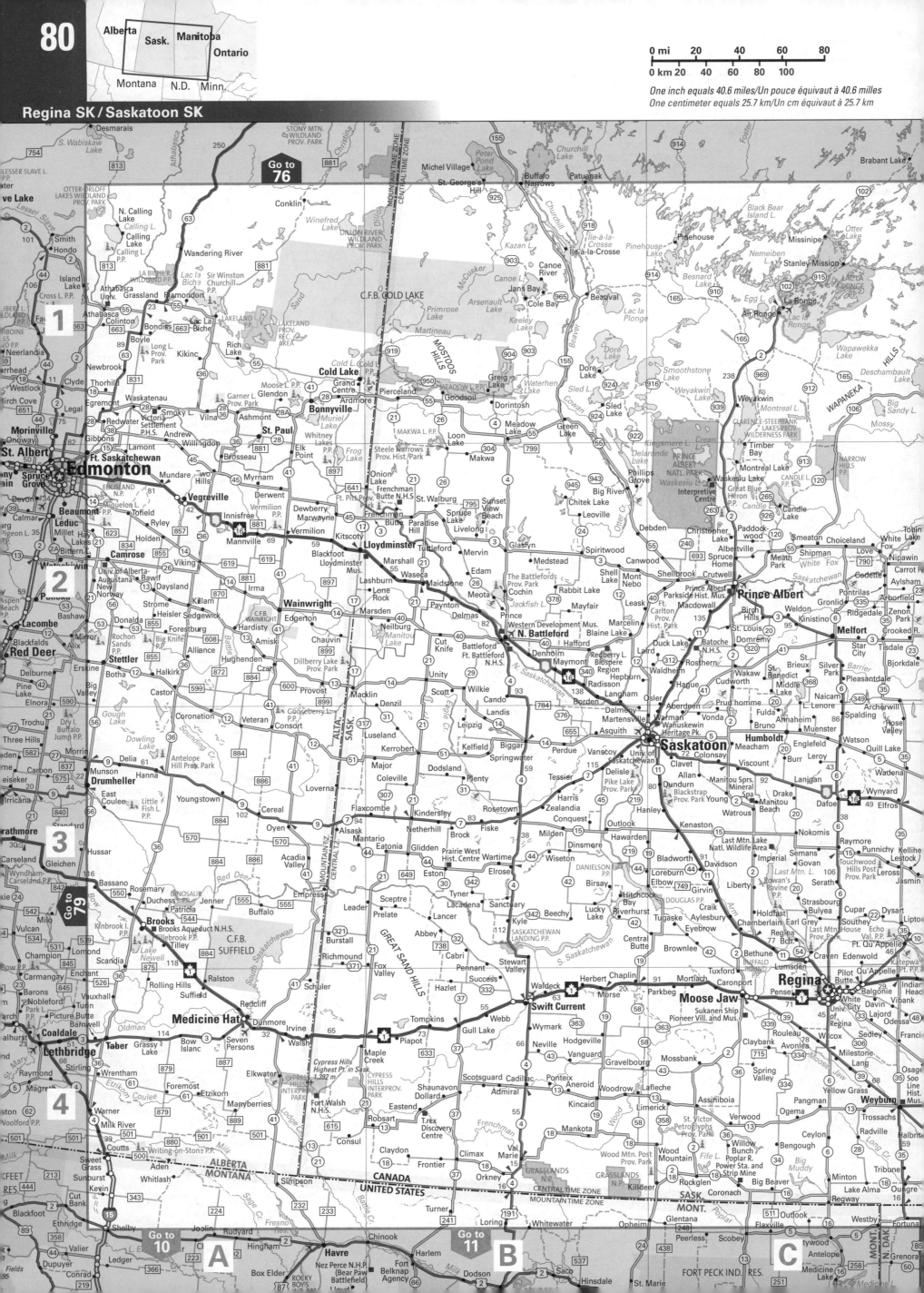

80

Alberta Sask. Manitoba Ontario
Montana N.D. Minn.

Regina SK / Saskatoon SK

0 mi   20   40   60   80
0 km 20   40   60   80   100

One inch equals 40.6 miles/Un pouce équivaut à 40.6 miles
One centimeter equals 25.7 km/Un cm équivaut à 25.7 km

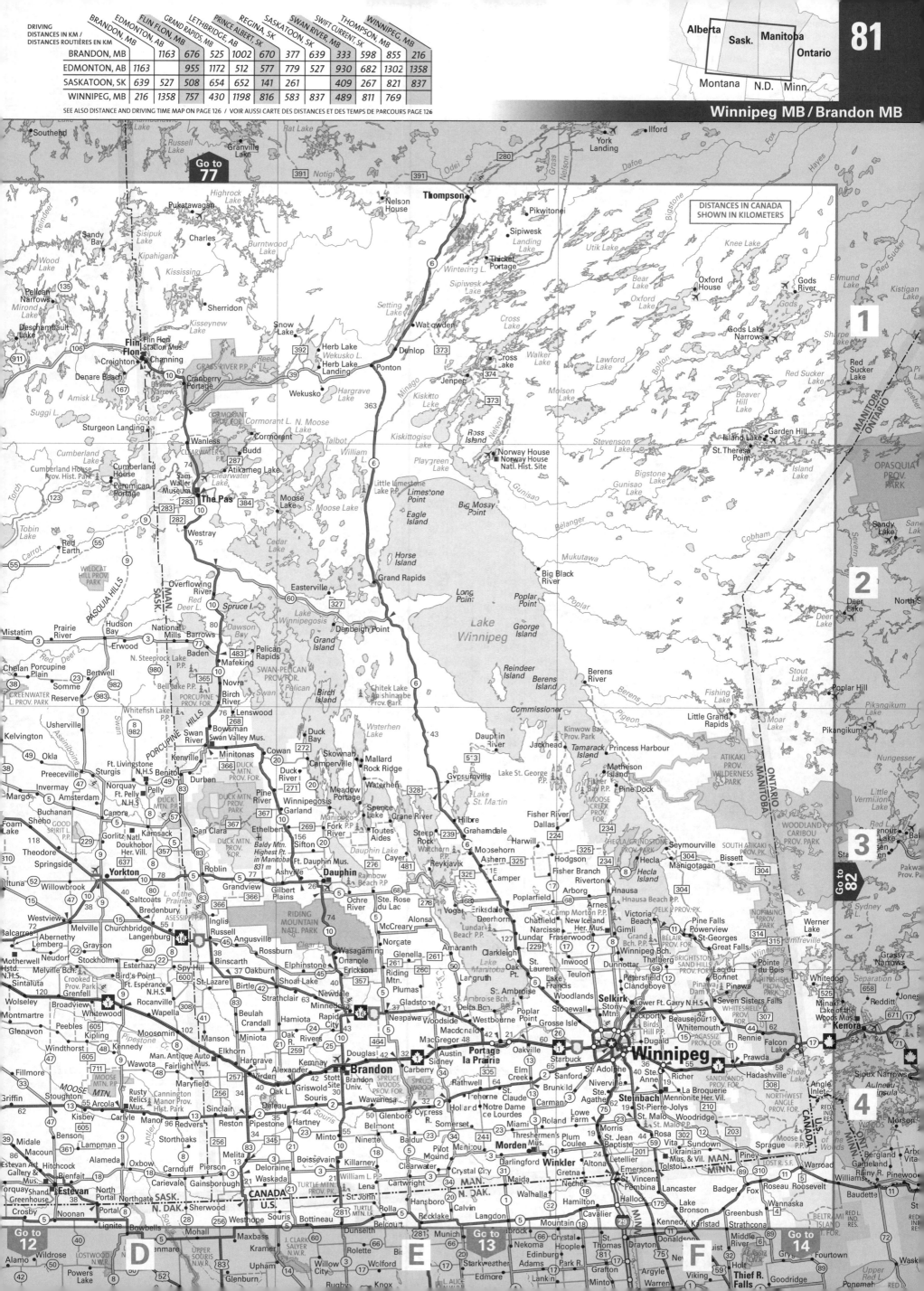

	BRANDON, MB	EDMONTON, AB	FLIN FLON, MB	GRAND RAPIDS, MB	LETHBRIDGE, AB	PRINCE ALBERT, SK	REGINA, SK	SASKATOON, SK	SWAN RIVER, MB	SWIFT CURRENT, SK	THOMPSON, MB	WINNIPEG, MB
BRANDON, MB		1163	676	525	1002	670	377	639	333	598	855	216
EDMONTON, AB	1163		955	1172	512	577	779	527	930	682	1302	1358
SASKATOON, SK	639	527	508	654	652	141	261		409	267	821	837
WINNIPEG, MB	216	1358	757	430	1198	816	583	837	489	811	769	

Alberta | Sask. | Manitoba | Ontario
Montana | N.D. | Minn.

DISTANCES IN CANADA
SHOWN IN KILOMETERS

Go to 77

Go to 82

Go to 12

Go to 13

Go to 14

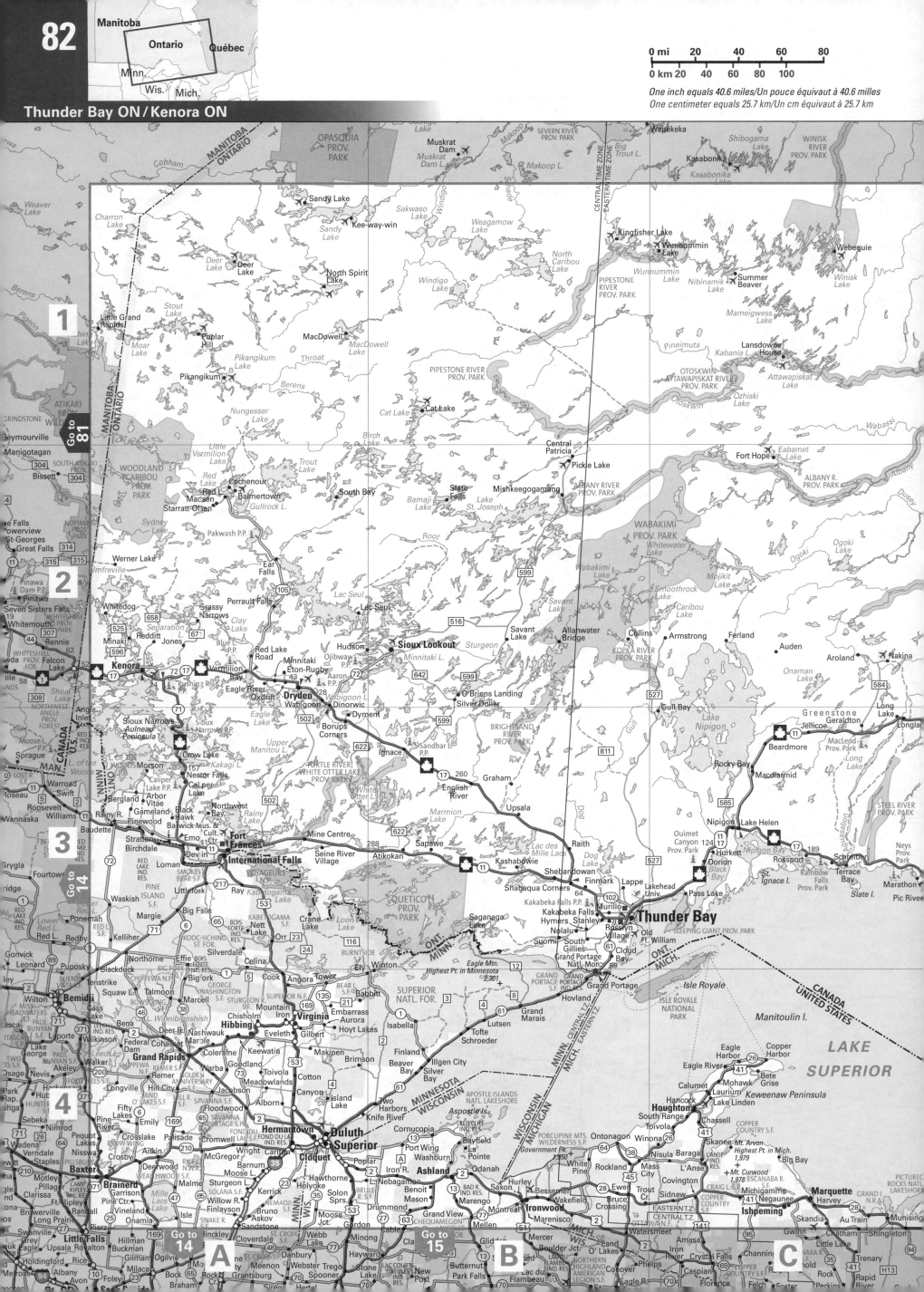

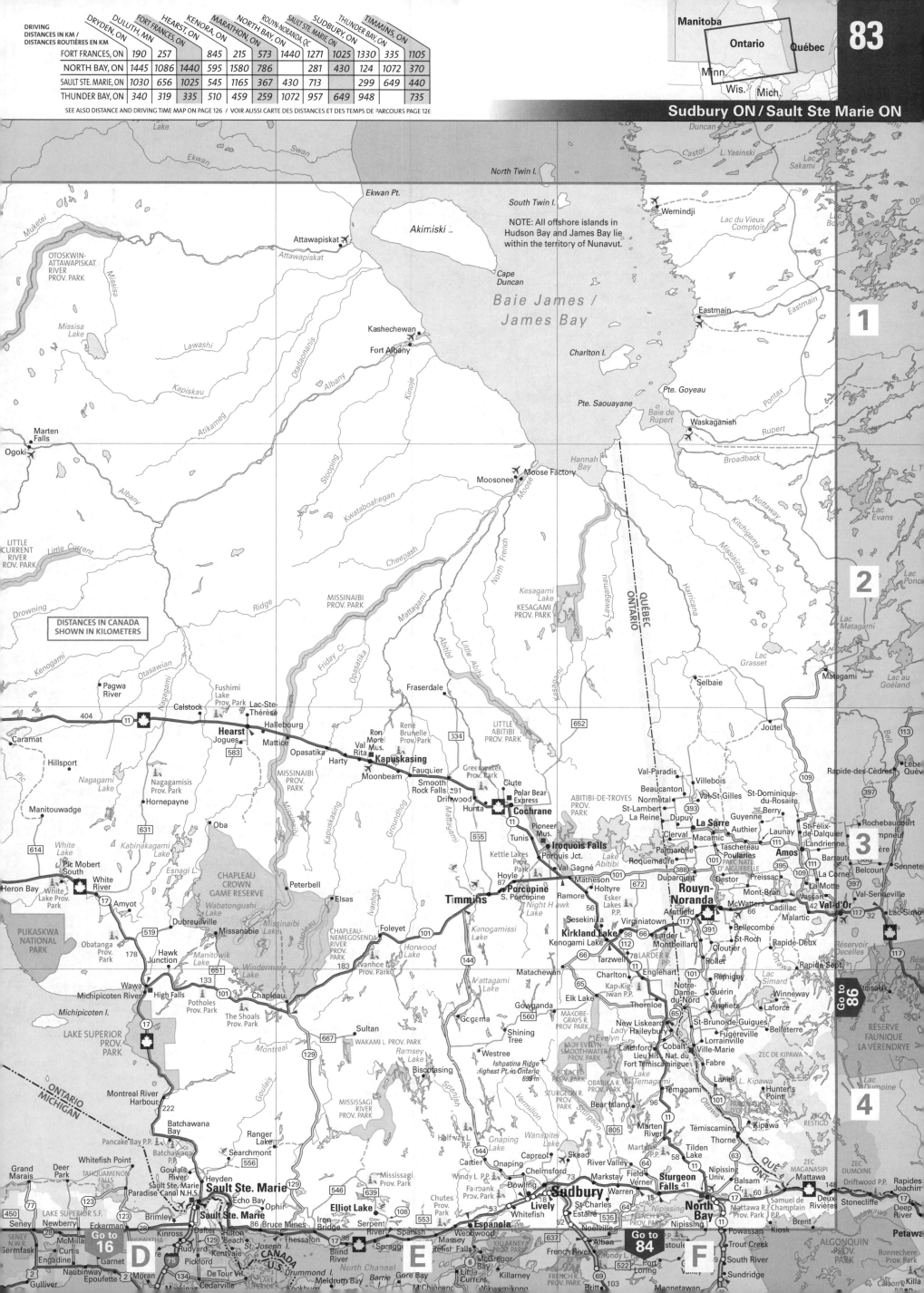

	DULUTH, MN	FORT FRANCES, ON	HEARST, ON	KENORA, ON	MARATHON, ON	NORTH BAY, ON	ROUYN-NORANDA, QC	SAULT STE. MARIE, ON	SUDBURY, ON	THUNDER BAY, ON	TIMMINS, ON	
FORT FRANCES, ON	190	257	845	215	573	1440	1271	1025	1330	335	1105	
NORTH BAY, ON	1445	1086	1440	595	1580	786		281	430	124	1072	370
SAULT STE. MARIE, ON	1030	656	1025	545	1165	367	430		713		299	649	440
THUNDER BAY, ON	340	319	335	510	459	259	1072	957	649	948		735

SEE ALSO DISTANCE AND DRIVING TIME MAP ON PAGE 126 / VOIR AUSSI CARTE DES DISTANCES ET DES TEMPS DE PARCOURS PAGE 126

NOTE: All offshore islands in
Hudson Bay and James Bay lie
within the territory of Nunavut.

Baie James /
James Bay

DISTANCES IN CANADA
SHOWN IN KILOMETERS

DRIVING DISTANCES IN KM / DISTANCES ROUTIÈRES EN KM

	BARRIE, ON	DETROIT, MI	KINGSTON, ON	LONDON, ON	MONTRÉAL, QC	NIAGARA FALLS ON	NORTH BAY, ON	OTTAWA, ON	SAULT STE. MARIE, ON	SUDBURY, ON	SYRACUSE, NY	TORONTO, ON
DETROIT, MI	436		613	212	899	389	663	807	563	741	692	573
KINGSTON, ON	330	613		434	290	390	460	179	875	600	211	251
MONTRÉAL, QC	610	899	290	715		670	544	194	967	685	404	531
TORONTO, ON	105	373	251	183	531	145	336	431	674	407	393	

SEE ALSO DISTANCE AND DRIVING TIME MAP ON PAGE 126 / VOIR AUSSI CARTE DES DISTANCES ET DES TEMPS DE PARCOURS PAGE 126

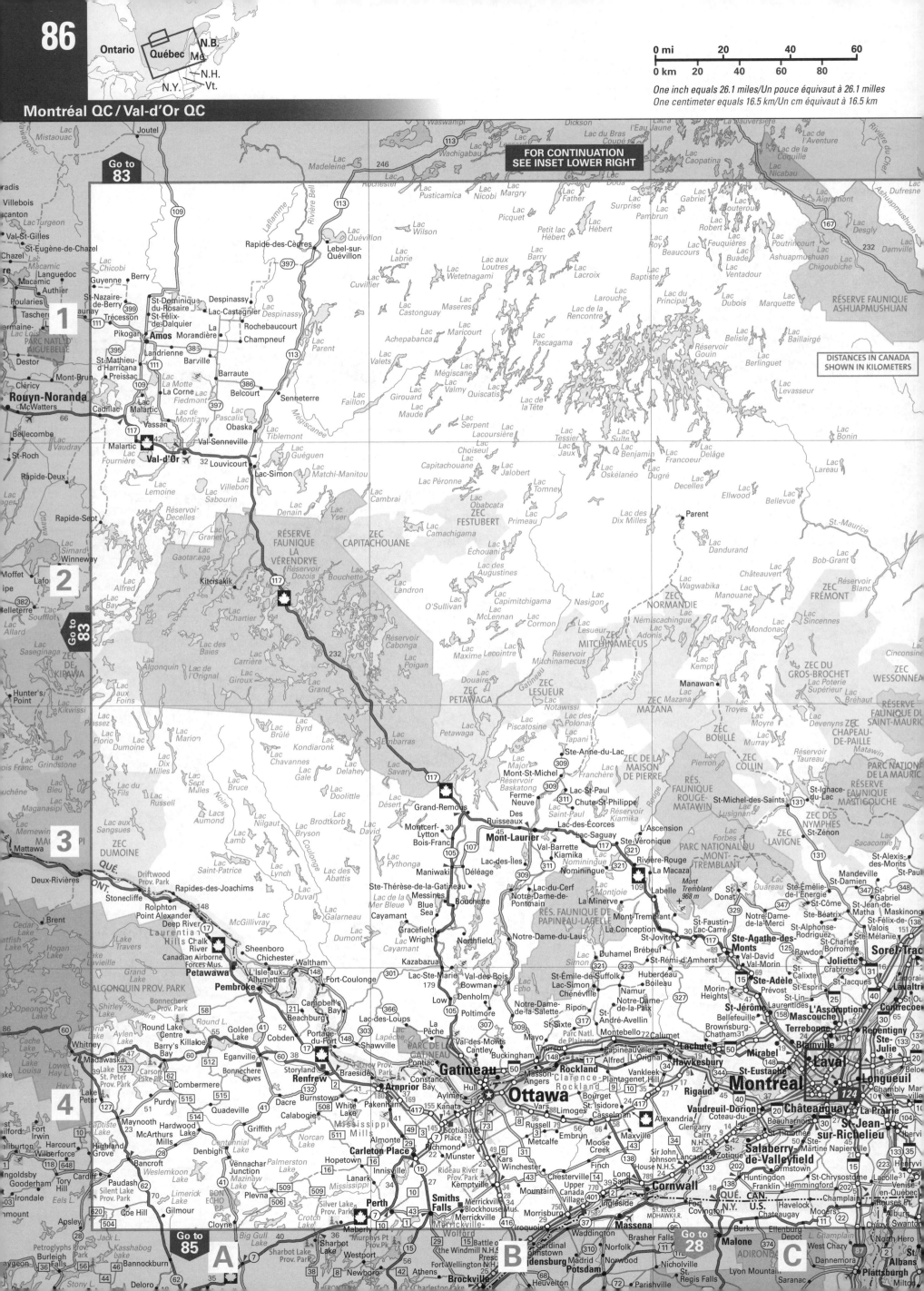

DRIVING DISTANCES IN KM / DISTANCES ROUTIÈRES EN KM	BAIE-COMEAU, QC	CHIBOUGAMAU, QC	CHICOUTIMI, QC	EDMUNDSTON, NB	MONTRÉAL, QC	OTTAWA, ON	PEMBROKE, ON	QUÉBEC, QC	RIMOUSKI, QC	SHERBROOKE, QC	TROIS-RIVIÈRES, QC	VAL-D'OR, QC	*DISTANCE INCLUDES FERRY TRAVEL / LA DISTANCE INCLUT LE VOYAGE EN TRAVERSIER
MONTRÉAL, QC	663	700	461	547		194	345	250	535	143	146	531	
QUÉBEC, QC	400	515	211	317	250	444	566		305	233	135	771	
RIMOUSKI, QC	93*	608*	264*	154	535	711	849	305		510	441	1060	
VAL-D'OR, QC	1183	396	747	1012	531	403	532	771	1060	677	638		

SEE ALSO DISTANCE AND DRIVING TIME MAP ON PAGE 126 / VOIR AUSSI CARTE DES DISTANCES ET DES TEMPS DE PARCOURS PAGE 126

Nfld. & Lab.
P.E.I.
N.B.
Québec   Me.
Nova Scotia

FOR CONTINUATION SEE INSET LOWER RIGHT

0 mi   20   40   60
0 km   20   40   60   80

One inch equals 26.1 miles/Un pouce équivaut à 26.1 milles
One centimeter equals 16.5 km/Un cm équivaut à 16.5 km

QUÉBEC

CANADA U.S.

1

2
Go to 30

3

4

A   B   C

Go to 87

Gulf of Maine

Bay of Fundy

NEW BRUNSWICK
NOVA SCOTIA

Chignecto Bay

Baie des Chaleurs / Chaleur Bay

HEURE DE L'EST/EASTERN TIME ZONE
HEURE DE L'ATLANTIQUE/ATLANTIC TIME ZONE

Edmundston
Grand Falls (Grand-Sault)
Campbellton
Bathurst
Miramichi
Moncton
Dieppe
Riverview
Sackville
Amherst
Fredericton
Oromocto
Saint John
Rothesay
Quispamsis
Sussex
Kentville
Bridgewater
Yarmouth
Bangor
Brewer
Old Town
Orono
Belfast
Rockland
Presque Isle
Caribou
Houlton
Woodstock
Rivière-du-Loup

Mt. Carleton Highest Pt. in New Brunswick 817 m
MT. CARLETON PROV. PARK

Gulf of Maine

to Portland, Maine (Seasonal)

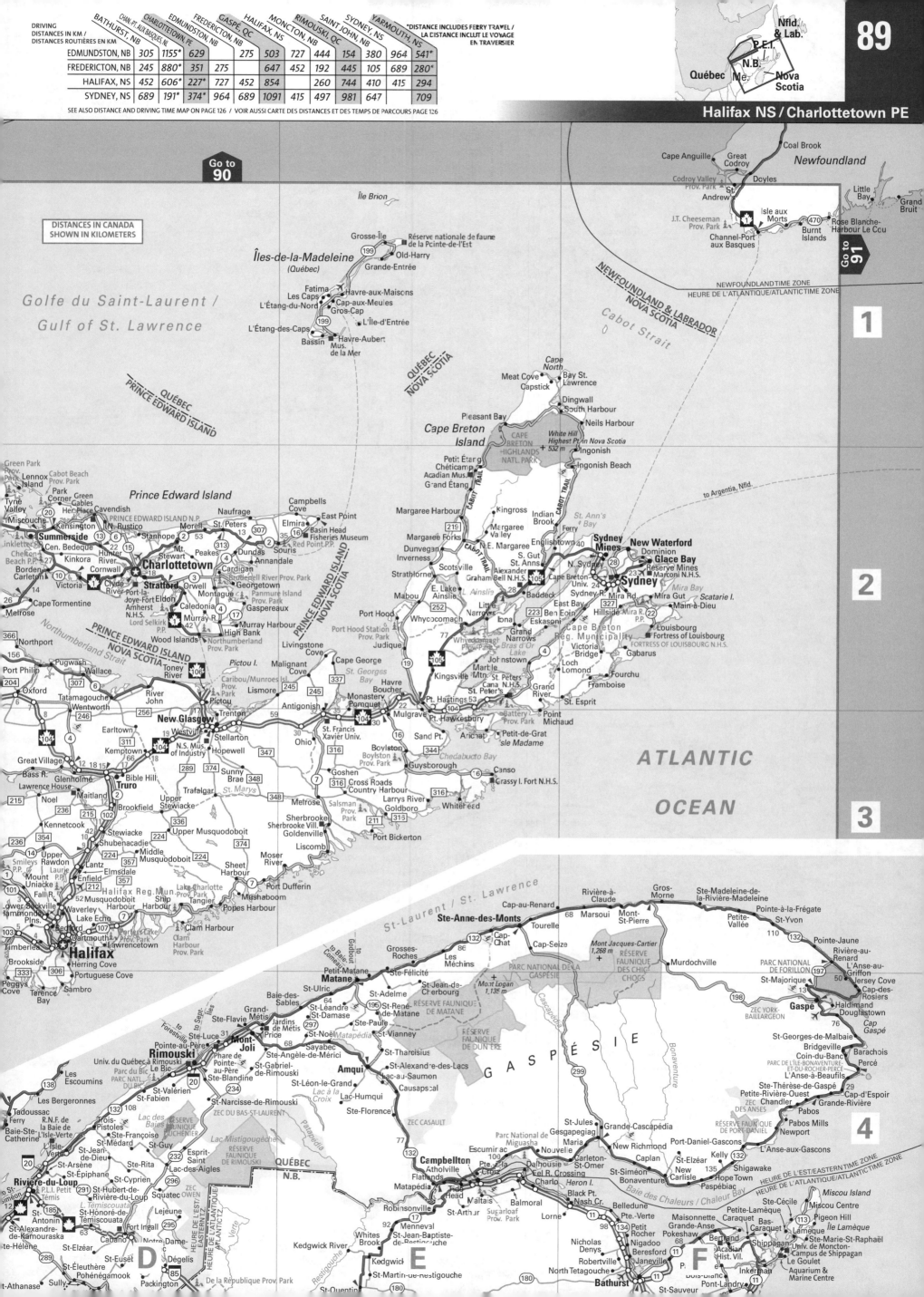

DRIVING DISTANCES IN KM / DISTANCES ROUTIÈRES EN KM

*DISTANCE INCLUDES FERRY TRAVEL / LA DISTANCE INCLUT LE VOYAGE EN TRAVERSIER

	BATHURST, NB	CHAN-PT AUX BASQUES, N.	CHARLOTTETOWN, PE	EDMUNDSTON, NB	FREDERICTON, NB	GASPE, QC	HALIFAX, NS	MONCTON, NB	RIMOUSKI, QC	SAINT JOHN, NB	SYDNEY, NS	YARMOUTH, NS
EDMUNDSTON, NB	305	1155*	629		275	503	727	444	154	380	964	541*
FREDERICTON, NB	245	880*	351	275		647	452	192	445	105	689	280*
HALIFAX, NS	452	606*	227*	727	452	854		260	744	410	415	290
SYDNEY, NS	689	191*	374*	964	689	1091	415	497	981	647		709

SEE ALSO DISTANCE AND DRIVING TIME MAP ON PAGE 126 / VOIR AUSSI CARTE DES DISTANCES ET DES TEMPS DE PARCOURS PAGE 126

DISTANCES IN CANADA SHOWN IN KILOMETERS

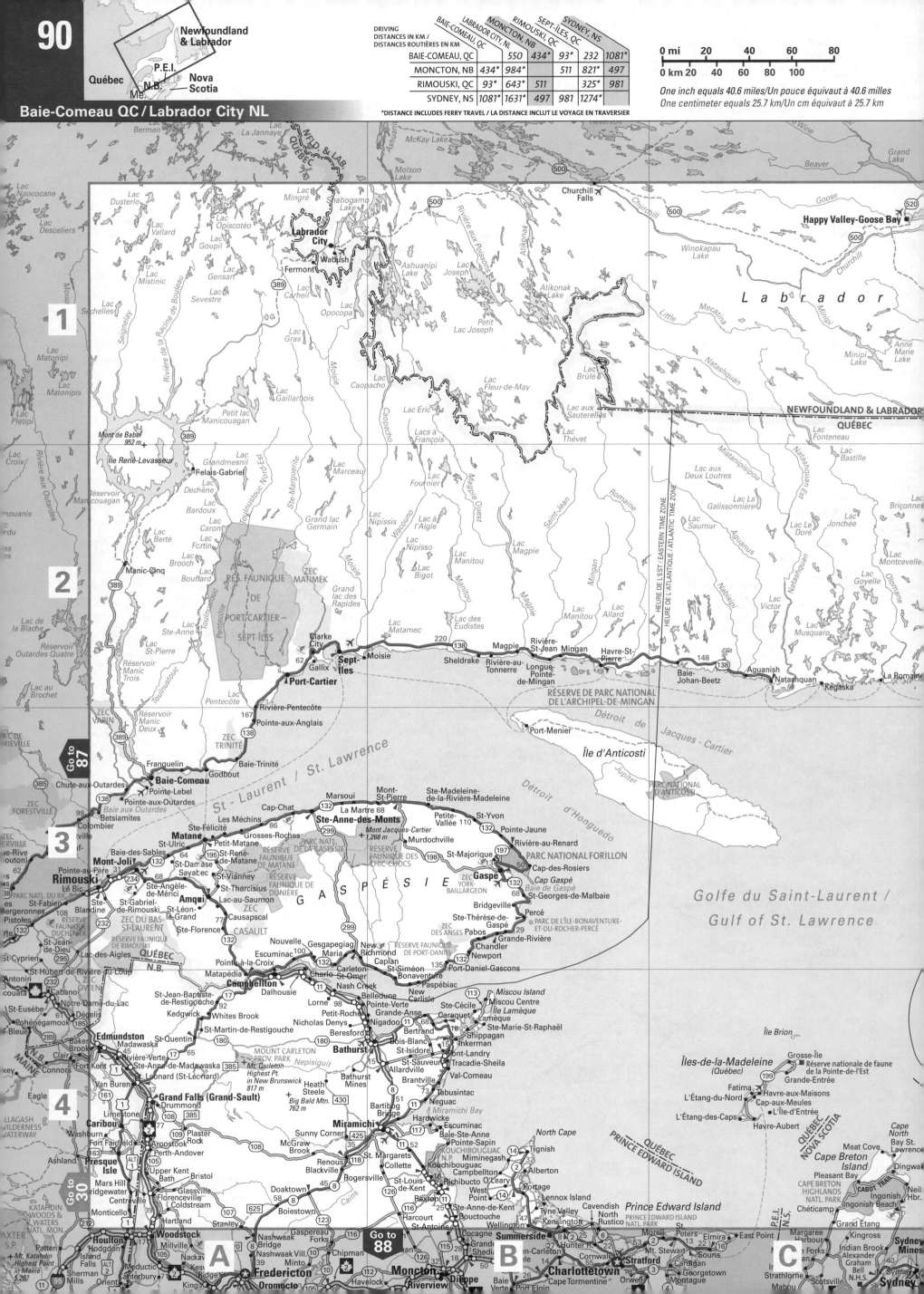

DRIVING DISTANCES IN KM / DISTANCES ROUTIÈRES EN KM

	BAIE-COMEAU, QC	LABRADOR CITY, NL	MONCTON, NB	RIMOUSKI, QC	SEPT-ÎLES, QC	SYDNEY, NS
BAIE-COMEAU, QC		550	434*	93*	232	1081*
MONCTON, NB	434*	984*		511	821*	497
RIMOUSKI, QC	93*	643*	511		325*	981
SYDNEY, NS	1081*	1631*	497	981	1274*	

*DISTANCE INCLUDES FERRY TRAVEL / LA DISTANCE INCLUT LE VOYAGE EN TRAVERSIER

0 mi 20 40 60 80
0 km 20 40 60 80 100

One inch equals 40.6 miles/Un pouce équivaut à 40.6 milles
One centimeter equals 25.7 km/Un cm équivaut à 25.7 km

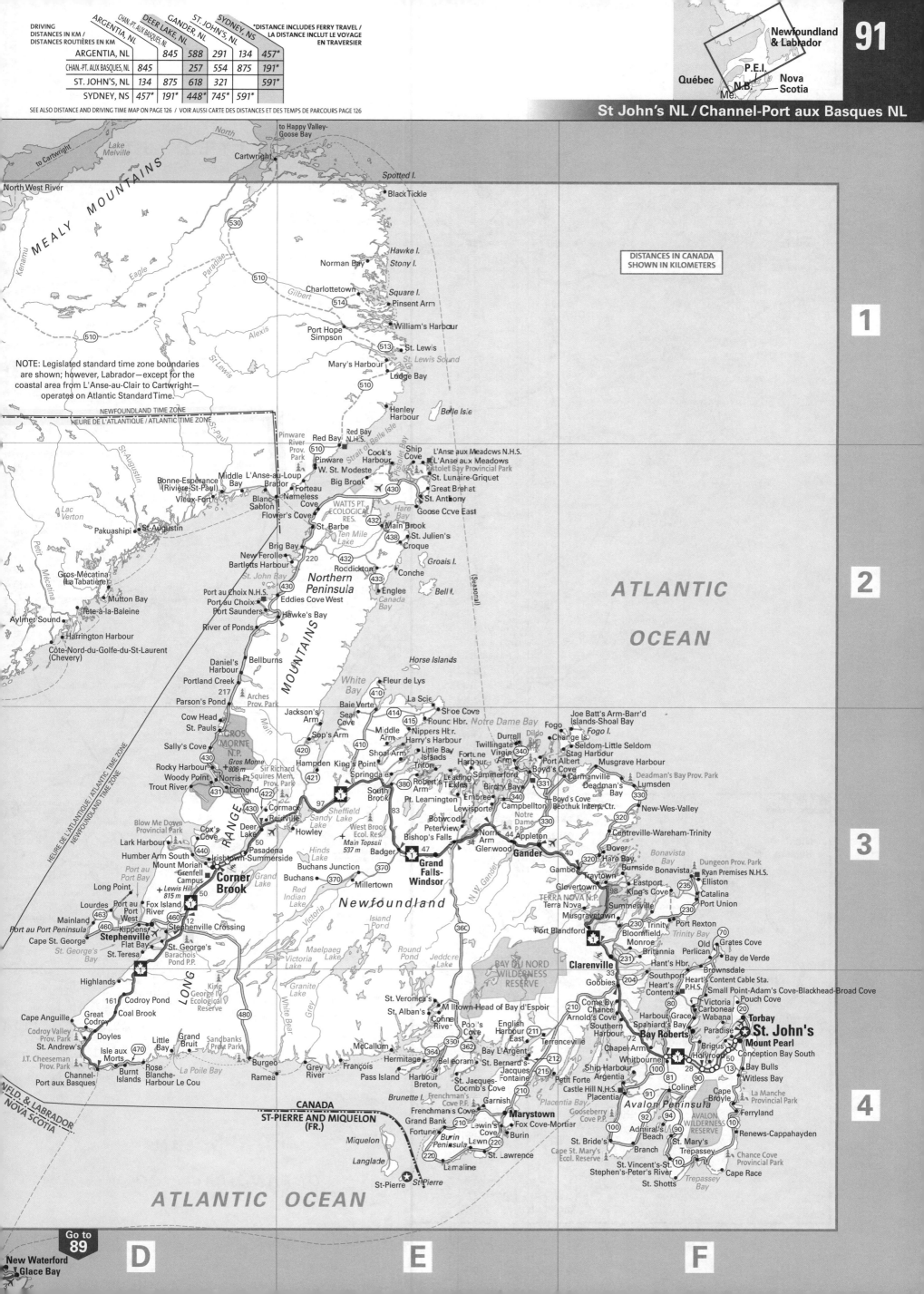

Newfoundland & Labrador

Québec P.E.I. Nova Scotia N.B.

DISTANCES IN CANADA SHOWN IN KILOMETERS

NOTE: Legislated standard time zone boundaries are shown; however, Labrador—except for the coastal area from L'Anse-au-Clair to Cartwright—operates on Atlantic Standard Time.

ATLANTIC OCEAN

ATLANTIC OCEAN

Newfoundland

CANADA
ST-PIERRE AND MIQUELON (FR.)

NFLD. & LABRADOR / NOVA SCOTIA

Go to 89

New Waterford Glace Bay

D   E   F

1   2   3   4

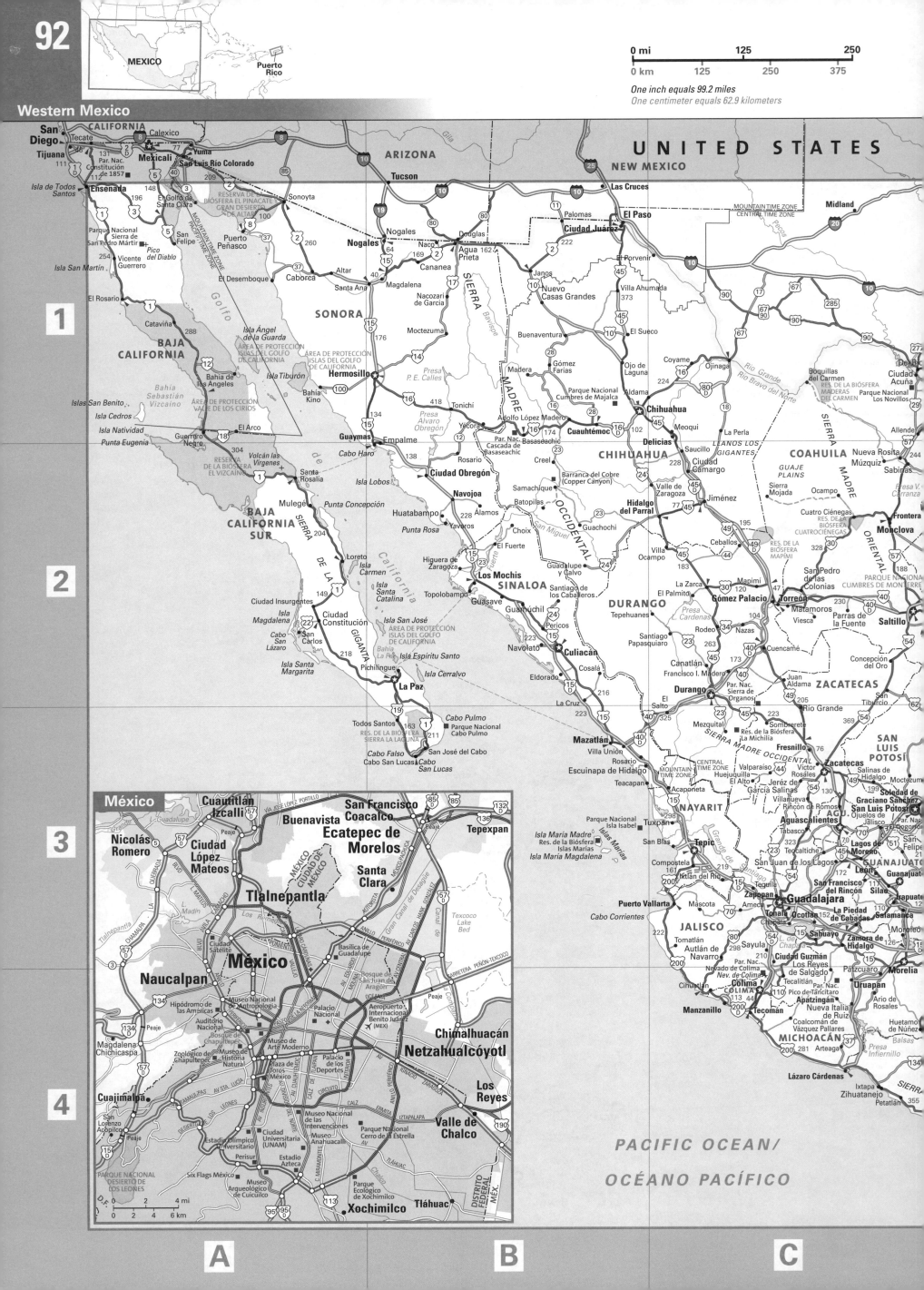

MEXICO

PUERTO Rico

DRIVING DISTANCES IN KILOMETERS

	ACAPULCO	CANCÚN	CHIHUAHUA	GUADALAJARA	LA PAZ	MAZATLÁN	MÉXICO	MONTERREY	PUEBLA	SAN LUIS POTOSÍ	TIJUANA	TUXTLA GUTIÉRREZ
CHIHUAHUA	1913	3290		1283	1432*	896	1538	808	1651	1155	1456	2417
GUADALAJARA	897	2275	1283		959*	523	578	758	691	336	2121	1510
MÉXICO	422	1736	1538	578	1537*	1081		892	133	381	2700	932
MONTERREY	1404	2416	808	758	1357*	901	892		1035	509	2362	1609

*DISTANCE INCLUDES FERRY TRAVEL

SEE ALSO DISTANCE AND DRIVING TIME MAP ON PAGE 126

PUERTO RICO

DISTANCES IN PUERTO RICO SHOWN IN KILOMETERS

DISTANCES IN MEXICO SHOWN IN KILOMETERS

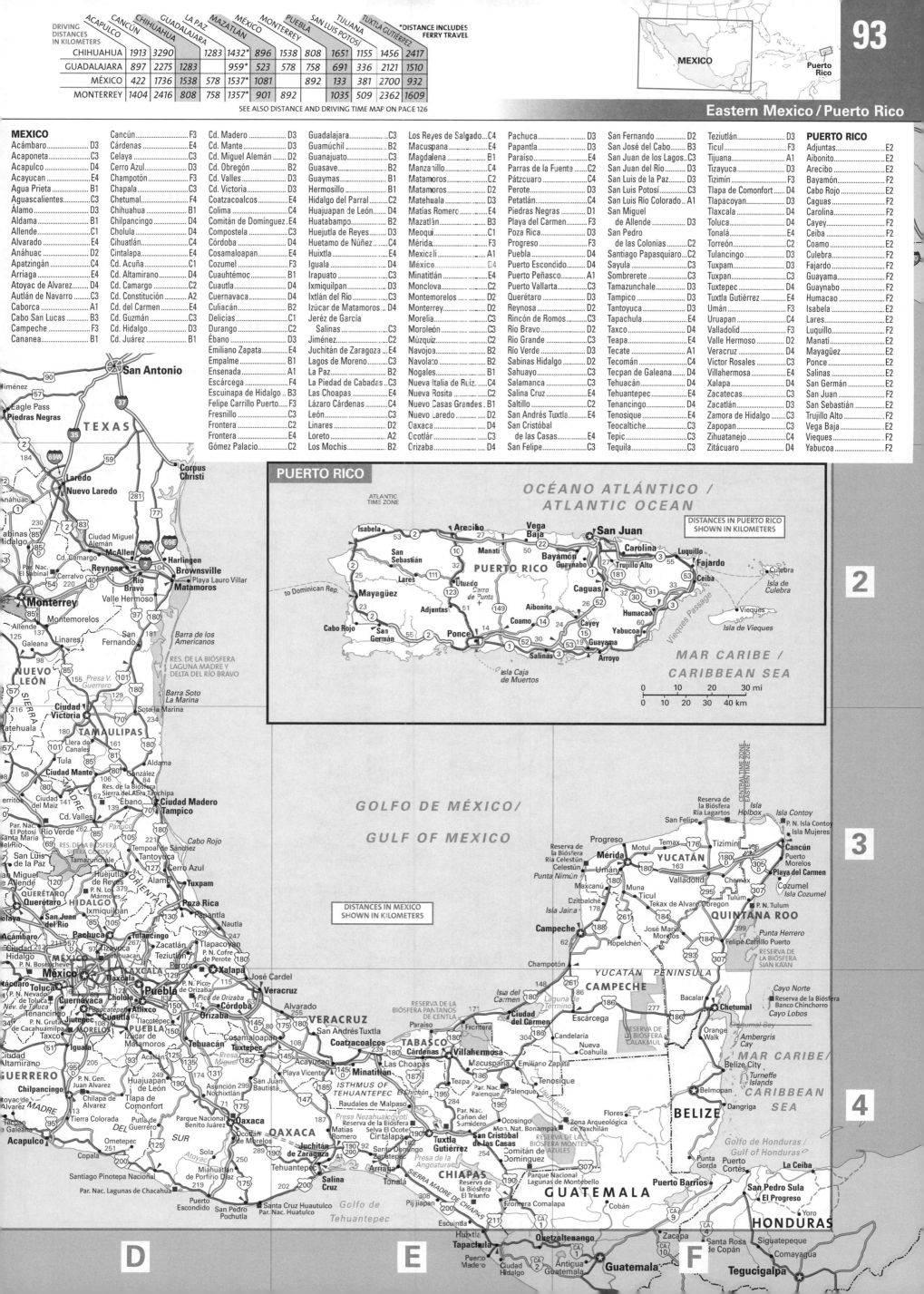

UNITED STATES

A

Abbeville AL	65	E2
Abbeville GA	65	F2
Abbeville LA	63	E4
Abbeville SC	54	A4
Abbotsford WI	25	D1
Aberdeen ID	19	F3
Albany MO	38	B1
Albany NY	70	A1
Albany OR	17	E1
Albany TX	59	E1
Albemarle NC	54	C2
Albertville AL	53	D3
Albertville MN	14	C4
Amboy WA	8	B4
Ambridge PA	41	F1
Amelia LA	63	F4
American Falls ID	19	F3
American Fork UT	34	A1
Americus GA	65	E2
Amery WI	15	D4
Amesbury MA	71	E1
Amherst MA	70	C2
Amherst NH	71	D1
Amherst VA	42	A4
Amherstdale WV	41	E4
Amite LA	63	F3
Ammon ID	20	A2
Amory MS	52	B4
Amsterdam NY	70	A1
Anaconda MT	10	B3
Anacortes WA	8	B1
Anadarko OK	49	F3
Anaheim CA	44	C4
Anahola HI	72	B1
Anahuac TX	61	F1
Anamosa IA	24	C4
Anchorage AK	74	C3
Anchor Pt. AK	74	C3
Andalusia AL	65	D2
Anderson CA	31	E1
Anderson IN	40	C3
Anderson MO	51	D1
Anderson SC	54	A3
Andover KS	37	F4
Andover MA	71	E1
Andrews SC	54	C4
Andrews TX	58	C1
Angel Fire NM	48	A1
Angels Camp CA	32	A4
Angier NC	55	D2
Angleton TX	61	F1
Angola IN	26	B4
Angoon AK	75	E4
Angwin CA	31	E3
Aniak AK	74	B3
Ankeny IA	24	B4
Anna IL	39	F4
Annandale MN	14	B4
Annandale VA	124	A3
Annapolis MD	68	B4
Ann Arbor MI	26	C3
Anniston AL	53	D4
Annville PA	68	B2
Anoka MN	14	C4
Anson TX	59	E1
Ansonia CT	70	B3
Ansted WV	41	F4
Antelope SD	22	C2
Anthony KS	37	E4
Anthony NM	57	E2
Anthony TX	57	E2
Antigo WI	15	F4
Antioch CA	31	E4
Antioch IL	25	E3
Antlers OK	50	C3
Apache OK	49	F3
Apache Jct. AZ	46	B4
Apex NC	55	D2
Appalachia VA	54	A1
Appleton MN	14	A4
Appleton WI	25	E1
Apple Valley CA	45	D3
Apple Valley MN	24	B1
Appomattox VA	42	B4
Aptos CA	31	D4
Arab AL	53	D3
Arapahoe NE	37	D1
Arapahoe WY	20	C3
Arcade CA	119	D1
Arcadia CA	106	E2
Arcadia FL	67	E2
Arcadia LA	63	D1
Arcadia WI	24	C1
Archbald PA	28	C4
Archbold OH	26	B4
Archer City TX	49	F4
Arco ID	19	F2
Arcola IL	40	A2
Arcola TX	61	F1
Arden CA	119	D2
Arden Hills MN	110	C1
Ardmore OK	50	B4
Ardmore PA	116	B3
Argentine MI	26	B3
Argo AL	53	D4
Argyle TX	62	A1
Arizona City AZ	56	A1
Arkadelphia AR	51	E4
Arkansas City KS	50	B1
Arkoma OK	51	D2
Arlee MT	10	A2
Arlington MA	96	D1
Arlington MN	24	A1
Arlington NE	23	F4
Arlington SD	23	E1
Arlington TN	52	B2
Arlington TX	62	A1
Arlington VT	29	D3
Arlington VA	68	A4
Arlington WA	8	B1
Arlington Hts. IL	98	B1
Arma KS	38	B4
Armona CA	44	B1
Armour SD	23	D2
Arnold CA	32	A3
Arnold MD	68	B4
Arnold MN	15	D4
Arroyo Grande CA	44	A3
Arroyo Hondo NM	48	A1
Arroyo Seco NM	48	A1
Artesia CA	106	D4
Artesia NM	58	A1
Arthur ND	13	E2
Arvada CO	35	F2
Arvin CA	44	C2
Asbury IA	25	D3
Asbury Park NJ	69	E2
Ashburn GA	65	F2
Ashburn VA	68	A4
Ashdown AR	51	D4
Asheboro NC	54	C2
Asheville NC	54	A2
Ashford AL	65	E3
Ash Grove MO	38	C4
Ashland AL	53	D4
Ashland CA	122	D3
Ashland KY	41	E3
Ashland MA	71	D1
Ashland MO	39	D3
Ashland MT	11	F4
Ashland NE	38	A1
Ashland OH	41	E1
Ashland OR	17	E3
Ashland PA	68	B1
Ashland VA	42	C4
Ashland WI	15	E3
Ashland City TN	52	C1
Ashley ND	13	E4
Ashtabula OH	27	E4
Ashton ID	20	A2
Aspen CO	35	E3
Aspen Hill MD	68	A4
Astoria OR	8	A3
Atascadero CA	44	A2
Atchison KS	38	A2
Athens AL	53	D3
Athens GA	54	B1
Athens OH	41	D3
Athens PA	28	B4
Athens TN	53	E2
Athens TX	62	B2
Athens WV	41	F4
Athol ID	9	F2
Athol MA	70	C1
Atkins AR	51	E2
Atkinson NE	23	D3
Atkinson NH	71	E1
Atlanta GA	53	E4
Atlantic IA	24	A4
Atlantic TX	62	C1
Atlantic Beach FL	66	B3
Atlantic City NJ	69	E3
Atlantic Highlands NJ	69	E2
Atmore AL	64	C3
Atoka OK	50	B3
Atoka TN	52	B2
Attalla AL	53	D4
Attica IN	40	A1
Attica NY	27	F3
Attleboro MA	71	E2
Atwater CA	32	A4

Albuquerque NM

Aberdeen MD	68	B3
Aberdeen MS	52	B4
Aberdeen NC	54	C3
Aberdeen SD	13	F4
Aberdeen WA	8	A3
Abernathy TX	49	D4
Abilene KS	37	F3
Abilene TX	59	E1
Abingdon IL	39	E1
Abingdon VA	54	B1
Abington MA	71	E2
Abita Sprs. LA	64	A3
Absarokee MT	11	D4
Absecon NJ	69	E3
Ackerman MS	52	B4
Ackley IA	24	B3
Acushnet MA	71	E3
Acworth GA	53	E4
Ada MN	14	A2
Ada OH	41	D1
Ada OK	50	B3
Adairsville GA	53	E3
Adams MA	70	B1
Adams WI	25	D2
Adamsville AL	53	D4
Adamsville TN	52	B2
Addis LA	63	F3
Addison IL	98	B4
Addison TX	100	F1
Adel GA	65	F3
Adel IA	24	A4
Adelanto CA	45	D3
Adelphi MD	124	D1
Adrian MI	26	B4
Adrian MO	38	B3
Affton MO	120	B3
Afton OK	50	C1
Afton WY	20	B3
Agawam MA	70	C2
Agua Fria NM	47	F2
Ahoskie NC	55	E1
Ahsahka ID	9	F3
Ahuimanu HI	72	A3
Aiken SC	54	B4
Ainsworth NE	22	C3
Airway Hts. WA	9	E2
Aitkin MN	14	C3
Ajo AZ	57	E4
Akiachak AK	74	B3
Akron CO	36	B2
Akron IA	23	F3
Akron NY	27	F3
Akron OH	41	F1
Akron PA	68	B2
Akutan AK	74	A4
Alabaster AL	53	D4
Alachua FL	66	A4
Alakanuk AK	74	A2
Alameda CA	122	B3
Alameda NM	47	F2
Alamo CA	122	D4
Alamo NM	47	E3
Alamo TN	52	B2
Alamogordo NM	57	F1
Alamosa CO	35	F4
Albany CA	122	B2
Albany GA	65	E2
Albany IN	40	C1
Albany KY	53	E1
Albany MN	14	B4
Albion IN	26	A4
Albion MI	26	B3
Albion NE	23	E4
Albion NY	27	F2
Albuquerque NM	47	F3
Alcester SD	23	F3
Alcoa TN	53	F2
Alcorn MS	63	F2
Alderwood Manor WA	123	B2
Aldine TX	102	E1
Aledo IL	25	D4
Aledo TX	59	F1
Alexander City AL	65	D1
Alexandria IN	40	C2
Alexandria KY	41	D3
Alexandria LA	63	E2
Alexandria MN	14	B4
Alexandria SD	23	E2
Alexandria VA	68	A4
Alfred NY	28	A3
Algodones NM	47	F2
Algoma WI	25	F1
Algona IA	24	A3
Algonac MI	26	C3
Algood TN	53	E2
Alhambra CA	106	D2
Alice TX	60	C3
Aliceville AL	64	B1
Aliquippa PA	41	F1
Aliso Viejo CA	107	G5
Allegan MI	26	A3
Allen TX	62	A1
Allendale MI	26	A3
Allendale SC	66	B1
Allen Park MI	101	E4
Allentown PA	68	C1
Allenton NE	22	A4
Alliance OH	41	F1
Allyn WA	8	A1
Alma AR	51	D2
Alma GA	66	A2
Alma MI	26	B2
Alma NE	37	D1
Almont MI	26	C3
Alpena MI	16	C4
Alpharetta GA	53	E4
Alpine CA	56	B4
Alpine TX	58	B3
Alpine WY	20	B2
Alsip IL	98	D6
Alta IA	23	F3
Altadena CA	106	D1
Altamont KS	38	A4
Altamont OR	17	E3
Altamonte Sprs. FL	67	E1
Altavista VA	55	D1
Alton IL	39	E3
Altoona IA	24	B4
Altoona PA	42	B1
Altoona WI	24	C1
Altus OK	49	F3
Alum Creek WV	41	E4
Alva OK	49	F1
Alvarado TX	62	A1
Alvin TX	61	F1
Ambler PA	69	D2
Amboy IL	25	E4

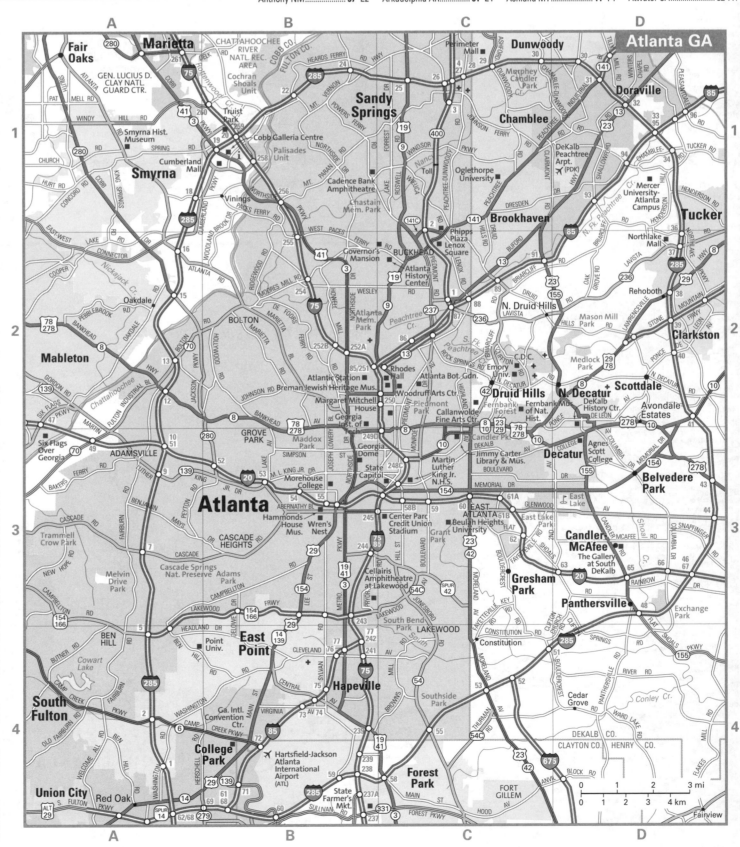

Atlanta GA

Entries in **bold color** indicate cities with detailed inset maps.

Atwood—Billerica **95**

Austin TX

(map inset)

Emma Long Metro. Park · Lake Austin · Wild Basin Wilderness Preserve · West Lake Hills · The Contemporary Austin-Laguna Gloria · Austin Nature & Science Center · Rollingwood · Camp Mabry · Blanton Mus. · State Capitol · State History Mus. · Austin Mus. of Art · UNIV. OF TEXAS AT AUSTIN · L.B.J. Pres. Lib. & Mus. · Erwin Center · Carver Museum · Umlauf Sculpture Garden · Barton Creek Square · Zilker Park · Barton Creek · Bat Colony · Texas St. School for the Deaf · St. Edward's University · Sunset Valley · Toney Burger Ctr. · Roy G. Guerrero Colorado R. Metro Park · Town Lake · Austin-Bergstrom Intl. Airport (AUS)

Baltimore MD

(map inset)

Gunpowder Falls State Park · Germantown · Lutherville · Hampton Natl. Hist. Site · Fire Museum · Providence · Brooklandville · Stevenson Univ. Greenspring Campus · Stevenson · Garrison · Chattolanee · Riderwood · Goucher College · Cub Hill · Towson · Towson Town Ctr. · Towson Univ. · Ruxton · Lake Roland Park · Perry Hall · Carney · Rodgers Forge · Putty Hill · White Marsh Mall · Pikesville · Hebbville · Milford · Lochearn · Woodmoor · Fullerton · Nottingham · Parkville · Overlea · Rossville · Cylburn Arboretum · Notre Dame of Maryland Univ. · Evergreen Mus. & Lib. · Loyola Univ. Maryland · Morgan St. Univ. · Kenwood · Woodlawn · Pimlico Race Course · Druid Hill Park · Maryland Zoo in Baltimore · Mus. of Art · Johns Hopkins University · Security Square Mall · Westview · Coppin State Univ. · Gwynns Falls Park · Univ. of Baltimore · Herring Run Park · Rosedale · Essex · Catonsville · Loudon Park Natl. Cem. · Edgar Allan Poe House & Mus. · Baltimore Natl. Cem. · Univ. of Md., Baltimore County · Mt. Clare Mus. House · M&T Bank Stadium · Oriole Park at Camden Yards · City Hall · Johns Hopkins Hosp. · Mus. of Industry · Ft. McHenry Natl. Mon. & Toll Hist. Shrine · Dundalk · Eastpoint Mall · Chesaco Park · North Point State Battlefield · North Point Village · Arbutus · Halethorpe · Lansdowne · Baltimore · Baltimore Highlands · Brooklyn Park · Pumphrey · Curtis Bay · Patapsco Valley State Park · Rockburn Branch Park · Elkridge · Harwood Park · Hanover · Dorsey · Linthicum · National Electronics Museum · Baltimore-Washington International Thurgood Marshall Airport (BWI) · Ferndale · Arundel Village · Fort Carroll · Sparrows Point · Fort Smallwood Park · Fort Howard · North Point · Solley · Patapsco River · Back River Neck · Middle Br.

Birmingham AL (inset map)

Boston MA (inset map)

Entries in **bold color** indicate cities with detailed inset maps.

Bryant—Cathedral City **97**

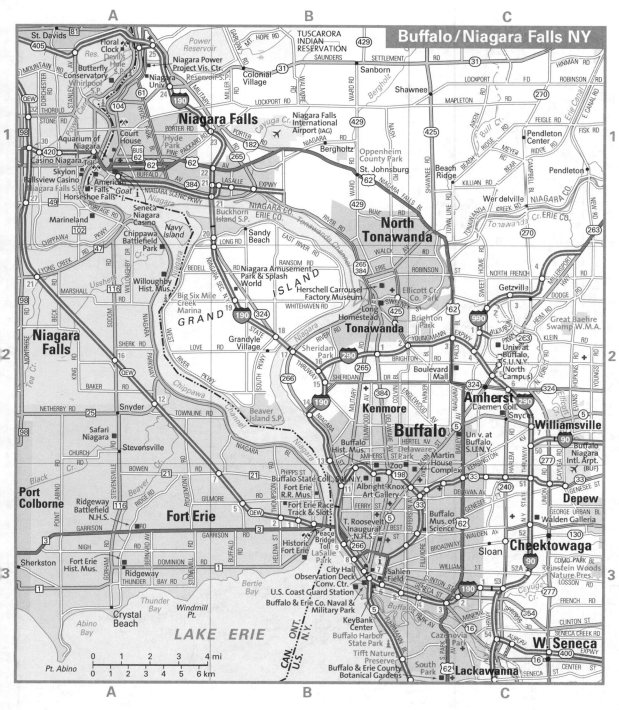

Buffalo/Niagara Falls NY

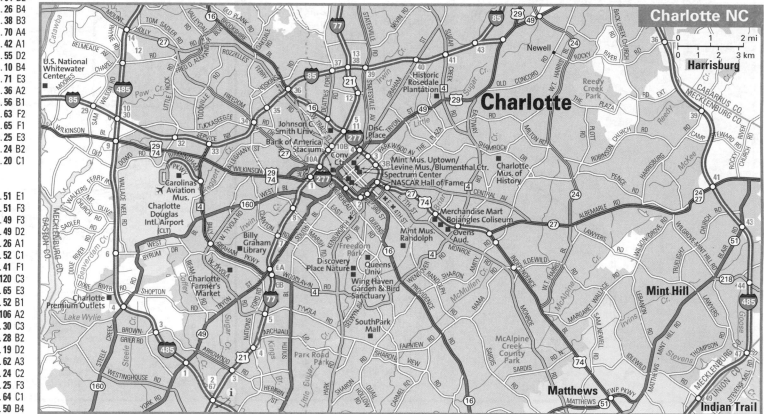

Charlotte NC

Charleston SC

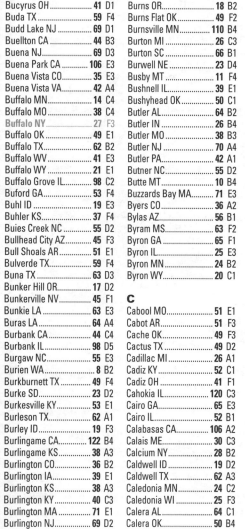

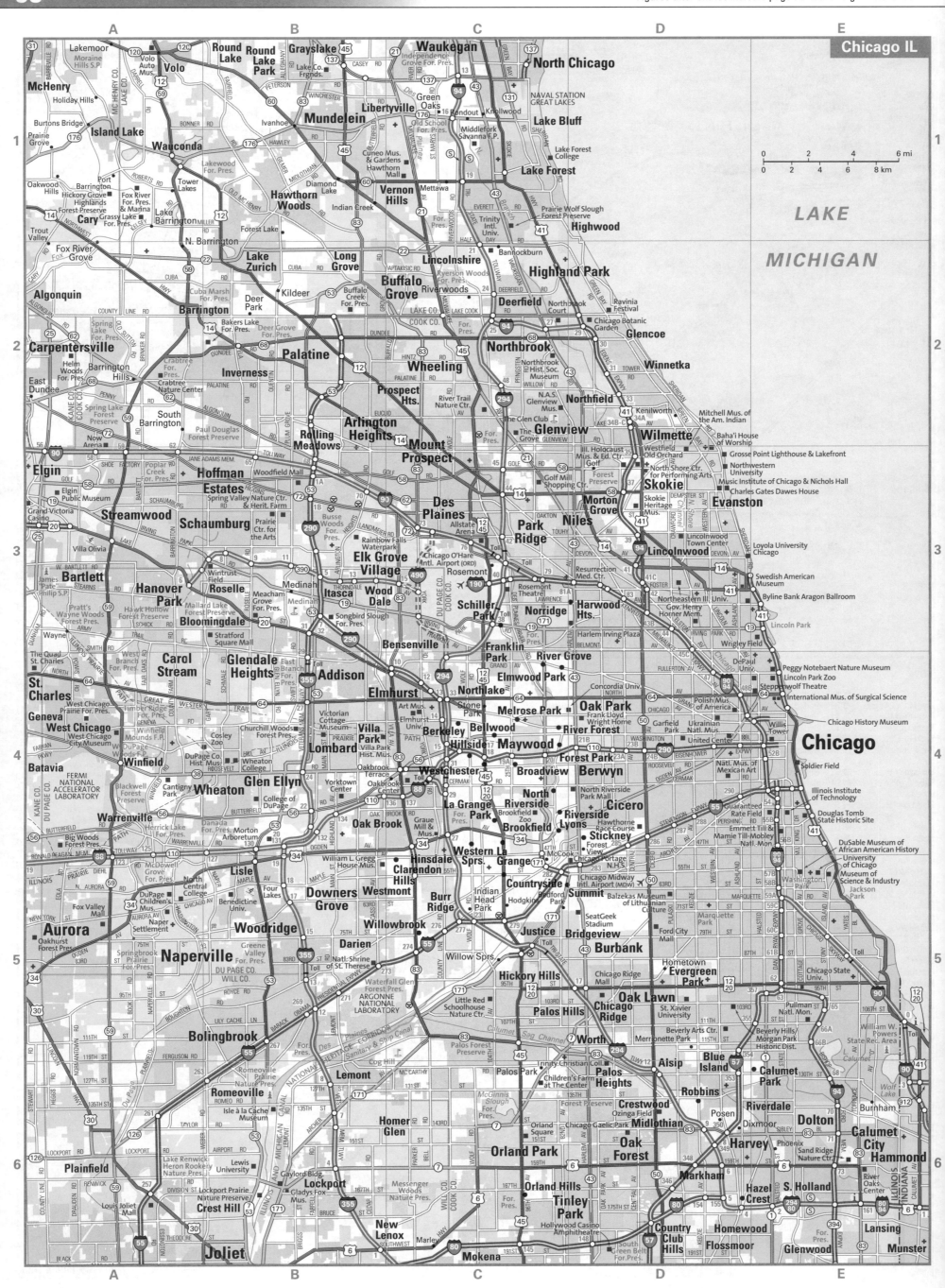

Chicago IL

Entries in **bold color** indicate cities with detailed inset maps.

Catlettsburg—Clintwood 99

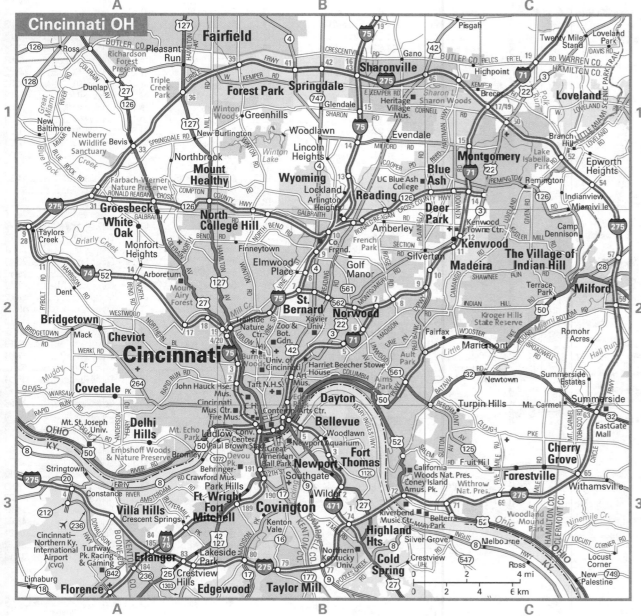

Cincinnati OH

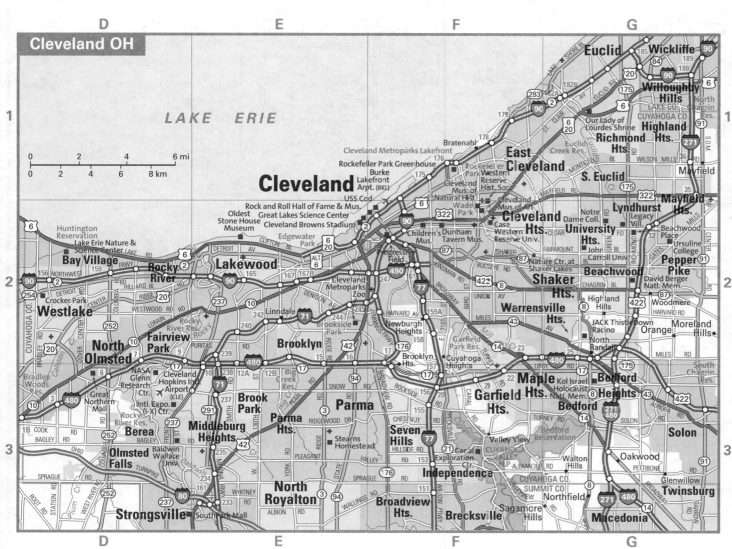

Cleveland OH

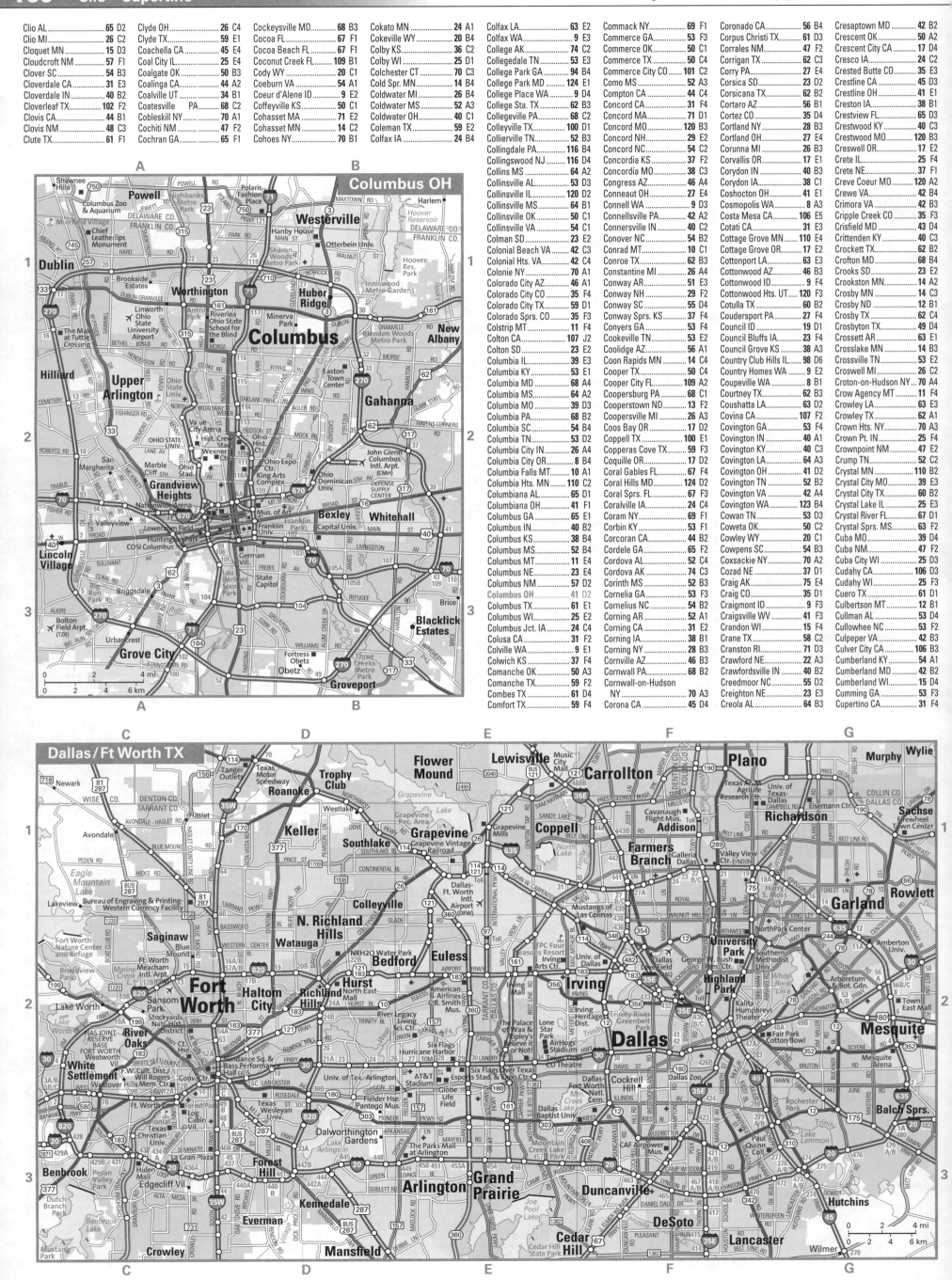

Columbus OH

Dublin, Powell, Westerville, Worthington, Huber Ridge, New Albany, Hilliard, Upper Arlington, Columbus, Gahanna, Grandview Heights, Bexley, Whitehall, Lincoln Village, Grove City, Blacklick Estates, Groveport

Dallas / Ft Worth TX

Newark, Avondale, Lakeview, Keller, Roanoke, Trophy Club, Flower Mound, Lewisville, Carrollton, Plano, Murphy, Wylie, Sachse, Richardson, Saginaw, Southlake, Grapevine, Coppell, Addison, Farmers Branch, Rowlett, Garland, Colleyville, N. Richland Hills, Watauga, Bedford, Euless, Irving, University Park, Highland Park, Fort Worth, Haltom City, Richland Hills, Hurst, Dallas, Mesquite, River Oaks, White Settlement, Benbrook, Forest Hill, Arlington, Grand Prairie, Duncanville, Balch Sprs., Crowley, Kennedale, Everman, Mansfield, Cedar Hill, DeSoto, Lancaster, Hutchins, Wilmer

Entries in **bold color** indicate cities with detailed inset maps.

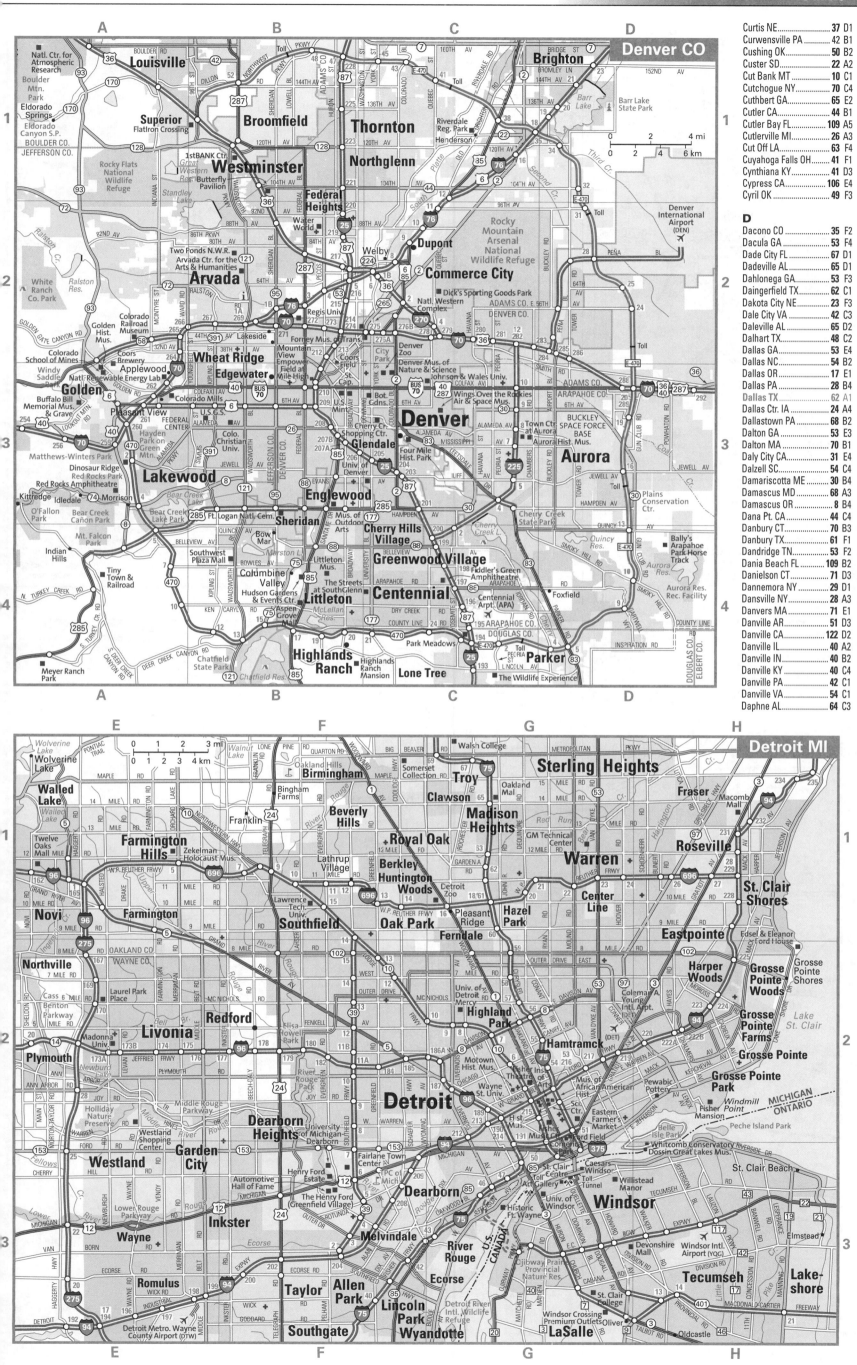

Denver CO

Detroit MI

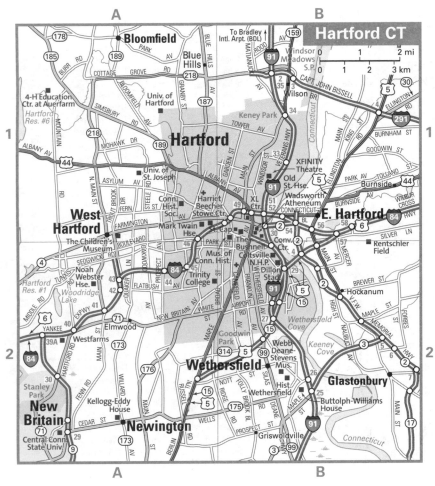

Hartford CT

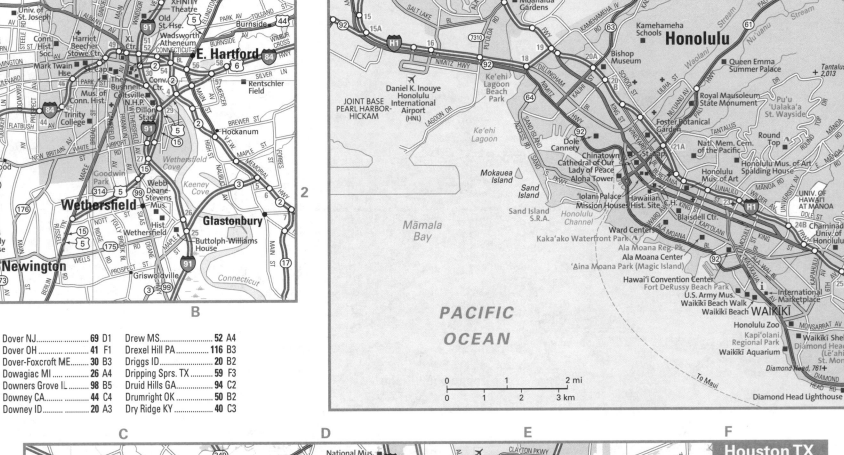

Honolulu HI

Houston TX

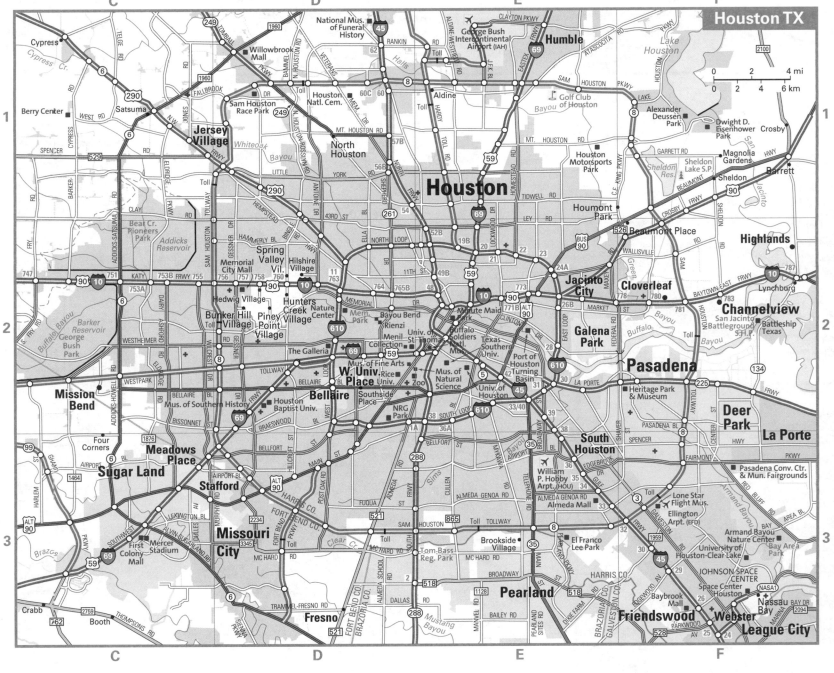

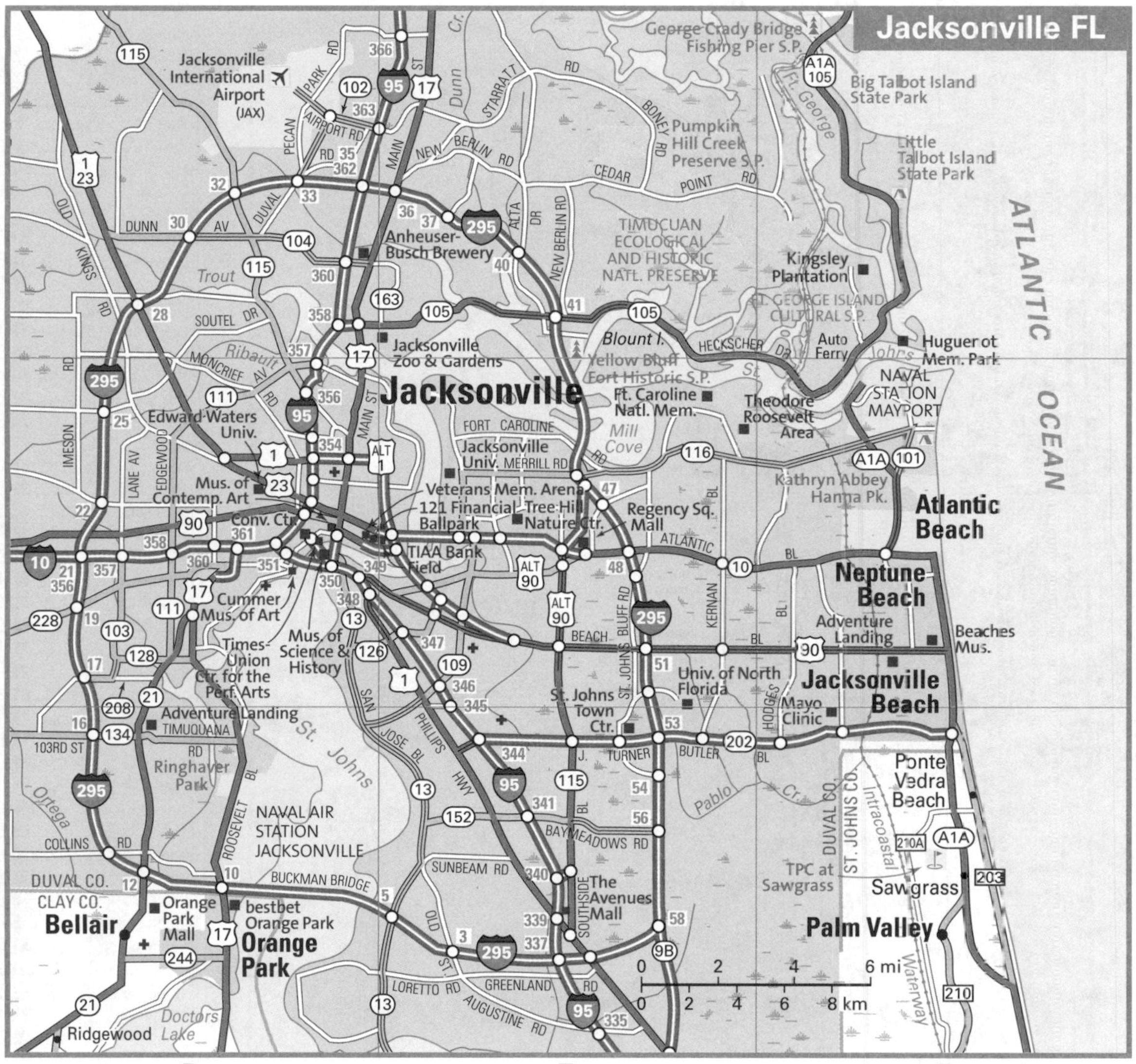

Entries in **bold color** indicate cities with detailed inset maps.

Indianapolis IN (inset map)

Jacksonville FL (inset map)

City	Pg	Grid
Easley SC	54	A3
E. Bernard TX	61	E1
E. Bethel MN	14	C4
E. Brewton AL	64	C3
E. Carbon UT	34	B2
E. Chicago IN	25	F4
E. Cleveland OH	99	F1
E. Dublin GA	65	F1
E. Falmouth MA	71	E3
E. Glenville NY	70	A1
E. Grand Forks MN	13	F2
E. Greenville PA	68	C1
E. Greenwich RI	71	D3
Easthampton MA	70	C2
E. Hartford CT	70	C3
E. Haven CT	70	C3
E. Helena MT	10	C3
E. Highland Park VA	119	B2
E. Jordan MI	16	B4
E. Lake FL	123	D1
E. Lansing MI	26	B3
E. Liverpool OH	41	F1
E. Los Angeles CA	106	D3
Eastman GA	65	F2
E. Millcreek UT	120	F2
E. Millinocket ME	30	B2
E. Moline IL	25	D4
E. Naples FL	67	E3
Easton MD	68	C4
Easton PA	69	D1
E. Orange NJ	69	E1
E. Palestine OH	41	F1
E. Palo Alto CA	122	C5
E. Peoria IL	39	F1
E. Petersburg PA	68	B2
E. Point GA	94	B4
Eastpointe MI	101	H1
Eastport ME	30	C3
E. Prairie MO	52	B1
E. Providence RI	71	D3
E. Ridge TN	53	E3
E. Rutherford NJ	112	B1
E. St. Louis IL	39	E3
E. Sandwich MA	71	F3
E. Stroudsburg PA	43	D1
E. Tawas MI	26	C1
E. Troy WI	25	E3
E. Wenatchee WA	8	C2
Eaton CO	35	F1
Eaton OH	40	C2
Eaton Rapids MI	26	B3
Eatonton GA	53	F4
Eatontown NJ	69	E2
Eatonville WA	8	B3
Eau Claire WI	24	C1
Ebensburg PA	42	B1
Ecorse MI	101	H4
Edcouch TX	60	C4
Ecdyville KY	52	C1
Eden NY	27	F3
Eden NC	54	C1
Eden TX	59	E1
Eden Prairie MN	110	A4
Edenton NC	55	F2
Edgard LA	63	F4
Edgefield SC	54	A4
Edgemere MD	95	D3
Edgemont SD	21	E2
Edgerton KS	38	B3
Edgerton WI	25	E3
Edgewater FL	67	E1
Edgewood KY	99	B3
Edgewood MD	68	B4
Edgewood NM	47	F3
Edgewood WA	123	B5
Edina MN	110	B3
Edinboro PA	27	E4
Edinburg TX	60	C4
Edinburgh IN	40	B2
Edison NJ	69	E1
Edmond OK	50	A2
Edmonds WA	8	B2
Edmonton KY	53	E1
Edna TX	61	E1
Edwards CO	35	E2
Edwards MS	63	F1
Edwardsville IL	39	E3
Effingham IL	39	F2
Egg Harbor City NJ	69	D3
Ehrenberg AZ	45	F4
Ekalaka MT	12	B4
Elba AL	65	D2
Elberton GA	54	A4
Elburn IL	25	E4
El Cajon CA	56	B4
El Campo TX	61	E1
El Cenizo TX	60	B3
El Centro CA	56	C4
El Cerrito CA	122	B2
Eldersburg MD	68	A3
Eldon MO	38	C3
El Dorado AR	51	E4
Eldorado IL	40	A4
El Dorado KS	37	F4
El Dorado Sprs. MO	38	B4
Eldorado TX	59	D3
Eldridge IA	25	D4
Eleanor WV	41	E3
Eleele HI	72	B1
Elephant Butte NM	57	E1
Elfers FL	67	D1
Elgin IL	25	E4
Elgin ND	12	C3
Elgin OK	49	F3
Elgin OR	9	E4
Elgin SC	54	B3
Elgin TX	62	A3
Elizabeth CO	36	A2
Elizabeth NJ	69	E1
Elizabeth City NC	55	F1
Elizabethton TN	54	A1
Elizabethtown KY	40	B4
Elizabethtown NC	55	D3
Elizabethtown PA	68	B2
El Jebel CO	35	E2
Elk City OK	49	F2
Elk Grove CA	31	F4
Elk Grove Vil. IL	98	B3
Elkhart IN	26	A4
Elkhart KS	49	D1
Elkhorn WI	25	E3
Elkin NC	54	B1
Elkins AR	63	F1
Elkins WV	42	A3
Elko NV	33	D1
Elk Pt. SD	23	F3
Elkridge MD	68	B4
Elk Ridge UT	34	B2
Elk River MN	14	C4
Elkton KY	52	C1
Elkton MD	68	C3
Elkton SD	23	F1
Elkton VA	42	B3
Elkview WV	41	F3
Ellendale ND	13	F4
Ellensburg WA	8	C3
Ellenville NY	70	A1
Ellettsville IN	40	B2
Ellicott City MD	68	B4
Ellinwood KS	37	E3
Ellis KS	37	D3
Ellisville MS	64	B2
Elma WA	8	A3
Elm Creek NE	37	D1
Elm Grove WI	109	C2
Elmhurst IL	98	C4
Elmira NY	28	B4
Elmira Hts. NY	28	B3
Elmont NY	113	G4
Elmwood Park IL	98	C4
Elmwood Park NJ	112	B1
Elnora NY	70	A1
Eloy AZ	56	A1
El Paso IL	39	F1
El Paso TX	57	E2
El Reno OK	50	A2
El Rio CA	44	B3
El Segundo CA	106	B3
Elroy WI	25	D2
Elsa TX	60	C4
Elsberry MO	39	E2
Elwood IN	40	B1
Ely MN	15	D2
Ely NV	33	E2
Elyria OH	27	D4
Emerado ND	13	F2
Emerald Isle NC	55	E3
Emerson NE	23	E3
Eminence KY	40	C3
Emmaus PA	68	C1
Emmetsburg IA	24	A2
Emmett ID	19	D2
Emmonak AK	74	B2
Emory VA	54	B1
Empire LA	64	A4
Empire NV	32	B1
Emporia KS	38	A3
Emporia VA	55	E1
Emporium PA	27	F4
Encampment WY	21	E4
Encinitas CA	56	A3
Enderlin ND	13	F3
Endicott NY	28	B4
Endwell NY	28	B4
Enfield CT	29	E4
Enfield NH	29	E2
Enfield NC	55	E2
England AR	51	F3
Englewood CO	35	F2
Englewood FL	67	D3
Englewood NJ	112	D1
Englewood TN	53	E2
Enid OK	50	A1
Ennis MT	10	C4
Ennis TX	62	A1
Enoch UT	33	F4
Enosburg Falls VT	29	D1
Ensley FL	64	C3
Enterprise AL	65	D2
Enterprise NV	105	A4
Enterprise OR	9	E4
Enterprise UT	33	F4
Epping NH	29	F3
Epworth IA	25	D3
Erath LA	63	E4
Erda UT	34	A1
Erie KS	38	B4
Erie PA	27	E4
Erlanger KY	99	A3
Erwin NC	55	D2
Erwin TN	54	A2
Escalon CA	31	F4
Escanaba MI	16	A4
Escobares TX	60	C4
Escondido CA	56	B4
Espanola NM	47	F2
Essex CT	70	D3
Essex MD	68	B3
Essex Jct. VT	29	D1
Essexville MI	26	C2
Estacada OR	8	B4
Estancia NM	47	F3
Estelle LA	111	C2
Estelline SD	23	F1
Ester AK	74	C2
Estero FL	67	E3
Estes Park CO	35	F1
Estherville IA	24	A2
Estill SC	66	B1
Estill Sprs. TN	53	D2
Ethete WY	20	C3
Etowah NC	54	A2
Etowah TN	53	E2
Euclid OH	27	D4
Eudora AR	63	F1
Eudora KS	38	B3
Eufaula AL	65	E2
Eufaula OK	50	C2
Eugene OR	17	E2
Euharlee GA	53	E4
Euless TX	100	C2
Eunice LA	63	E3
Eunice NM	58	B1
Eupora MS	52	B4
Eureka CA	31	D1
Eureka IL	39	F1
Eureka KS	38	A4
Eureka MO	39	E3
Eureka MT	10	A1
Eureka SD	13	E4
Eureka Sprs. AR	51	D1
Eustis FL	67	E1
Eutaw AL	64	C1
Evadale TX	62	C3
Evans CO	35	F1
Evans GA	54	A4
Evansdale IA	24	C3
Evanston IL	25	F4
Evanston WY	20	B4
Evansville IN	40	A4
Evansville WI	25	E3
Evansville WY	21	E3
Eveleth MN	14	C2
Everett MA	96	E1
Everett WA	8	B2
Evergreen AL	64	C2
Evergreen CO	35	F2
Evergreen MT	10	A1
Evergreen Park IL	98	D5
Everson WA	8	B1
Ewa Beach HI	72	A3
Ewa Villages HI	72	A3
Excelsior Sprs. MO	38	B2
Exeter CA	44	B1
Exeter NH	71	E1
Experiment GA	53	F4
Exton PA	68	C2
Eyota MN	24	C2

F

City	Pg	Grid
Fabens TX	57	F2
Fairacres NM	57	E1
Fairbanks AK	74	C2
Fairborn OH	41	D2
Fairburn GA	53	E4
Fairbury IL	39	F1
Fairbury NE	37	F1
Fairfax CA	31	E4
Fairfax OK	50	B1
Fairfax SC	66	B1
Fairfax VA	54	B4
Fairfield AL	53	D4
Fairfield CA	31	F3
Fairfield CT	70	B4
Fairfield IL	40	A3
Fairfield IA	39	D1
Fairfield MT	10	C2
Fairfield OH	40	C2
Fairfield TX	62	B2
Fairfield Bay AR	51	E2
Fairfield Glade TN	53	E2
Fairhaven MA	71	E3
Fair Haven NJ	69	E2
Fair Haven VT	29	D2
Fairhope AL	64	B3
Fair Lawn NJ	112	B1
Fairmont MN	24	A2
Fairmont NC	55	D3
Fairmont WV	42	A2
Fairmount IN	40	C1
Fairmount NY	28	B3
Fairmount ND	14	A4
Fair Oaks Ranch TX	59	F4

Bottom index (continued):

City	Pg	Grid
Durant MS	64	A1
Durant OK	50	B4
Durham CA	31	F2
Durham CT	70	C3
Durham NH	29	F2
Durham NC	55	D2
Dushore PA	28	B4
Duvall WA	8	B2
Dwight IL	39	F1
Dyer TN	52	B2
Dyersburg TN	52	B2
Dyersville IA	24	C3

E

City	Pg	Grid
Eagan MN	110	D4
Eagar AZ	47	D4
Eagle WI	25	E3
Eagle CO	35	E2
Eagle ID	19	D2
Eagle NE	38	A1
Eagle Butte SD	22	B1
Eagle Grove IA	24	B3
Eagle Lake MN	24	B1
Eagle Lake TX	61	E1
Eagle Mtn. UT	34	A1
Eagle Pass TX	60	A2
Eagle Pt. OR	17	E3
Earle AR	52	A2
Earlimart CA	44	B2
Earlington KY	40	A4
Early TX	59	E2

Kansas City MO/KS

Map labels include: Smithville, Ferrelview, Kansas City International Airport (MCI), Zona Rosa, Gladstone, Pleasant Valley, Liberty, Glenaire, Claycomo, Avondale, Randolph, Birmingham, River Bend, Parkville, Park Univ., Riverside, Northmoor, North Kansas City, Kansas City (MO), Kansas City (KS), Independence, Sugar Creek, Edwardsville, Waldron, Farley, Lakeside Speedway, Kansas Speedway, Legends Field, Shawnee, Merriam, Mission, Roeland Park, Fairway, Westwood, Mission Hills, Prairie Village, Overland Park, Lenexa, Olathe, Raytown, Lee's Summit.

Entries in bold color indicate cities with detailed inset maps.

Garner—Henagar 105

Garner NC 55 D2
Garnett KS 38 B3
Garretson SD 23 F2
Garrett IN 26 B4
Garrison ND 13 D2
Gary IN 25 F4
Gas City IN 40 C1
Gassville AR 51 E1
Gastonia NC 54 B2
Gate City VA 54 A1
Gatesville TX 59 F2
Gatlinburg TN 53 F2
Gautier MS 64 B3
Gaylord MI 26 B1
Gaylord MN 24 A1
Geary OK 49 F2
Genesee ID 9 E3
Geneseo IL 25 D4
Geneseo NY 28 A3
Geneva AL 65 D3
Geneva IL 25 E4
Geneva NE 37 F1
Geneva NY 28 B3
Geneva OH 27 D4
Geneva WA 8 B1
Genoa IL 25 E4
Genoa NE 23 E4
Genoa City WI 25 E3
Gentry AR 51 D1
Georgetown CO 35 F2
Georgetown DE 43 D3
Georgetown ID 20 A3
Georgetown IL 40 A2
Georgetown IN 40 B3
Georgetown KY 40 C3
Georgetown MA 71 E1
Georgetown OH 41 D3
Georgetown SC 55 D4
Georgetown TX 59 F3
George West TX 60 C2
Georgiana AL 64 C2
Gering NE 22 A4
Gerlach NV 32 B1
Germantown MD 68 A4
Germantown OH 41 D2
Germantown TN 52 A3
Germantown WI 25 E2
Gettysburg PA 68 A3
Gettysburg SD 22 C1
Gibbon NE 37 E1
Gibsonburg OH 26 C4
Gibson City IL 39 F1
Gibsonton FL 67 D2
Giddings TX 62 A4
Gifford FL 67 F2
Gig Harbor WA 8 B2
Gila Bend AZ 57 E3
Gilbert AZ 46 B4
Gilbert MN 15 D2
Gilcrest CO 35 F1
Gillespie IL 39 E3
Gillette WY 21 E1
Gilmer TX 62 C1
Gilroy CA 44 A1
Girard KS 38 B4
Girard PA 27 E4
Gladewater TX 62 C1
Gladstone MI 16 A4
Gladstone MO 104 C2
Gladstone OR 118 B3
Gladwin MI 26 B2
Glasgow DE 68 C3
Glasgow KY 53 D1
Glasgow MT 11 F1
Glassboro NJ 69 D3
Glassmanor MD 124 D3
Glastonbury CT 70 C3
Glen Allen VA 119 A1
Glen Burnie MD 68 B4
Glencoe AL 53 D4
Glencoe MN 24 A1
Glen Cove NY 69 F1
Glendale AZ 46 B4
Glendale CA 44 C4
Glendale WI 109 D1
Glendale Hts. IL 98 B4
Glendive MT 12 B2
Glendora CA 107 F2
Glen Ellyn IL 98 B4
Glenmora LA 63 E3
Glennallen AK 74 C3
Glenns Ferry ID 19 E3
Glennville GA 66 A2
Glenpool OK 50 C2
Glenrock WY 21 E3
Glen Rose TX 59 F1
Glens Falls NY 29 D2
Glen Ullin ND 12 C3
Glenview IL 98 C2
Glenville WV 41 F3
Glenwood AR 51 D3
Glenwood IA 38 A1
Glenwood MN 14 B4
Glenwood Sprs. CO 35 E2
Glide OR 17 E2
Globe AZ 46 C4
Glorieta NM 48 A2
Gloucester MA 71 E1
Gloucester VA 42 C4
Gloucester City NJ 116 D4
Gloucester Pt. VA 42 C4
Gloversville NY 28 C3
Goddard KS 37 F4
Godfrey IL 39 E3
Goffstown NH 29 E3
Gold Bar WA 8 B2
Gold Beach OR 17 D3
Golden CO 35 F2
Goldendale WA 8 C4
Golden Gate FL 67 E3
Golden Meadow LA 64 A4
Golden Valley MN 110 B2
Goldsboro NC 55 D2
Goldsby OK 50 A3
Goldthwaite TX 59 F2
Goleta CA 44 B3
Goliad TX 61 D2
Gonzales CA 44 A1
Gonzales LA 63 F3
Gonzales TX 61 D1
Gonzalez FL 64 C3
Good Hope AL 53 D4
Gooding ID 19 E3
Goodland KS 36 C2
Goodlettsville TN 53 D1
Goodman MS 64 A1
Goodview MN 24 C2
Goodwater AL 65 D1
Goodwell OK 49 D1
Goodyear AZ 46 B4
Goose Creek SC 66 C1
Gordo AL 52 C4
Gordon GA 65 F1
Gordon NE 22 B3
Gordonsville VA 42 B4
Gorham NH 29 F1
Goshen IN 26 A4
Goshen NY 70 A3
Gosnell AR 52 A2
Gothenburg NE 37 D1
Gould AR 51 F4
Goulds FL 67 F4
Gouverneur NY 28 C1
Gowanda NY 27 F3
Grace ID 20 A3
Grafton ND 13 F1
Grafton WV 42 A2
Grafton WI 25 F2
Graham NC 54 C2
Graham TX 59 F1
Grambling LA 63 E1
Gramercy LA 63 F4
Granbury TX 59 F1
Granby CO 35 F2
Granby MO 51 D1
Grand Bay AL 64 B3
Grand Blanc MI 26 C3
Grand Canyon AZ 46 B2
Grandfield OK 49 F3
Grand Forks ND 13 F2
Grand Haven MI 26 A3
Grand Island NE 37 E1
Grand Isle LA 64 A4
Grand Jct. CO 35 D3
Grand Ledge MI 26 B3
Grand Prairie TX 100 E3
Grand Rapids MI 26 A3
Grand Rapids MN 14 C2
Grand Saline TX 62 B1
Grandview WA 8 C3
Grandview Plaza KS 37 F3
Granger WA 8 C3
Grangeville ID 9 F4
Granite OK 49 F3
Granite City IL 39 E3
Granite Falls MN 23 F1
Granite Falls NC 54 B2
Granite Falls WA 8 B2
Granite Quarry NC 54 C2
Granite Shoals TX 59 F3
Graniteville SC 54 B4
Grant NE 36 C1
Grants NM 47 E3
Grantsdale MT 10 A3
Grants Pass OR 17 E3
Grantsville UT 34 A1
Granville NY 29 D2
Granville OH 41 E2
Grapeland TX 62 B2
Grapevine TX 62 A1
Grass Valley CA 31 F2
Gravette AR 51 D1
Gray LA 63 F4
Grayslake IL 98 B1
Grayson KY 41 E3
Great Bend KS 37 E3
Great Falls MT 10 C2
Great Falls SC 54 B3
Great Neck NY 69 F1
Greece NY 28 A2
Greeley CO 35 F1
Green OR 17 E2
Greenacres CA 44 B2
Greenacres FL 67 F3
Green Bay WI 25 E1
Greenbelt MD 68 A4
Greenbrier AR 51 E2
Greenbrier TN 53 D1
Greencastle IN 40 B2
Greencastle PA 68 A3
Green Cove Sprs. FL 66 B4
Greendale WI 109 C3
Greeneville TN 54 A2
Greenfield CA 44 A1
Greenfield IN 40 C2
Greenfield IA 24 A4
Greenfield MA 70 C1
Greenfield OH 41 D2
Greenfield TN 52 B2
Greenfield WI 109 C3
Green Forest AR 51 D1
Green River WY 20 C4
Greensboro AL 64 C1
Greensboro GA 53 F4
Greensboro NC 54 C2
Greensburg IN 40 C2
Greensburg KS 37 E4
Greensburg KY 40 C4
Greensburg PA 42 A1
Greentown IN 40 B1
Green Valley AZ 56 B2
Green Valley MD 68 A3
Greenville AL 65 D2
Greenville IL 39 F3
Greenville KY 40 A4
Greenville ME 30 B3
Greenville MI 26 B2
Greenville MS 51 F4
Greenville NC 55 E2
Greenville OH 40 C2
Greenville PA 27 E4
Greenville RI 71 D3
Greenville SC 54 A3
Greenville TX 62 B1
Greenwich CT 70 B4
Greenwood AR 51 D3
Greenwood IN 40 B2
Greenwood LA 63 D1
Greenwood MS 52 A4
Greenwood SC 54 A3
Greenwood Lake NY 70 A4
Greenwood Vil. CO 101 C4
Greer SC 54 A3
Gregory SD 23 D2
Grenada MS 52 A4
Gresham OR 8 B4
Gresham Park GA 94 C3
Gretna LA 64 A4
Gretna NE 23 F4
Greybull WY 21 D1
Gridley CA 31 F2
Griffin GA 53 F4
Grifton NC 55 E2
Grimes IA 24 B4
Grinnell IA 24 B4
Groesbeck TX 62 B2
Grosse Pointe MI 101 H2
Grosse Pointe Farms MI 101 H2
Grosse Pointe Park MI 101 H2
Grosse Pointe Woods MI 101 H2
Groton CT 71 D3
Groton SD 13 F4
Grottoes VA 42 B3
Grove OK 50 C1
Grove City OH 41 D2
Grove City PA 27 E4
Groveland CA 32 A4
Groveland MA 71 E1
Grover Beach CA 44 A3
Groves TX 63 D4
Grovetown GA 54 A4
Gruetli-Laager TN 53 E2
Grundy Ctr. IA 24 B3
Guadalupe CA 44 A3
Gueydan LA 63 E4
Guilford CT 70 C4
Guernsey WY 21 F3
Guin AL 52 C4
Gulf Breeze FL 64 C3
Gulfport MS 64 B3
Gulf Shores AL 64 C3
Gun Barrel City TX 62 B1
Gunnison CO 35 E3
Gunnison UT 34 A2
Guntersville AL 53 D3
Guntown MS 52 B3
Gurdon AR 51 E4
Gustine CA 31 F4
Guthrie KY 52 C1
Guthrie OK 50 A2
Guthrie Ctr. IA 24 A4
Guttenberg IA 24 C3
Guttenberg NJ 112 D2
Guymon OK 49 D1
Gwinner ND 13 F3
Gypsum CO 35 E2

H

Hacienda Hts. CA 106 E3
Hackberry LA 63 D4
Hackensack NJ 69 E1
Hackettstown NJ 69 D1
Hackleburg AL 52 C3
Haddonfield NJ 116 D4
Hagerman ID 19 E3
Hagerman NM 58 A1
Hagerstown MD 42 B2
Hahnville LA 63 F4
Haiku HI 73 D1
Hailey ID 19 E2
Haines AK 75 D3
Haines City FL 67 E2
Halawa HI 72 C3
Hale Ctr. TX 49 D4
Haleiwa HI 72 A2
Haleyville AL 52 C3
Half Moon NC 55 E3
Half Moon Bay CA 31 E4
Hallandale Beach FL 67 F4
Hallettsville TX 61 D1
Hallowell ME 29 F1
Halls TN 52 B2
Halls Crossroads TN 53 F2
Hallsville TX 62 C1
Halstead KS 37 F4
Haltom City TX 100 D2
Hamburg AR 51 F4
Hamburg NY 27 F3
Hamburg PA 68 C1
Hamden CT 70 C3
Hamilton AL 52 C4
Hamilton IL 39 D1
Hamilton MO 38 B2
Hamilton MT 10 A3
Hamilton NY 28 C3
Hamilton OH 40 C2
Hamilton TX 59 F2
Ham Lake MN 14 C4
Hamlet NC 54 C3
Hamlin TX 59 E1
Hamlin WV 41 E3
Hammond IN 25 F4
Hammond LA 63 F3
Hammonton NJ 69 D3
Hampden ME 30 B3
Hampshire IL 25 E4
Hampstead MD 68 B3
Hampton AR 51 E4
Hampton GA 53 F4
Hampton IA 24 B3
Hampton NH 71 E1
Hampton SC 66 B1
Hampton VA 55 F1
Hampton Bays NY 70 C4
Hampton Beach NH 71 E1
Hamtramck MI 101 G2
Hanahan SC 66 C1
Hanamaulu HI 72 B1
Hanapepe HI 72 B1
Hanceville AL 53 D4
Hancock MI 15 F2
Hanford CA 44 B1
Hankinson ND 14 A3
Hanna WY 21 E4
Hannibal MO 39 D2
Hanover IN 40 C3
Hanover NH 29 E2
Hanover PA 68 A3
Hanover Park IL 98 A3
Hansen ID 19 E3
Harahan LA 111 B2
Harbor OR 17 D4
Hardeeville SC 66 B1
Hardin MT 11 F4
Hardinsburg KY 40 B4
Hardwick VT 29 E1
Harker Hts. TX 59 F3
Harlan IA 23 F4
Harlan KY 53 F1
Harlem MT 11 E1
Harlingen TX 61 D4
Harlowton MT 11 D3
Harold KY 41 E4
Harper KS 37 E4
Harpersville AL 53 D4
Harper Woods MI 101 H2
Harrah OK 50 B2
Harriman TN 53 E2
Harrington DE 68 C4
Harrisburg AR 51 F2
Harrisburg IL 39 F4
Harrisburg NC 54 B2
Harrisburg OR 17 E1
Harrisburg PA 68 B2
Harrisburg SD 23 E2
Harrison AR 51 E1
Harrison MI 26 B2
Harrison NJ 112 B3
Harrison TN 53 E3
Harrisonburg VA 42 B3
Harrisonville MO 38 B3
Harrisville WV 41 F2
Harrodsburg KY 40 C4
Harrogate TN 53 F1
Hartford AL 65 D3
Hartford CT 70 C3
Hartford KY 40 B4
Hartford MI 26 A3
Hartford SD 23 E2
Hartford WI 25 E2
Hartford City IN 40 C1
Hartington NE 23 E3
Hartley IA 23 F2
Harts WV 41 E4
Hartselle AL 53 D3
Hartshorne OK 50 C3
Hartsville SC 54 C3
Hartsville TN 53 D1
Hartwell GA 54 A3
Harvard IL 25 E3
Harvard NE 37 E1
Harvest AL 53 D3
Harvey IL 98 D6
Harvey LA 111 C2
Harvey ND 13 E2
Harveys Lake PA 28 B4
Harwinton CT 70 B3
Harwood ND 14 A3
Hasbrouck Hts. NJ 112 C1
Haskell AR 51 E3
Haskell OK 50 C2
Haskell TX 59 E1
Hastings MI 26 B3
Hastings MN 24 B1
Hastings NE 37 E1
Hatch NM 57 E1
Hattiesburg MS 64 A2
Hatton ND 13 F2
Haughton LA 63 D1
Hauula HI 72 A2
Havana IL 39 E1
Havelock NC 55 E3
Haven KS 37 F4
Haverhill MA 71 E1
Haverstraw NY 70 A4
Havre MT 11 D1
Havre de Grace MD 68 B3
Hawarden IA 23 F3
Hawkinsville GA 65 F1
Hawley MN 14 A3
Hawthorne CA 106 C3
Hawthorne NV 32 B3
Hayden CO 35 E1
Hayden ID 9 E2
Hayesville OR 17 E1
Haynesville LA 63 D1
Hays KS 37 E3
Hays MT 11 E2
Haysville KS 37 F4
Hayti MO 52 B1
Hayward CA 31 F4
Hayward WI 15 D4
Hazard KY 41 D4
Hazel Green AL 53 D3
Hazel Park MI 101 G1
Hazelton ID 19 E3
Hazelwood MO 120 A1
Hazen AR 51 F3
Hazen ND 13 D2
Hazlehurst GA 66 A2
Hazlehurst MS 63 F2
Hazleton PA 68 C1
Headland AL 65 E2
Healdsburg CA 31 E3
Healdton OK 50 A3
Healy AK 74 C2
Hearne TX 62 A3
Heart Butte MT 10 B1
Heath OH 41 E2
Heavener OK 51 D3
Hebbronville TX 60 C3
Heber AZ 46 C3
Heber City UT 34 B1
Heber Sprs. AR 51 E2
Hebron IN 25 F4
Hebron NE 37 F1
Hebron ND 12 C3
Heeia HI 72 A3
Heflin AL 53 E4
Helena AL 53 D4
Helena-W. Helena AR 52 A3
Helena GA 65 F2
Helena MT 10 C3
Hellertown PA 68 C1
Helotes TX 59 F4
Helper UT 34 B2
Hemet CA 45 D4
Hemingford NE 22 A3
Hempstead NY 69 F1
Hempstead TX 62 B4
Henagar AL 53 D3

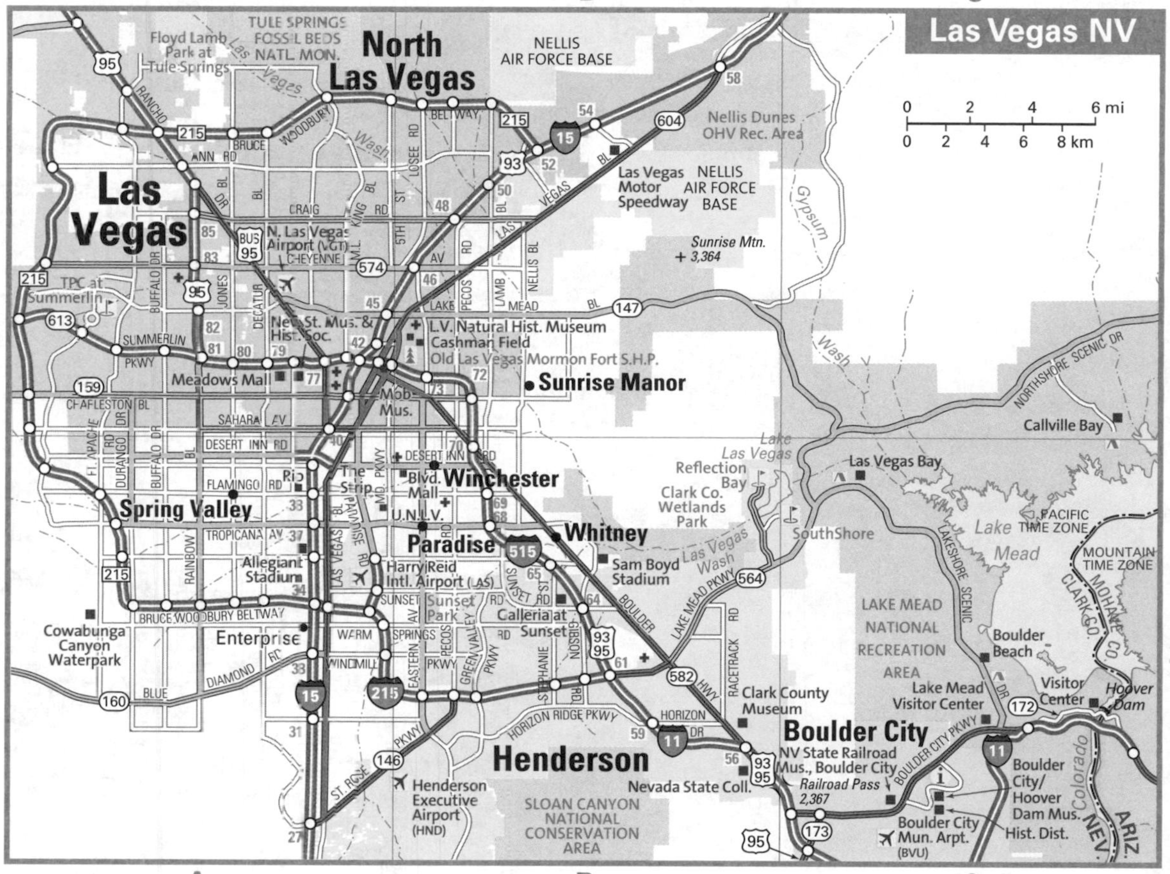
Las Vegas NV
A
B
C
1
2
North Las Vegas
NELLIS AIR FORCE BASE
TULE SPRINGS FOSSIL BEDS NATL. MON.
Floyd Lamb Park at Tule Springs
Nellis Dunes OHV Rec. Area
Las Vegas
Las Vegas Motor Speedway
NELLIS AIR FORCE BASE
Sunrise Mtn. 3,364
N. Las Vegas Airport (VGT)
TPC at Summerlin
L.V. Natural Hist. Museum
Cashman Field
Old Las Vegas Mormon Fort S.H.P.
Sunrise Manor
Meadows Mall
Callville Bay
Las Vegas Bay
Reflection Bay
Clark Co. Wetlands Park
Spring Valley
Winchester
Paradise
Whitney
Sam Boyd Stadium
Harry Reid Intl. Airport (LAS)
SouthShore
Lake Mead
PACIFIC TIME ZONE
MOUNTAIN TIME ZONE
LAKE MEAD NATIONAL RECREATION AREA
Boulder Beach
Lake Mead Visitor Center
Visitor Center
Hoover Dam
Cowabunga Canyon Waterpark
Enterprise
Galleria at Sunset
Clark County Museum
Boulder City
Henderson
NV State Railroad Mus., Boulder City
Railroad Pass 2,367
Nevada State Coll.
Henderson Executive Airport (HND)
SLOAN CANYON NATIONAL CONSERVATION AREA
Boulder City Mun. Arpt. (BVU)
Boulder City/Hoover Dam Mus.
Hist. Dist.
ARIZ.
NEV.
0 2 4 6 mi
0 2 4 6 8 km

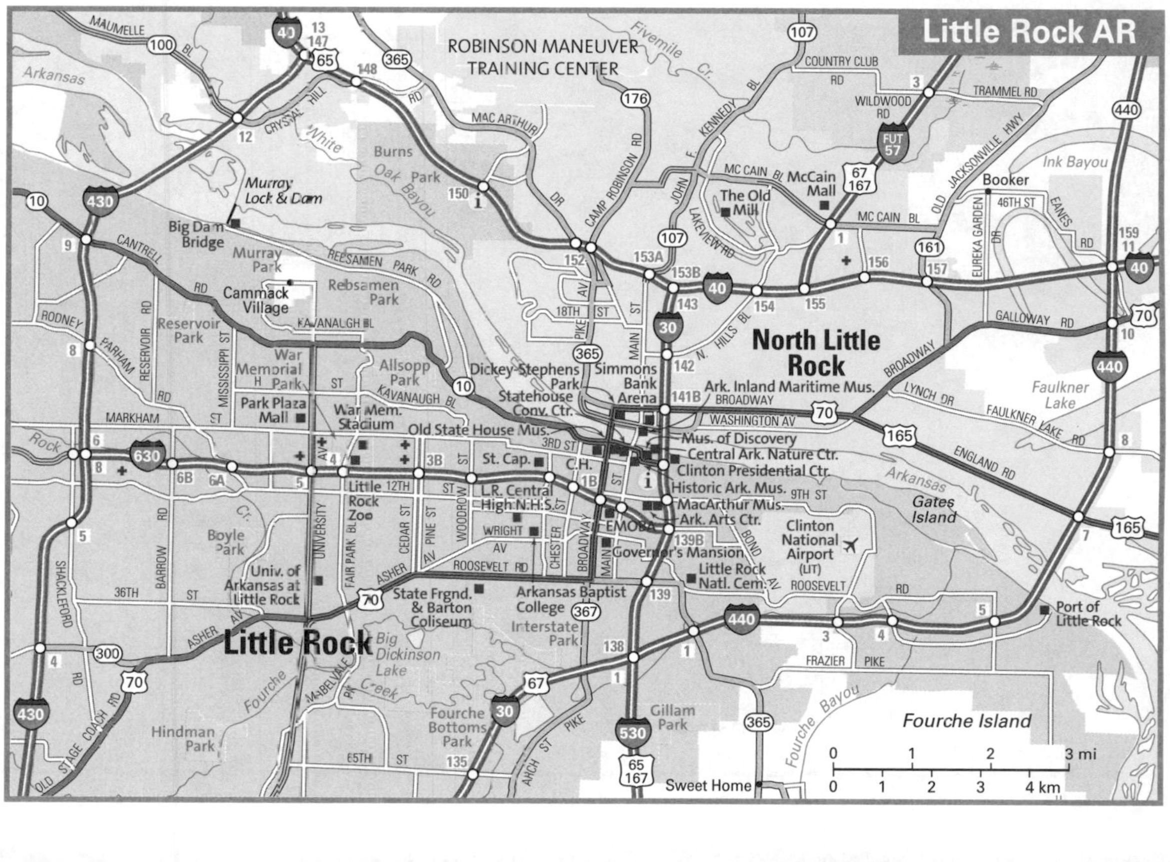
Little Rock AR
ROBINSON MANEUVER TRAINING CENTER
Arkansas
Burns Park
Murray Lock & Dam
Big Dam Bridge
Murray Park
Rebsamen Park
Cammack Village
Reservoir Park
McCain Mall
The Old Mill
North Little Rock
War Memorial Park
Allsopp Park
Dickey-Stephens Park
Statehouse Conv. Ctr.
Simmons Bank Arena
Ark. Inland Maritime Mus.
Faulkner Lake
Park Plaza Mall
War Mem. Stadium
Old State House Mus.
Mus. of Discovery
Central Ark. Nature Ctr.
Clinton Presidential Ctr.
Historic Ark. Mus.
MacArthur Mus.
Ark. Arts Ctr.
Little Rock Zoo
L.R. Central High N.H.S.
Boyle Park
Univ. of Arkansas at Little Rock
Governor's Mansion
Clinton National Airport (LIT)
Little Rock Natl. Cem.
Gates Island
State Frgnd. & Barton Coliseum
Arkansas Baptist College
Interstate Park
Little Rock
Big Dickinson Lake
Fourche Bottoms Park
Gillam Park
Hindman Park
Port of Little Rock
Fourche Island
Sweet Home
0 1 2 3 mi
0 1 2 3 4 km

Entries in **bold color** indicate cities with detailed inset maps.

107

Los Angeles CA

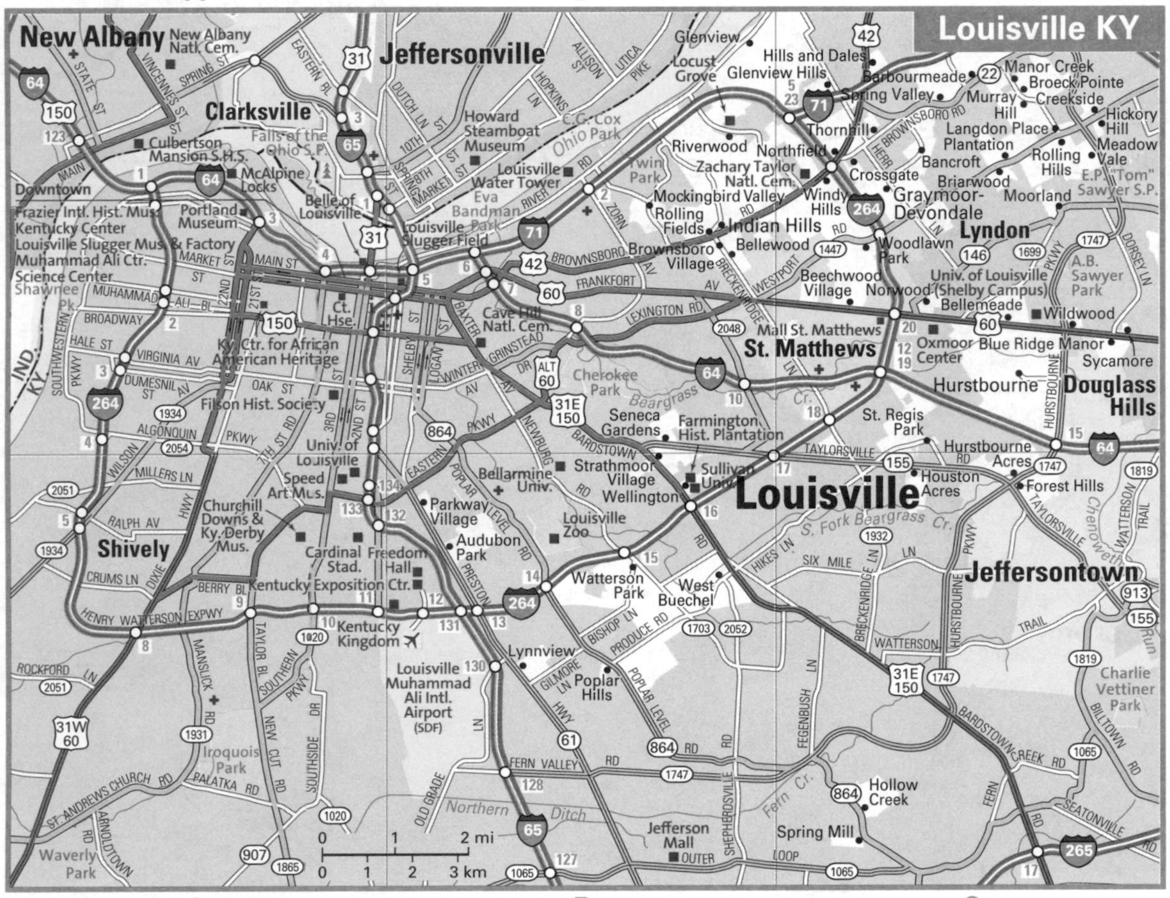
A
B
C
1
2
Louisville KY
New Albany
Jeffersonville
Clarksville
Downtown
Louisville
St. Matthews
Lyndon
Douglass Hills
Hurstbourne
Jeffersontown
Shively
Indian Hills
Graymoor-Devondale
Louisville Muhammad Ali Intl. Airport (SDF)
Kentucky Exposition Ctr.
Churchill Downs & Ky. Derby Mus.
Univ. of Louisville
Jefferson Mall
Hollow Creek
Spring Mill
0 1 2 mi
0 1 2 3 km

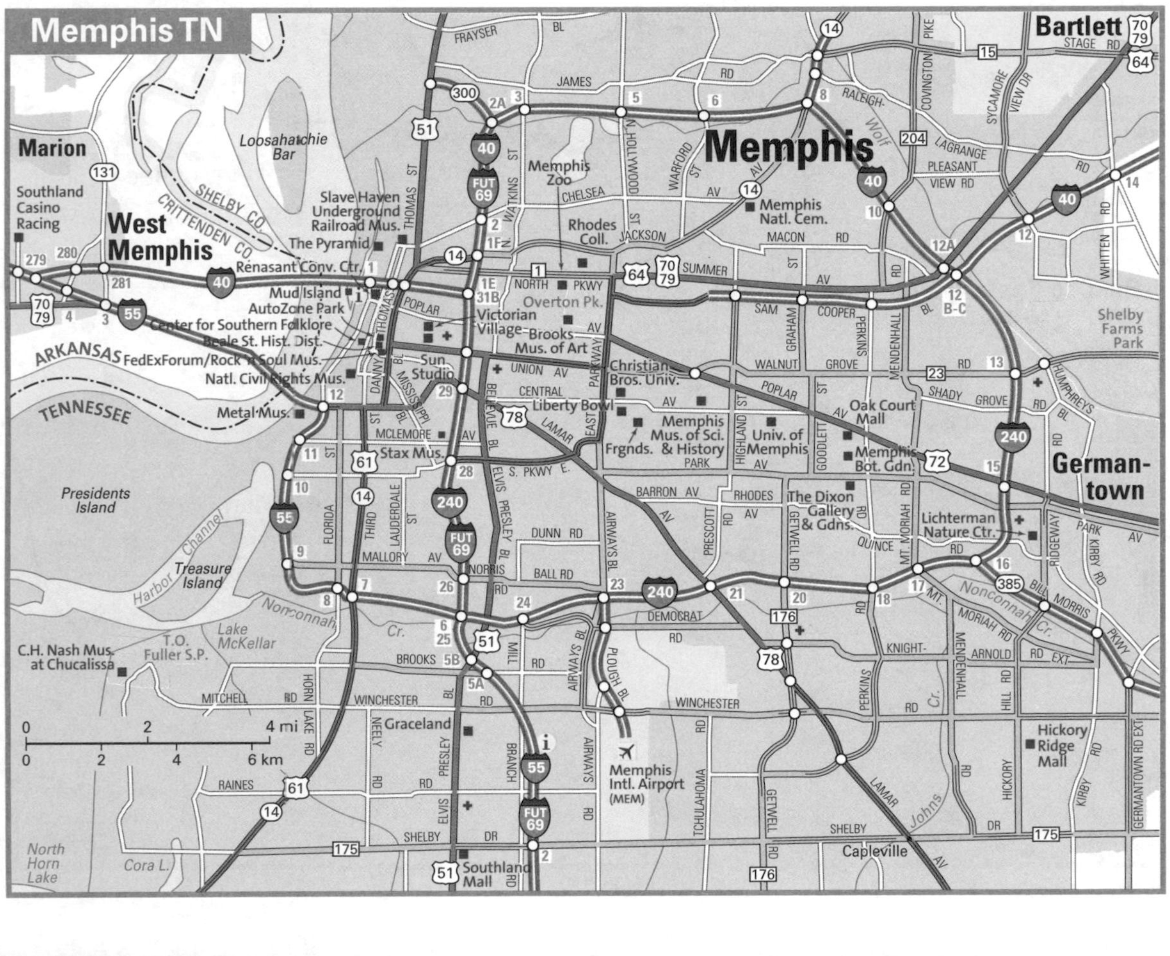
Memphis TN
Memphis
West Memphis
Marion
Bartlett
Germantown
Southland Casino Racing
Presidents Island
Treasure Island
Memphis Zoo
Overton Pk.
Rhodes Coll.
Memphis Natl. Cem.
Graceland
Memphis Intl. Airport (MEM)
Capleville
Hickory Ridge Mall
Southland Mall
C.H. Nash Mus. at Chucalissa
T.O. Fuller S.P.
Shelby Farms Park
Oak Court Mall
Lichterman Nature Ctr.
The Dixon Gallery & Gdns.
Memphis Bot. Gdn.
Univ. of Memphis
Liberty Bowl
Memphis Mus. of Sci. & History
Victorian Village
Brooks Mus. of Art
Sun Studio
Stax Mus.
Metal Mus.
Natl. Civil Rights Mus.
FedExForum/Rock 'n' Soul Mus.
Beale St. Hist. Dist.
Center for Southern Folklore
AutoZone Park
Mud Island
Renasant Conv. Ctr.
The Pyramid
Slave Haven Underground Railroad Mus.
ARKANSAS
TENNESSEE
0 2 4 mi
0 2 4 6 km

Miami/Fort Lauderdale FL

Milwaukee WI

Minneapolis/St Paul MN

Entries in **bold color** indicate cities with detailed inset maps.
Louisville–Minneota 111

Louisville MS 64 B1
Louisville NE 38 A1
Louisville OH 41 F1
Loup City NE 23 D4
Loveland CO 35 F1
Loveland OH 41 D2
Lovell WY 20 C1
Lovelock NV 32 B1
Loves Park IL 25 E3
Loving NM 58 A1
Lovington NM 58 B1
Lowell AR 51 D1
Lowell IN 25 F4
Lowell MA 71 E1
Lowell MI 26 A3
Lower Brule SD 23 D2
Lowville NY 28 C2
Lubbock TX 49 D4
Lucedale MS 64 B3
Lucerne WY 21 D2
Ludington MI 26 A2
Ludlow MA 70 C2
Ludlow VT 29 E2
Lufkin TX 62 C2
Lugoff SC 54 B3
Lukachukai AZ 47 D1
Luling LA 111 A2
Luling TX 61 D1
Lumberton MS 64 A3
Lumberton NC 55 D3
Lumberton TX 62 C3
Luray VA 42 B3
Lusk WY 21 F3
Lutcher LA 63 F4
Lutz FL 67 D1
Luverne AL 65 D2
Luverne MN 23 F2
Luxemburg WI 25 F1
Luxora AR 52 A2
Lyford TX 61 D4
Lyman WY 20 B4
Lynchburg TN 53 D2
Lynchburg VA 42 A4
Lynden WA 8 B1
Lyndhurst NJ 112 B2
Lyndhurst OH 99 G2
Lyndhurst VA 42 B4
Lyndon KS 38 A3
Lyndon KY 108 C1
Lyndonville VT 29 E1
Lynn MA 71 E1
Lynn Haven FL 65 D3
Lynnwood WA 8 B2
Lynwood CA 106 D3
Lyons CO 35 F1
Lyons GA 66 A1
Lyons KS 37 E3
Lyons NE 23 F4
Lyons NY 28 B3
Lytle TX 59 F4

M

Mabank TX 62 B1
Mableton GA 53 E4
Mabton WA 8 C3
Macclenny FL 66 A3
Macedonia OH 99 G3
Machesney Park IL 25 E3
Machias ME 30 C3
Mackay ID 19 F2
Macomb IL 39 E1
Macon GA 65 F1
Macon MS 64 B1
Macon MO 39 D2
Macungie PA 68 C1
Macy NE 23 F3
Madawaska ME 30 B1
Maddock ND 13 E2
Madeira OH 99 C2
Madeira Beach FL 67 D2
Madelia MN 24 A2
Madera CA 44 B1
Madill OK 50 B4
Madison AL 53 D3
Madison FL 65 F3
Madison GA 53 F4
Madison IN 40 C3
Madison ME 29 F1
Madison MN 23 F1
Madison MS 64 A1
Madison NE 23 E4
Madison NJ 69 E1
Madison NC 54 C1
Madison SD 23 E2
Madison WV 41 E4
Madison WI 25 E3
Madison Hts. MI 101 G1
Madisonville KY 40 A4
Madisonville TN 53 F2
Madisonville TX 62 B3
Madras OR 17 F1
Madrid IA 24 B4
Maeser UT 34 C1
Magalia CA 31 F2
Magdalena NM 47 F4
Magee MS 64 A2
Magna UT 34 A1
Magnolia AR 51 E4
Magnolia MS 63 F3
Mahanoy City PA 68 B1
Mahomet IL 39 F1
Mahopac NY 70 B3
Mahwah NJ 70 A4
Maiden NC 54 B2
Maili HI 72 A3
Maize KS 37 F4
Makaha HI 72 A3
Makakilo City HI 72 A3
Makawao HI 73 D1
Makena HI 73 D1
Malad City ID 20 A3
Malakoff TX 62 B2
Malden MA 71 E1
Malden MO 52 A1
Malibu CA 44 C4
Malone NY 28 C1
Malta MT 11 E1
Malvern AR 51 E3
Malvern PA 68 C2
Mammoth AZ 56 B1
Mammoth Lakes CA 32 B4
Mamou LA 63 E3
Manasquan NJ 69 E2
Manassa CO 35 F4
Manassas VA 68 A4
Manassas Park VA 68 A4
Manchester CT 70 C3
Manchester GA 65 E1
Manchester IA 24 C3
Manchester KY 53 F1
Manchester MD 68 A3
Manchester MI 26 B3
Manchester MO 120 A3
Manchester NH 29 E3
Manchester TN 53 D2
Manchester-by-the-Sea MA 71 E1
Mancos CO 35 D4
Mandan ND 13 D3
Mandaree ND 12 C2
Manderson SD 22 B2
Mandeville LA 64 A3
Mangum OK 49 E3
Manhattan IL 25 F4
Manhattan KS 37 F2
Manhattan MT 10 C4
Manhattan Beach CA 106 B3
Manheim PA 68 B2
Manila AR 52 A2
Manistee MI 26 A1
Manistique MI 16 B4
Manitou Beach MI 26 B4
Manitou Sprs. CO 35 F3
Manitowoc WI 25 F2
Mankato MN 24 B1
Manlius NY 28 B3
Mannford OK 50 B2
Manning IA 24 A4
Manning SC 54 C4
Mannington WV 41 F2
Manomet MA 71 E2
Mansfield LA 63 D2
Mansfield MA 71 E2
Mansfield OH 41 E1
Mansfield PA 28 B4
Mansfield TX 62 A1
Manson IA 24 A3
Mansura LA 63 E3
Mantachie MS 52 B3
Manteca CA 31 F4
Manteno IL 25 F4
Manti UT 34 B2
Manvel TX 61 F1
Manville NJ 69 D1
Manville RI 71 D2
Many LA 63 D2
Many Farms AZ 47 D1
Maple Grove MN 14 C4
Maple Hts. OH 99 G3
Maple Lake MN 14 C4
Mapleton IA 23 F3
Mapleton MN 24 B2
Mapleton ND 13 F3
Mapleton UT 34 B2
Maple Valley WA 8 B2
Maplewood MN 110 D2
Maplewood MO 120 B2
Maquoketa IA 25 D4
Marana AZ 56 B1
Marathon FL 67 D4
Marathon City WI 25 D1
Marble Falls TX 59 F3
Marblehead MA 71 E1
Marble Hill MO 39 E4
Marbleton WY 20 B3
Marceline MO 38 C2
Marco Island FL 67 E4
Marengo IL 25 E3
Marengo IA 24 C4
Marfa TX 58 A3
Margate FL 109 A1
Margate City NJ 69 E3
Marianna AR 51 F3
Marianna FL 65 E3
Maricopa AZ 56 A1
Marietta GA 53 E4
Marietta OH 41 F2
Marietta OK 50 B4
Marietta PA 68 B2
Marietta SC 54 A3
Marietta WA 8 B1
Marina CA 31 D4
Marine City MI 26 C3
Marinette WI 16 A4
Marion AL 64 C1
Marion AR 52 A2
Marion IL 39 F4
Marion IN 40 C1
Marion IA 24 C4
Marion KS 37 F3
Marion KY 40 A4
Marion MS 64 B1
Marion NC 54 A2
Marion OH 41 D1
Marion SC 54 C4
Marion SD 23 E2
Marion VA 54 B1
Marionville MO 51 D1
Marked Tree AR 52 A2
Marks MS 52 A3
Marksville LA 63 E3
Marlborough MA 71 D2
Marlette MI 26 C2
Marlin TX 62 A2
Marlinton WV 42 A3
Marlow OK 50 A3
Marlton NJ 69 D2
Marmet WV 41 F3
Marquette MI 16 A3
Marrero LA 64 A4
Marseilles IL 25 E4
Marshall AR 51 E2
Marshall IL 40 A2
Marshall MI 26 B3
Marshall MN 23 F1
Marshall MO 38 C3
Marshall TX 62 C1
Marshalltown IA 24 B4
Marshfield MA 71 E2
Marshfield MO 38 C4
Marshfield WI 25 D1
Mars Hill ME 30 C1
Marshville NC 54 C3
Marsing ID 19 D2
Mart TX 62 A2
Martha Lake WA 123 B2
Martin SD 22 B2
Martin TN 52 B1
Martinez CA 31 F4
Martinsburg WV 42 B2
Martins Ferry OH 41 F2
Martinsville IN 40 B2
Martinsville VA 54 C1
Marvell AR 51 F3
Mary Esther FL 64 C3
Maryland Hts. MO 120 A1
Marysville CA 31 F2
Marysville KS 37 F2
Marysville MI 26 C3
Marysville OH 41 D1
Marysville WA 8 B2
Maryville MO 38 B1
Maryville TN 53 F2
Mascot TN 53 F2
Mascoutah IL 39 E3
Mason MI 26 B3
Mason NV 32 B3
Mason OH 41 D2
Mason TX 59 E3
Mason City IL 39 F1
Mason City IA 24 B2
Masontown PA 42 A2
Massapequa NY 69 F1
Massena NY 28 C1
Massillon OH 41 F1
Mastic NY 43 F1
Mastic Beach NY 43 F1
Matawan NJ 69 E2
Mathews LA 63 F4
Mathis TX 61 D2
Mattapoisett MA 71 E3
Mattawa WA 8 C3
Mattawan MI 26 A3
Matthews NC 54 B3
Mattituck NY 70 C4
Mattoon IL 39 F2
Maud OK 50 B3
Mauldin SC 54 A3
Maumee OH 26 C4
Maumelle AR 51 E3
Maunawili HI 72 A3
Mauriceville TX 63 D4
Mauston WI 25 D2
Maxton NC 54 C3
Maybrook NY 70 A3
Mayer AZ 46 B3
Mayfield KY 52 B1
Mayfield Hts. OH 99 G2
Mayflower AR 51 E3
Maynard MA 71 D1
Maynardville TN 53 F1
Mayo MD 68 B4
Mayo SC 54 B3
Mayodan NC 54 C1
Maysville KY 41 D3
Maysville OK 50 A3
Mayville ND 13 F2
Mayville WI 25 E2
Maywood CA 106 D3
Maywood IL 98 C4
Maywood NJ 112 C1
McAlester OK 50 C3
McAllen TX 60 C4
McCall ID 19 D1
McCamey TX 58 C3
McCammon ID 20 A3
McCandless PA 42 A1
McClusky ND 13 D2
McColl SC 54 C3
McComb MS 63 F2
McCook NE 37 D1
McCrory AR 51 F2
McDonough GA 53 F4
McEwen TN 52 C2
McFarland CA 44 B2
McFarland WI 25 E3
McGehee AR 51 F4
McGill NV 33 E2
McGregor TX 62 A2
McHenry IL 25 E3
McKeesport PA 42 A1
McKenzie TN 52 B2
McKinleyville CA 31 D1
McKinney TX 50 B4
McLaughlin SD 13 D4
McLean VA 68 A4
McLeansboro IL 39 F4
McLoud OK 50 B2
McMechen WV 41 F2
McMinnville OR 8 A4
McMinnville TN 53 D2
McPherson KS 37 F3
McRae GA 65 F2
McSherrystown PA 68 A3
McVille ND 13 F2
Mead CO 35 F1
Mead WA 9 E2
Meade KS 37 D4
Meadowview VA 54 B1
Meadville PA 27 E4
Mebane NC 55 D2
Mecca CA 45 E4
Mechanic Falls ME 29 F1
Mechanicsburg PA 68 A2
Mechanicsville VA 42 C4
Mechanicville NY 70 B1
Medfield MA 71 E2
Medford MA 29 F3
Medford NJ 69 D2
Medford NY 69 F1
Medford OK 50 A1
Medford OR 17 E3
Medford WI 15 E4
Medford Lakes NJ 69 D3
Media PA 68 C2
Mediapolis IA 39 D1
Medical Lake WA 9 E2
Medicine Lodge KS 37 E4
Medina NY 27 F2
Medina OH 41 E1
Medulla FL 67 E2
Meeker CO 35 D2
Mehlville MO 120 B3
Meiners Oaks CA 44 B3
Melbourne AR 51 F2
Melbourne FL 67 F2
Melrose MN 14 B4
Melrose NM 48 B3
Melrose Park IL 98 C4
Melvindale MI 101 F3
Memphis MO 39 D1
Memphis TN 52 A3
Memphis TX 49 E3
Mena AR 51 D3
Menan ID 20 A2
Menard TX 59 E3
Menasha WI 25 E1
Mendenhall MS 64 A2
Mendham NJ 69 D1
Mendota CA 44 A1
Mendota IL 25 E4
Mendota Hts. MN 110 D3
Menifee CA 45 D4
Menlo Park CA 122 C5
Menno SD 23 E2
Menominee MI 16 A4
Menomonee Falls WI 25 E2
Menomonie WI 24 C1
Mentone CA 45 D4
Mentor OH 27 D4
Mequon WI 25 F2
Meraux LA 111 D2
Merced CA 32 A4
Mercedes TX 60 C4
Mercer Island WA 123 B3
Mercerville NJ 69 D2
Meredith NH 29 E2
Meriden CT 70 C3
Meridian ID 19 D2
Meridian MS 64 B1
Meridian PA 42 A1
Meridian TX 59 F2
Meridianville AL 53 D3
Merkel TX 59 E1
Merriam KS 104 B4
Merrifield VA 124 A2
Merrill WI 15 E4
Merrillville IN 25 F4
Merrimack NH 71 D1
Merritt Island FL 67 F1
Mesa AZ 46 B4
Mescalero NM 48 A4
Mesilla NM 57 E1
Mesita NM 47 E3
Mesquite NV 45 F1
Mesquite NM 57 E2
Mesquite TX 62 B1
Metairie LA 64 A4
Metamora IL 39 F1
Metcalfe MS 51 F4
Methuen MA 71 E1
Metlakatla AK 75 E4
Metropolis IL 39 F4
Metter GA 66 A1
Mexia TX 62 B2
Mexico ME 29 F1
Mexico MO 39 D3
Miami AZ 46 C4
Miami FL 67 F4
Miami OK 50 C1
Miami Beach FL 67 F4
Miami Lakes FL 109 A3
Micco FL 67 F2
Michigan Ctr. MI 26 B3
Michigan City IN 25 F4
Middleboro MA 71 E2
Middleburg FL 66 A4
Middleburg Hts. OH 99 E3
Middlebury IN 26 A4
Middlebury VT 29 D2
Middle River MD 68 B3
Middlesboro KY 53 F1
Middlesex NJ 69 E1
Middleton ID 19 D2
Middleton WI 25 E3
Middletown CT 70 C3
Middletown DE 68 C3
Middletown IN 40 C2
Middletown KY 40 C3
Middletown MD 68 A3
Middletown NY 70 A3
Middletown OH 40 C2
Middletown PA 68 B2
Middletown RI 71 E3
Middleville MI 26 A3
Midland MI 26 B2
Midland PA 41 F1
Midland TX 58 C2
Midland City AL 65 D2
Midlothian TX 62 A1
Midvale UT 120 E3
Midway KY 40 C4
Midway NM 48 B4
Midwest WY 21 E2
Midwest City OK 50 A2
Mifflinburg PA 68 A1
Milaca MN 14 C4
Milan MI 26 C4
Milan MO 38 C1
Milan NM 47 E3
Milan TN 52 B2
Milbank SD 14 A4
Miles City MT 12 A3
Milford CT 70 B4
Milford DE 68 C4
Milford IA 24 A2
Milford ME 30 B3
Milford MD 95 A2
Milford MA 71 D2
Milford MI 26 C3
Milford NE 37 F1
Milford NH 71 D1
Milford UT 33 F3
Mililani Town HI 72 A3
Millbrae CA 122 B4
Millbrook AL 65 D1
Millbury MA 71 D2
Mill City OR 17 E1
Millcreek UT 120 F2
Mill Creek WA 123 B2
Milledgeville GA 65 F1
Millen GA 66 A1
Miller SD 23 D1
Millersburg OH 41 E1
Millersburg PA 68 A1
Millersville PA 68 B2
Millersville TN 53 D1
Milliken CO 35 F1
Millington TN 52 A2
Millinocket ME 30 B2
Mills WY 21 E3
Millsboro DE 43 D3
Mill Valley CA 31 E4
Millville NJ 69 D3
Milnor ND 13 F3
Milo ME 30 B3
Milpitas CA 31 F4
Milton DE 68 C4
Milton FL 64 C3
Milton MA 96 E3
Milton PA 42 C1
Milton VT 29 D1
Milton WV 41 E3
Milton WI 25 E3
Milton-Freewater OR 9 D4
Milwaukee WI 25 F3
Milwaukie OR 118 B2
Mims FL 67 F1
Minatare NE 22 A4
Minco OK 50 A2
Minden LA 63 D1
Minden NE 37 E1
Minden NV 32 B3
Mineola NY 69 F1
Mineola TX 62 B1
Mineral Pt. WI 25 D3
Mineral Sprs. AR 51 D4
Mineral Wells TX 59 F1
Mineral Wells WV 41 F2
Minersville PA 68 B1
Minerva OH 41 F1
Minneapolis KS 37 F3
Minneapolis MN 24 B1
Minneota MN 23 F1

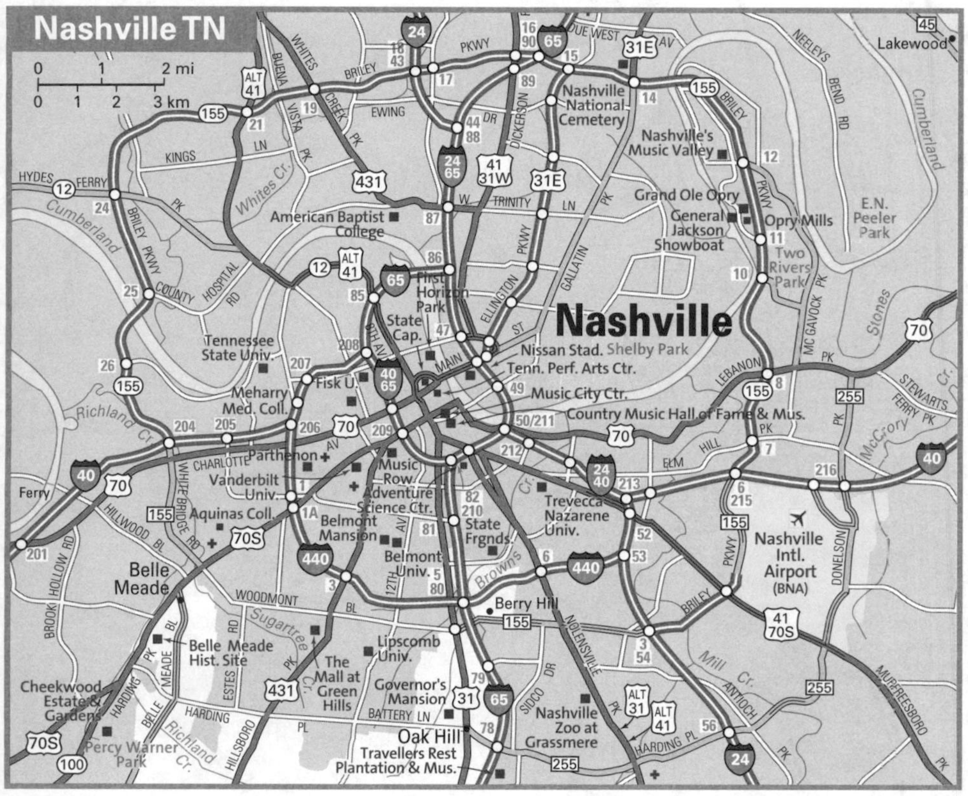
Nashville TN
0 1 2 mi
0 1 2 3 km
Nashville
Nashville National Cemetery
Nashville's Music Valley
Grand Ole Opry
Opry Mills
General Jackson Showboat
E.N. Peeler Park
Two Rivers Park
American Baptist College
Tennessee State Univ.
Fisk U.
Meharry Med. Coll.
State Cap.
Nissan Stad.
Shelby Park
Tenn. Perf. Arts Ctr.
Music City Ctr.
Country Music Hall of Fame & Mus.
Parthenon
Vanderbilt Univ.
Music Row
Adventure Science Ctr.
Aquinas Coll.
Belmont Mansion
Belmont Univ.
Trevecca Nazarene Univ.
State Frgds.
Nashville Intl. Airport (BNA)
Berry Hill
Belle Meade
Belle Meade Hist. Site
Lipscomb Univ.
The Mall at Green Hills
Governor's Mansion
Cheekwood Estate & Gardens
Percy Warner Park
Oak Hill
Travellers Rest Plantation & Mus.
Nashville Zoo at Grassmere
Lakewood
Cumberland
Richland Cr.
Whites Cr.
Mill Cr.
Stones
Ferry

A B C D

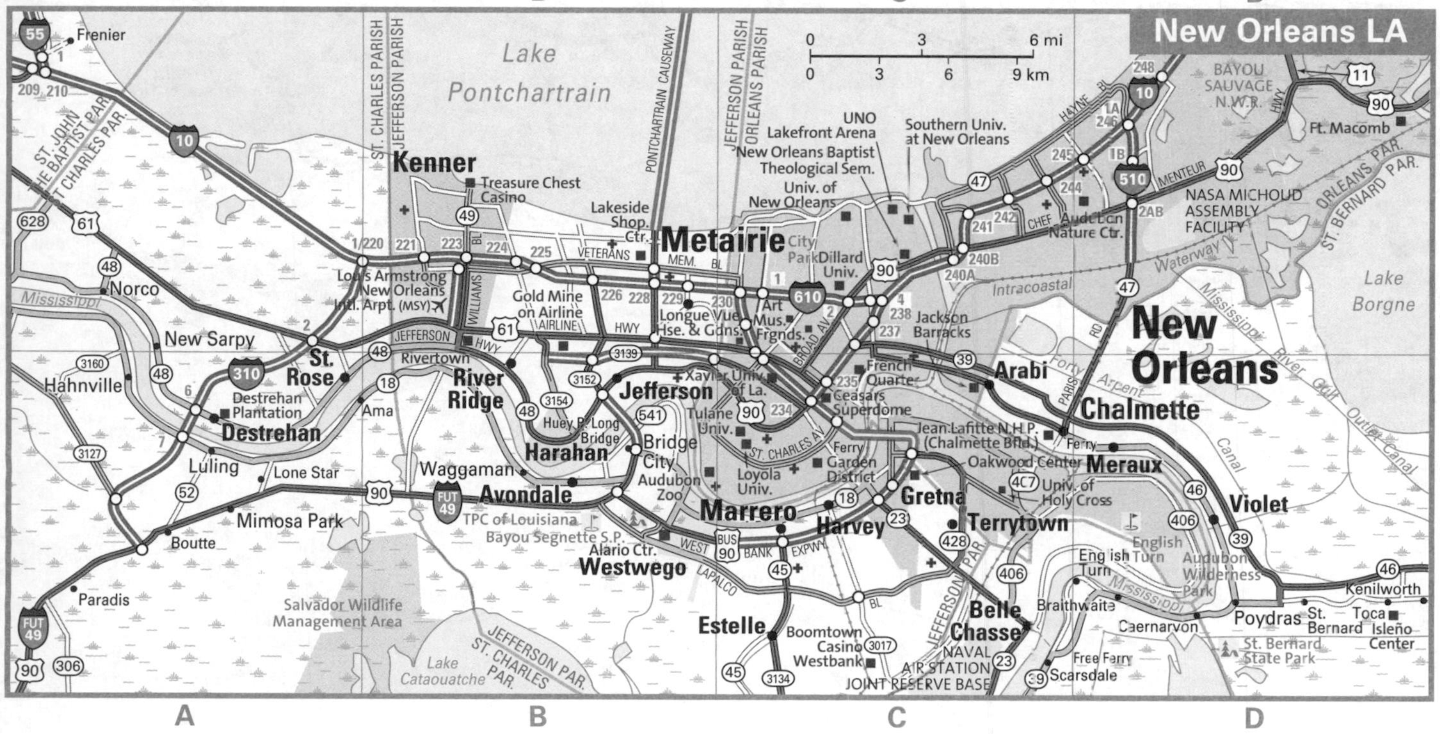
New Orleans LA
0 3 6 mi
0 3 6 9 km
Lake Pontchartrain
Kenner
Metairie
New Orleans
Chalmette
Meraux
Violet
Arabi
Jefferson
Harahan
River Ridge
St. Rose
Destrehan
Luling
Boutte
Paradis
Norco
New Sarpy
Hahnville
Frenier
Avondale
Waggaman
Westwego
Marrero
Harvey
Gretna
Terrytown
Estelle
Belle Chasse
Braithwaite
Caernarvon
Poydras
St. Bernard
Toca
Kenilworth
Mimosa Park
Lake Borgne
Lake Cataouatche
Salvador Wildlife Management Area
Bayou Sauvage N.W.R.
Ft. Macomb
UNO Lakefront Arena
Southern Univ. at New Orleans
New Orleans Baptist Theological Sem.
Univ. of New Orleans
Treasure Chest Casino
Lakeside Shop. Ctr.
Louis Armstrong New Orleans Intl. Arpt. (MSY)
Gold Mine on Airline
Longue Vue Hse. & Gdns.
Dillard Univ.
Jackson Barracks
French Quarter
Caesars Superdome
Xavier Univ. of La.
Tulane Univ.
Loyola Univ.
Audubon Zoo
Ferry Garden District
Jean Lafitte N.H.P. (Chalmette Btfld.)
Oakwood Center
Univ. of Holy Cross
NASA Michoud Assembly Facility
Audubon Louisiana Nature Ctr.
TPC of Louisiana
Bayou Segnette S.P.
Alario Ctr.
Boomtown Casino Westbank
Naval Air Station Joint Reserve Base
Destrehan Plantation
English Turn
Scarsdale
Free Ferry
Isleño Center
Audubon Wilderness Park
Intracoastal Waterway
Mississippi River
St. Bernard State Park
St. Charles Parish
Jefferson Parish
Orleans Parish
Pontchartrain Causeway
1 2
A B C D

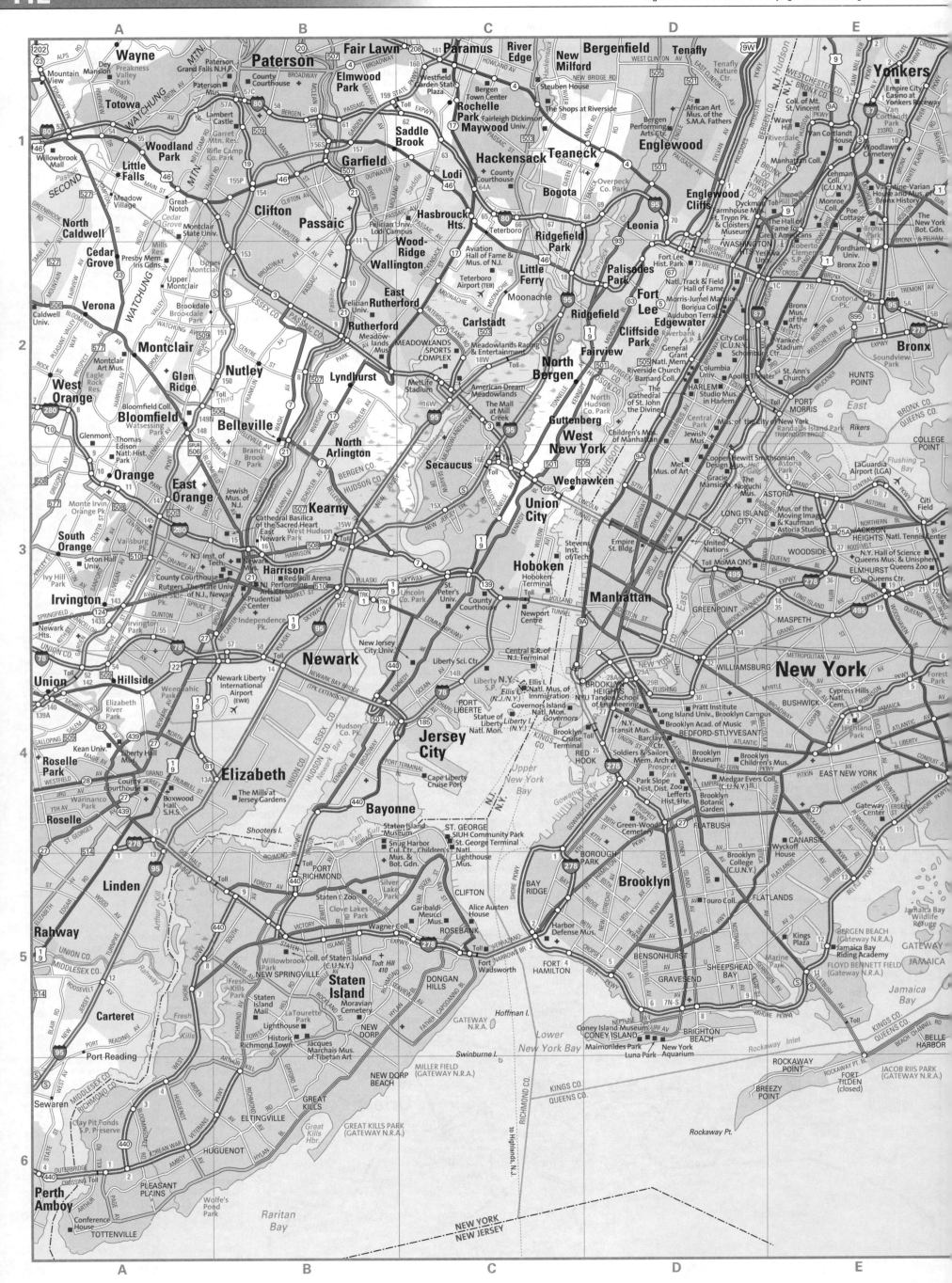

Entries in bold color indicate cities with detailed inset maps.
Minnetonka—North Palm Beach 113

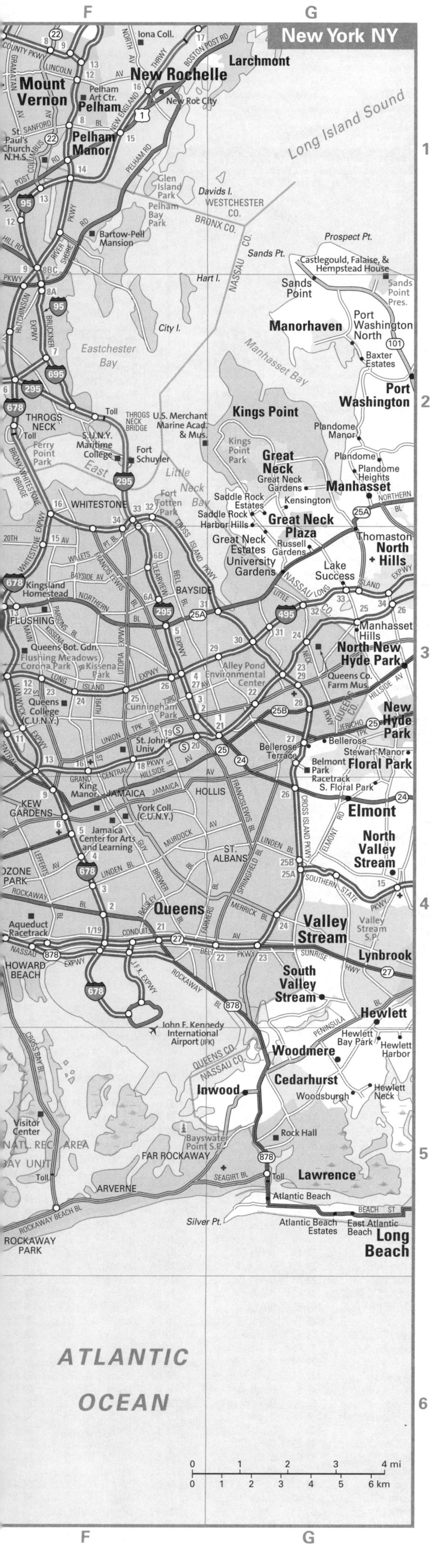
New York NY
F
G
1
2
3
4
5
6
Mount Vernon
New Rochelle
Larchmont
Pelham
Pelham Manor
Long Island Sound
Manorhaven
Port Washington
Port Washington North
Sands Point
Kings Point
Great Neck
Manhasset
Great Neck Plaza
North Hills
Lake Success
Queens
New Hyde Park
North New Hyde Park
Floral Park
Elmont
North Valley Stream
Valley Stream
South Valley Stream
Lynbrook
Hewlett
Woodmere
Cedarhurst
Inwood
Lawrence
Long Beach
Atlantic Beach
ATLANTIC OCEAN
John F. Kennedy International Airport (JFK)
Eastchester Bay
Manhasset Bay
Little Neck Bay
City I.
Hart I.
Davids I.
Whitestone
Flushing
Kew Gardens
Jamaica
Hollis
St. Albans
Rockaway Park
Howard Beach
Far Rockaway
0 1 2 3 4 mi
0 1 2 3 4 5 6 km

Minnetonka MN 110 A3
Minooka IL 25 E4
Minot ND 13 D1
Minster OH 41 D1
Mint Hill NC 54 B3
Minto ND 13 F1
Minturn CO 35 E2
Mio MI 26 B1
Miramar FL 67 F4
Mishawaka IN 25 A4
Mission KS 104 B3
Mission SD 22 C2
Mission TX 60 C4
Mission Bend TX 102 C2
Mission Viejo CA 44 C4
Mississippi State MS 52 B4
Missoula MT 10 A3
Missouri City TX 61 E1
Missouri Valley IA 23 F4
Mitchell IN 40 B3
Mitchell NE 22 A4
Mitchell SD 23 E2
Moab UT 34 C3
Moapa NV 45 F1
Moberly MO 39 D2
Mobile AL 64 B3
Mobridge SD 13 D4
Mocksville NC 54 C2
Modesto CA 31 F4
Mohall ND 13 D1
Mohave Valley AZ 45 F3
Mohawk NY 28 C3
Mojave CA 44 C3
Mokuleia HI 72 A2
Molalla OR 8 B4
Moline IL 25 D4
Momence IL 25 F4
Monahans TX 58 E2
Moncks Corner SC 66 C1
Mondovi WI 24 C1
Monee IL 25 F4
Monessen PA 42 A1
Monett MO 51 D1
Monmouth IL 39 E1
Monmouth OR 17 E1
Monmouth Beach NJ 69 E2
Monona IA 24 C3
Monona WI 25 E3
Monroe CT 70 B3
Monroe GA 53 F4
Monroe IA 24 B4
Monroe LA 63 E1
Monroe MI 26 C4
Monroe NY 70 A3
Monroe NC 54 C3
Monroe OH 41 D2
Monroe UT 34 A3
Monroe WA 8 B2
Monroe WI 25 D3
Monroe City MO 39 D2
Monroeville AL 64 C2
Monroeville PA 42 A1
Monrovia CA 106 E2
Montague MI 26 A2
Montana City MT 10 C3
Montauk NY 71 D4
Mont Belvieu TX 62 C4
Montclair CA 107 G2
Montclair NJ 112 A2
Monte Alto TX 60 C4
Montebello CA 106 D3
Montecito CA 44 B3
Montegut LA 63 F4
Monterey CA 31 D4
Monterey TN 53 E2
Monterey Park CA 106 D2
Montesano WA 8 A3
Montevallo AL 64 C1
Montevideo MN 23 F1
Monte Vista CO 35 F4
Montezuma GA 65 F1
Montezuma IA 24 B4
Montgomery AL 65 D1
Montgomery MN 24 B1
Montgomery NY 70 A3
Montgomery OH 99 C1
Montgomery WV 41 F3
Montgomery City MO 39 D3
Montgomery Vil. MD 68 A4
Montgomeryville PA 69 D2
Monticello AR 51 F4
Monticello GA 53 F4
Monticello IL 39 F2
Monticello IN 40 B1
Monticello IA 24 C3
Monticello KY 53 E1
Monticello MN 14 C4
Monticello MS 64 A2
Monticello NY 28 C4
Monticello UT 34 C4
Montoursville PA 28 B4
Montpelier ID 20 A3
Montpelier OH 26 B4
Montpelier VT 29 E1
Montrose CA 106 D1
Montrose CO 35 D3
Monument CO 35 F2
Moody TX 62 A2
Moorcroft WY 21 F1
Moore OK 50 A2
Moorefield WV 42 B3
Mooreland OK 49 F1
Moorestown NJ 43 D2
Mooresville IN 40 B2
Mooresville NC 54 B2
Moorhead MN 14 A3
Moorhead MS 52 A4
Moorpark CA 44 C3
Moose Lake MN 14 C3
Moosup CT 71 D3
Mora MN 14 C4
Moraga CA 122 D2
Morehead KY 41 D3
Morehead City NC 55 E3
Morenci AZ 56 C1
Morenci MI 26 B4
Moreno Valley CA 45 D4
Morgan UT 34 B1
Morgan City LA 63 F4
Morganfield KY 40 A4
Morgan Hill CA 31 F4
Morganton NC 54 B2
Morgantown KY 40 B4
Morgantown WV 42 A2
Moriarty NM 47 F3
Moroni UT 34 B2
Morrill NE 21 F4
Morrilton AR 51 E3
Morris AL 53 D4
Morris IL 25 E4
Morris MN 14 A4
Morris OK 50 C2
Morrison IL 25 D4
Morris Plains NJ 69 E1
Morristown NJ 69 E1
Morristown TN 53 F1
Morrisville NC 55 D2
Morrisville VT 29 E1
Morro Bay CA 44 A2
Morton IL 39 F1
Morton MS 64 A1
Morton TX 48 C4
Morton Grove IL 98 D3
Moscow ID 9 E3
Moscow Mills MO 39 E3
Moses Lake WA 9 D2
Mosheim TN 54 A1
Mosinee WI 25 D1
Moss Bluff LA 63 D3
Moss Pt. MS 64 B3
Mott ND 12 C3
Moulton AL 52 C3
Moultrie GA 65 F3
Mound MN 24 B1
Mound Bayou MS 52 A4
Moundridge KS 37 F3
Mounds OK 50 B2
Mounds View MN 110 C1
Moundsville WV 41 F2
Moundville AL 64 C1
Mountainair NM 47 F3
Mountainaire AZ 46 B3
Mtn. Brook AL 96 B2
Mtn. City TN 54 B1
Mtn. Grove MO 51 E1
Mtn. Home AR 51 E1
Mtn. Home ID 19 D3
Mtn. Home NC 54 A2
Mtn. Iron MN 14 C2
Mtn. Lake MN 24 A2
Mtn. View AR 51 E2
Mtn. View CA 122 D5
Mtn. View HI 73 F3
Mtn. View MO 51 F1
Mtn. View WY 20 B4
Mtn. Vil. AK 74 B2
Mt. Airy MD 68 A3
Mt. Airy NC 54 C1
Mt. Angel OR 17 E1
Mt. Ayr IA 38 B1
Mt. Carmel IL 40 A3
Mt. Carmel PA 68 B1
Mt. Clemens MI 26 C3
Mt. Dora FL 67 E1
Mt. Gay WV 41 E4
Mt. Gilead OH 41 E1
Mt. Holly NJ 69 D2
Mt. Holly NC 54 B2
Mt. Hope WV 41 F4
Mt. Horeb WI 25 D3
Mt. Jackson VA 42 B3
Mt. Joy PA 68 B2
Mt. Juliet TN 53 D2
Mt. Kisco NY 70 B4
Mountlake Terrace WA 123 B2
Mt. Lebanon PA 117 F3
Mt. Morris IL 25 E4
Mt. Morris MI 26 C3
Mt. Morris NY 28 A3
Mt. Olive NC 55 D3
Mt. Pleasant IA 39 D1
Mt. Pleasant MI 26 B2
Mt. Pleasant PA 42 A1
Mt. Pleasant SC 66 C1
Mt. Pleasant TN 52 C2
Mt. Pleasant TX 62 C1
Mt. Pleasant UT 34 B2
Mt. Pocono PA 43 D1
Mt. Prospect IL 98 C3
Mt. Shasta CA 17 E4
Mt. Sterling KY 41 D4
Mt. Union PA 42 B1
Mt. Vernon GA 66 A2
Mt. Vernon IL 39 F3
Mt. Vernon IN 40 A4
Mt. Vernon IA 24 C4
Mt. Vernon KY 41 D4
Mt. Vernon MO 51 D1
Mt. Vernon NY 27 F3
Mt. Vernon NY 69 E1
Mt. Vernon OH 41 E1
Mt. Vernon TX 62 C1
Mt. Vernon WA 8 B1
Mt. Washington KY 40 C4
Moville IA 23 F3
Moyie Sprs. ID 9 F1
Muenster TX 50 A4
Mukilteo WA 8 B2
Mulberry AR 51 D2
Mulberry FL 67 E2
Mulberry NC 54 B1
Muldrow OK 51 D2
Muleshoe TX 48 C3
Mullan ID 8 A4
Mullens WV 41 F4
Mullins SC 55 D4
Mulvane KS 37 F4
Muncie IN 40 C1
Muncy PA 28 B4
Munday TX 49 E4
Mundelein IL 98 B1
Munds Park AZ 46 B3
Munford AL 53 D4
Munford TN 52 A2
Munfordville KY 40 B4
Munhall PA 117 G3
Munising MI 16 A3
Munster IN 98 E6
Murdo SD 22 C2
Murfreesboro AR 51 D4
Murfreesboro NC 55 E1
Murfreesboro TN 53 D2
Murphy MO 120 A3
Murphysboro IL 39 F4
Murray KY 52 C1
Murray UT 34 A1
Murrells Inlet SC 55 D4
Murrieta CA 45 D4
Muscatine IA 24 C4
Muscle Shoals AL 52 C3
Muskego WI 25 E3
Muskegon MI 26 A2
Muskegon Hts. MI 26 A2
Muskogee OK 50 C2
Mustang OK 50 A2
Myerstown PA 68 B2
Myrtle Beach SC 55 D4
Myrtle Creek OR 17 E3
Myrtle Pt. OR 17 D3
Mystic CT 71 D3
Mystic Island NJ 69 E3

N

Nacogdoches TX 62 C2
Nags Head NC 55 F2
Naknek AK 74 B3
Nampa ID 19 D2
Nanakuli HI 72 A3
Nanticoke PA 28 B4
Nantucket MA 71 F4
Nanty Glo PA 42 B1
Napa CA 31 E3
Naperville IL 25 E4
Naples FL 67 E3
Naples TX 50 C4
Naples UT 34 C1
Naples Manor FL 67 E4
Naples Park FL 67 E3
Napoleon ND 13 E3
Napoleon OH 26 B4
Nappanee IN 26 A4
Naranja FL 67 F4
Narragansett Pier RI 71 D3
Narrows VA 41 F4
Nashua IA 24 B3
Nashua NH 71 D1
Nashville AR 51 D4
Nashville GA 65 F2
Nashville IL 39 F3
Nashville NC 55 D2
Nashville TN 53 D2
Natalbany LA 63 F3
Natalia TX 59 F4
Natchez MS 63 F2
Natchitoches LA 63 D2
Natick MA 71 D2
National City CA 121 E2
Naugatuck CT 70 B3
Navajo NM 47 D2
Navasota TX 62 B3
Nazareth PA 69 D1
Nebraska City NE 38 A1
Neche ND 13 F1
Nederland CO 35 F2
Nederland TX 63 D4
Needham MA 71 E2
Needles CA 45 F3
Needville TX 61 E1
Neenah WI 25 E1
Negaunee MI 16 A3
Neillsville WI 25 D1
Nekoosa WI 25 D1
Neligh NE 23 E3
Nelsonville OH 41 E2
Neodesha KS 38 A4
Neosho MO 51 D1
Nephi UT 34 A2
Neptune Beach FL 66 B3
Neptune City NJ 69 E2
Nesquehoning PA 68 C1
Ness City KS 37 D3
Nettleton MS 52 B4
Nevada IA 24 B4
Nevada MO 38 B4
Nevada City CA 31 F2
New Albany IN 40 B3
New Albany MS 52 B3
Newark AR 51 F2
Newark CA 122 D5
Newark DE 68 C3
Newark NJ 69 E1
Newark NY 28 B3
Newark OH 41 E2
New Baden IL 39 F3
New Baltimore MI 26 C3
New Bedford MA 71 E3
Newberg OR 8 A4
New Berlin WI 25 E3
New Bern NC 55 E3
Newbern TN 52 B2
Newberry FL 66 A4
Newberry MI 16 B3
Newberry SC 54 B3
New Boston TX 51 D4
New Braunfels TX 59 F4
New Bremen OH 41 D1
New Brighton MN 110 C1
New Britain CT 70 C3
New Brunswick NJ 69 E1
New Buffalo MI 25 F4
Newburgh IN 40 A4
Newburgh NY 70 A3
Newburyport MA 71 E1
New Canaan CT 70 B4
New Carlisle OH 41 D2
New Carrollton MD 124 E1
New Castle CO 35 D2
New Castle DE 68 C3
New Castle IN 40 C2
Newcastle OK 50 A2
New Castle PA 41 F1
Newcastle WY 21 F2
New City NY 70 A4
Newcomerstown OH 41 E1
New Concord OH 41 E2
New Cordell OK 49 F2
Newell SD 22 A1
New Ellenton SC 54 B4
New England ND 12 C3
New Fairfield CT 70 B3
Newfane NY 27 F2
New Freedom PA 68 B3
New Glarus WI 25 D3
New Hampton IA 24 C3
New Haven CT 70 C4
New Haven IN 40 C1
New Haven MI 26 C3
New Haven MO 39 D3
New Haven WV 41 E3
New Holland PA 68 C2
New Holstein WI 25 E2
New Hope AL 53 D3
New Hope MN 110 B2
New Hope MS 52 C4
New Hyde Park NY 113 G3
New Iberia LA 63 E4
Newington CT 70 C3
New Johnsonville TN 52 C2
New Kensington PA 42 A1
Newkirk OK 50 B1
New Lebanon OH 41 D2
New Lenox IL 98 B6
New Lexington OH 41 E2
New Llano LA 63 D3
New London CT 71 D3
New London IA 39 D1
New London OH 41 E1
New London WI 25 E1
New Madrid MO 52 B1
Newman CA 31 F4
New Market AL 53 D3
Newmarket NH 29 F3
New Market VA 42 B3
New Martinsville WV 41 F2
New Meadows ID 19 D1
New Milford CT 70 B3
New Milford NJ 112 C1
Newnan GA 53 E4
New Orleans LA 64 A4
New Paltz NY 70 A3
New Philadelphia OH 41 F1
New Plymouth ID 19 D2
Newport AR 51 F2
Newport KY 99 B3
Newport ME 30 B3
Newport NH 29 E2
Newport NC 55 E3
Newport OR 17 D1
Newport RI 71 E3
Newport TN 53 F2
Newport VT 29 E1
Newport WA 9 E1
Newport Beach CA 44 C4
Newport News VA 55 F1
New Port Richey FL 67 D1
New Prague MN 24 B1
New Richmond WI 14 C4
New River AZ 46 B4
New Roads LA 63 F3
New Rochelle NY 69 E1
New Rockford ND 13 E2
New Salem ND 13 D3
New Smyrna Beach FL 67 E1
New Tazewell TN 53 F1
Newton AL 65 D2
Newton IL 40 A3
Newton IA 24 B4
Newton KS 37 F4
Newton MA 71 E2
Newton MS 64 B1
Newton NJ 43 E1
Newton NC 54 B2
Newton TX 63 D3
New Town ND 12 C2
New Ulm MN 24 A1
New Underwood SD 22 A2
New Whiteland IN 40 B2
New Windsor NY 70 A3
New York NY 69 E1
Nezperce ID 9 F3
Niagara WI 15 F4
Niagara Falls NY 27 F3
Niantic CT 70 C3
Niceville FL 65 D3
Nicholasville KY 40 C4
Nicholson MS 64 A3
Nickerson KS 37 E3
Nikiski AK 74 C3
Niles IL 98 D3
Niles MI 26 A4
Niles OH 27 E4
Ninety Six SC 54 A4
Nipomo CA 44 A3
Nisswa MN 14 B3
Nitro WV 41 E3
Niwot CO 35 F2
Nixa MO 51 E1
Nixon NV 32 B2
Nixon TX 59 F4
Noble OK 50 A3
Noblesville IN 40 B2
Nocona TX 50 A4
Noel MO 51 D1
Nogales AZ 56 B2
Nolanville TX 62 A3
Nolensville TN 53 D2
Nome AK 74 B2
Noorvik AK 74 B2
Nora Sprs. IA 24 B2
Norco CA 45 D4
Norfolk NE 23 E4
Norfolk VA 55 F1
Normal IL 39 F1
Norman OK 50 A2
Norridgewock ME 29 F1
Norristown PA 68 C2
N. Adams MA 70 B1
N. Amherst MA 70 C2
Northampton MA 70 C2
Northampton PA 68 C1
N. Arlington NJ 112 B3
N. Atlanta GA 94 C1
N. Attleboro MA 71 E2
N. Augusta SC 54 A4
N. Baltimore OH 26 C4
N. Bend NE 23 E4
N. Bend OR 17 D2
N. Bend WA 8 B2
N. Bennington VT 70 B1
N. Bergen NJ 112 C2
N. Berwick ME 29 F2
Northborough MA 71 D2
N. Branch MN 14 C4
Northbridge MA 71 D2
Northbrook IL 98 C2
Northbrook OH 99 A1
N. Brunswick NJ 69 E1
N. Canton OH 41 F1
N. Cape May NJ 69 D4
N. Charleston SC 66 C1
N. Chicago IL 25 F3
N. College Hill OH 99 A2
N. Conway NH 29 F2
N. Crossett AR 51 F4
Northdale FL 123 E1
N. Decatur GA 94 D2
N. Druid Hills GA 94 C2
North East MD 68 C3
N. East PA 27 E3
N. Fair Oaks CA 122 C5
Northfield MN 24 B1
Northfield NJ 69 D3
Northfield VT 29 E1
N. Fond du Lac WI 25 E2
N. Ft. Myers FL 67 E3
Northglenn CO 101 B1
N. Haven CT 70 C3
N. Highlands CA 31 F3
N. Kingsville OH 27 E4
N. Las Vegas NV 45 E1
N. Lauderdale FL 109 A2
N. Liberty IA 24 C4
N. Little Rock AR 51 E3
N. Manchester IN 40 C1
N. Mankato MN 24 A1
N. Miami FL 67 F4
N. Miami Beach FL 67 F4
N. Muskegon MI 26 A2
N. Myrtle Beach SC 55 D4
N. Naples FL 67 E3
N. Ogden UT 20 A4
N. Olmsted OH 27 D4
N. Palm Beach FL 67 F3

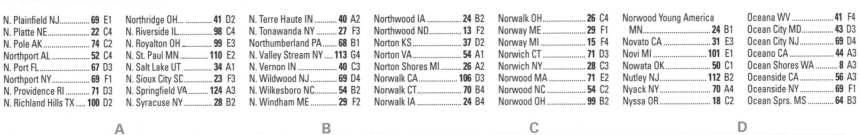

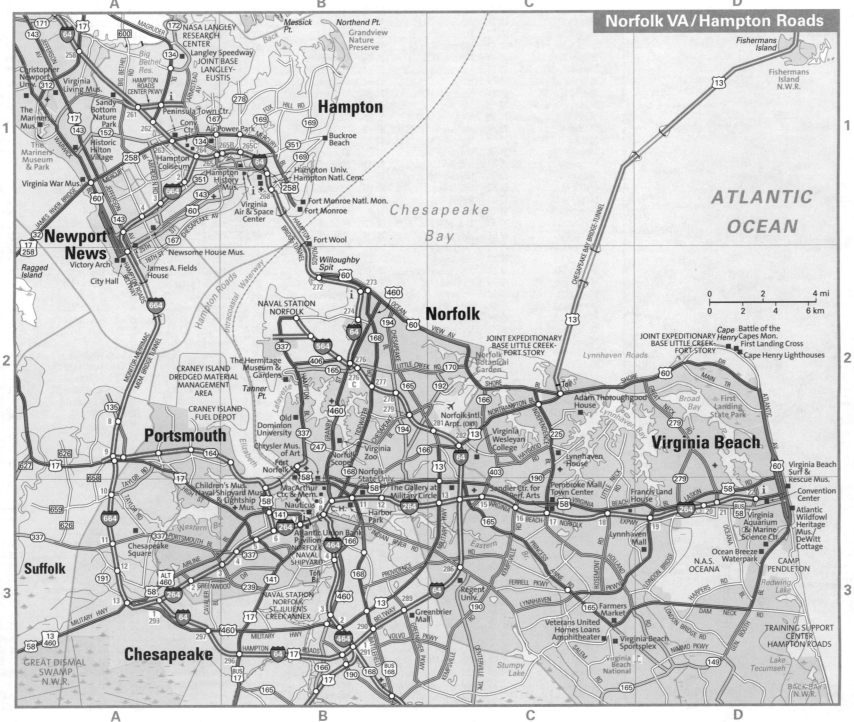

Norfolk VA / Hampton Roads

ATLANTIC OCEAN

Chesapeake Bay

Oklahoma City OK

Entries in **bold color** indicate cities with detailed inset maps.

Owensville—Portsmouth 115

Owensville MO 39 D3
Owenton KY 40 C3
Owings Mills MD 68 B3
Owingsville KY 41 D4
Owosso MI 26 B3
Owyhee NV 19 D4
Oxford AL 53 D4
Oxford KS 37 F4
Oxford ME 29 F1
Oxford MA 71 D2
Oxford MI 26 C3
Oxford MS 52 B3
Oxford NE 37 D1
Oxford NC 55 D1
Oxford PA 68 C3
Oxnard CA 44 B4
Oxon Hill MD 68 A4
Oyster Bay NY 69 F1
Ozark AL 65 D2
Ozark AR 51 D2
Ozark MO 51 E1
Ozona TX 59 D3

P

Pablo MT 10 A2
Pace FL 64 C3
Pacific MO 39 E3
Pacifica CA 31 E4
Pacific Grove CA 31 D4
Pacolet SC 54 B3
Paddock Lake WI 25 E3
Paden City WV 41 F2
Paducah KY 52 B1
Paducah TX 49 E4
Page AZ 46 B1
Pageland SC 54 C3
Pagosa Sprs. CO 35 E4
Pahokee FL 67 F3
Pahrump NV 45 E2
Paia HI 73 D1
Painesville OH 27 D4
Paintsville KY 41 E4
Palacios TX 61 E2
Palatine IL 25 F3
Palatka FL 66 B4
Palermo CA 31 F2
Palestine TX 62 B2
Palisade CO 35 D3
Palisades Park NJ 112 D2
Palm Bay FL 67 F2
Palm Beach FL 67 F3
Palm Beach Gardens FL 67 F3
Palm Coast FL 66 B4
Palmdale CA 44 C3
Palm Desert CA 45 D4
Palmer AK 74 C3
Palmer MA 70 C2
Palmer TX 62 A1
Palmer Lake CO 35 F2
Palmerton PA 68 C1
Palmetto FL 67 D2
Palmetto GA 53 E4
Palmetto Bay FL 109 A5
Palm Harbor FL 67 D2
Palm River FL 123 E2
Palm Sprs. CA 45 D4
Palm Valley FL 66 B3
Palmyra MO 39 D2
Palmyra NJ 69 D2
Palmyra NY 28 A3
Palmyra PA 68 B2
Palmyra WI 25 E3
Palo Alto CA 31 F4
Palos Hills IL 98 C5
Pampa TX 49 D2
Pana IL 39 F2
Panaca NV 33 E4
Panama OK 50 C3
Panama City FL 65 D4
Panama City Beach FL 65 D4
Panguitch UT 34 A4
Panhandle TX 48 A1
Panthersville GA 94 D3
Paola KS 38 B3
Paoli IN 40 B3
Paoli PA 68 C2
Paonia CO 35 D3
Papillion NE 23 F4
Parachute CO 35 D2
Paradise CA 31 F2
Paradise NV 105 B2
Paradise Valley AZ 46 B4
Paragould AR 52 A2
Paramount CA 106 D3
Paramus NJ 112 C1
Pardeeville WI 25 E2
Paris AR 51 D2
Paris ID 20 A3
Paris IL 40 A2
Paris KY 41 D3
Paris MO 39 D2
Paris TN 52 C1
Paris TX 50 C4
Park City KS 37 F4
Park City MT 11 E4
Park City UT 34 B1
Parker AZ 45 F4
Parker CO 35 F2
Parker FL 65 D4
Parker SD 23 E2
Parkersburg IA 24 B3
Parkersburg WV 41 F2
Parkesburg PA 68 C2
Park Falls WI 15 E4
Park Hill OK 50 C2
Park Hills MO 39 E4
Parkin AR 52 A2
Parkland FL 109 A1
Parkland WA 8 B2
Park Rapids MN 14 B3
Park Ridge IL 98 C3
Park River ND 13 F1
Parks AZ 46 B2
Parkston SD 23 E2
Parkville MD 95 C1
Parlier CA 44 B1
Parma ID 18 C2
Parma OH 27 D4
Parma Hts. OH 99 E3
Parmelee SD 22 C2
Parowan UT 34 A4
Parshall ND 12 C2
Parsons KS 38 B4
Parsons TN 52 C2
Parsons WV 42 A3
Pasadena CA 44 C4
Pasadena TX 61 F1
Pascagoula MS 64 B3
Pasco WA 9 D3
Pascoag RI 71 D2
Paso Robles CA 44 A2
Passaic NJ 69 E1
Pass Christian MS 64 A3
Patchogue NY 69 F1
Paterson NJ 69 E1
Patrick Sprs. VA 54 C1
Patterson CA 31 F4
Patterson LA 63 F4
Paul ID 19 F3
Paulden AZ 46 B3
Paulding OH 26 B4
Pauls Valley OK 50 B3
Pauwela HI 73 D1
Pawcatuck CT 71 D3
Pawhuska OK 50 B1
Pawnee IL 39 F2
Pawnee OK 50 B1
Pawnee City NE 38 A2
Paw Paw MI 26 A3
Pawtucket RI 71 D2
Paxton IL 40 A1
Payette ID 18 C2
Paynesville MN 14 B4
Payson AZ 46 B3
Payson UT 34 B2
Peabody KS 37 F3
Peabody MA 71 E1
Peachtree City GA 53 E4
Pea Ridge AR 51 D1
Pearisburg VA 41 F4
Pearl MS 64 A1
Pearland TX 61 F1
Pearl City HI 72 A3
Pearlington MS 64 A3
Pearl River LA 64 A3
Pearsall TX 60 C1
Pecos NM 48 A2
Pecos TX 58 B2
Peculiar MO 38 B3
Peekskill NY 70 A4
Pegram TN 53 D2
Pekin IL 39 F1
Pelahatchie MS 64 A1
Pelham AL 53 D4
Pelham GA 65 E3
Pelican Rapids MN 14 A3
Pella IA 24 B4
Pell City AL 53 D4
Pembina ND 13 F1
Pembroke GA 66 B2
Pembroke NC 55 D3
Pembroke Pines FL 109 A3
Pena Blanca NM 47 F2
Pen Argyl PA 69 D1
Peñasco NM 48 A1
Pender NE 23 E3
Pendleton IN 40 C2
Pendleton OR 9 D4
Pendleton SC 54 A3
Penn Hills PA 117 H1
Pennington Gap VA 53 F1
Pennsauken NJ 116 D3
Pennsboro WV 41 F2
Pennsburg PA 68 C2
Penns Grove NJ 43 D2
Pennsville NJ 68 C3
Penn Yan NY 28 B3
Penrose CO 35 F3
Pensacola FL 64 C3
Peoria AZ 46 B4
Peoria IL 39 F1
Peotone IL 25 F4
Pepeekeo HI 73 F3
Peralta NM 47 F3
Perham MN 14 B3
Peridot AZ 46 C4
Perkasie PA 69 D2
Perkins OK 50 B2
Perrine FL 109 A5
Perris CA 45 D4
Perry FL 65 F4
Perry GA 65 F1
Perry IA 24 A4
Perry MI 26 B3
Perry NY 27 F3
Perry OK 50 B1
Perry UT 20 A4
Perry Hall MD 68 B3
Perrysburg OH 26 C4
Perryton TX 49 D1
Perryville AR 51 E3
Perryville MD 68 C3
Perryville MO 39 E4
Perth Amboy NJ 69 E1
Peru IL 25 E4
Peru IN 40 B1
Peshtigo WI 16 A4
Petal MS 64 A2
Petaluma CA 31 E3
Peterborough NH 71 D1
Petersburg AK 75 E4
Petersburg IN 40 A3
Petersburg VA 42 C4
Petersburg WV 42 A3
Petersville AL 52 C3
Petoskey MI 16 B4
Pevely MO 39 E3
Pflugerville TX 62 A3
Pharr TX 60 C4
Phenix City AL 65 E1
Philadelphia MS 64 B1
Philadelphia PA 69 D2
Philip SD 22 B2
Philippi WV 42 A2
Philipsburg MT 10 B3
Philipsburg PA 42 B1
Phillips WI 15 E4
Phillipsburg KS 37 D2
Phillipsburg NJ 69 D1
Philomath OR 17 E1
Phoenix AZ 46 B4
Phoenix OR 17 E3
Phoenixville PA 68 C2
Picayune MS 64 A3
Picher OK 50 C1
Pickens MS 64 A1
Pickens SC 54 A3
Pickerington OH 41 E2
Pico Rivera CA 106 D3
Piedmont AL 53 E4
Piedmont MO 51 F1
Piedmont OK 50 A2
Piedmont SC 54 A3
Piedmont SD 22 A1
Pierce ID 9 F3
Pierce NE 23 E3
Pierre SD 22 C1
Pierre Part LA 63 F4
Pigeon Forge TN 53 F2
Piggott AR 52 A1
Pikesville MD 95 A1
Pikeville KY 41 E4
Pikeville TN 53 E2
Pilot Pt. TX 50 B4
Pilot Rock OR 9 D4
Pilot Sta. AK 74 B3
Pima AZ 56 C1
Pinckney MI 26 B3
Pinckneyville IL 39 F4
Pine AZ 46 B3
Pine Bluff AR 51 F3
Pine Bluffs WY 21 F4
Pine City MN 14 C4
Pinecrest FL 109 A5
Pinedale WY 20 B3
Pine Hills FL 115 B2
Pinehurst ID 9 F2
Pinehurst NC 54 C3
Pinehurst TX 62 B4
Pine Island MN 24 B1
Pine Knot KY 53 E1
Pinellas Park FL 67 D2
Pine Ridge SD 22 B3
Pinesdale MT 10 A3
Pinetop-Lakeside AZ 46 C4
Pineville KY 53 F1
Pineville LA 63 E2
Piney Green NC 55 E3
Pink OK 50 B2
Pinole CA 122 C1
Pinon AZ 46 C2
Pinson AL 53 D4
Pioche NV 33 E4
Pipestone MN 23 F2
Piqua OH 41 D2
Pirtleville AZ 56 C2
Pismo Beach CA 44 A3
Pitman NJ 69 D3
Pittsboro NC 55 D2
Pittsburg CA 31 F4
Pittsburg KS 38 B4
Pittsburg TX 62 C1
Pittsburgh PA 42 A1
Pittsfield IL 39 E2
Pittsfield ME 30 B3
Pittsfield MA 70 B1
Pittsfield NH 29 E2
Pittston PA 28 B4
Placentia CA 107 F4
Placerville CA 31 F3
Placitas NM 47 F2
Plain City OH 41 D2
Plain City UT 20 A4
Plainfield CT 71 D3
Plainfield IL 25 E4
Plainfield IN 40 B2
Plainfield NJ 69 E1
Plainfield VT 29 E1
Plains KS 37 D4
Plains MT 10 A2
Plains TX 58 B1
Plainview MN 24 C1
Plainview NE 23 E3
Plainview TX 49 D4
Plainville KS 37 E2
Plainville MA 71 E2
Plainwell MI 26 A3
Plaistow NH 71 E1
Planada CA 32 A4
Plankinton SD 23 D2
Plano IL 25 E4
Plano TX 62 A1
Plantation FL 67 F3
Plant City FL 67 D2
Plantersville MS 52 B4
Plaquemine LA 63 F3
Platte SD 23 D2
Platte City MO 38 B2
Platteville CO 35 F1
Platteville WI 25 D3
Plattsburg MO 38 B2
Plattsburgh NY 29 D1
Plattsmouth NE 38 A1
Pleasant Garden NC 54 C2
Pleasant Grove AL 96 A1
Pleasant Grove UT 34 B1
Pleasant Hill CA 122 D2
Pleasant Hill MO 38 B3
Pleasant Hills MD 68 B3
Pleasanton CA 31 F4
Pleasanton KS 38 B3
Pleasanton TX 60 C1
Pleasant Prairie WI 25 F3
Pleasant View TN 53 D1
Pleasant View UT 20 A4
Pleasantville IA 24 B4
Pleasantville NJ 69 E3
Pleasantville NY 70 A4
Plentywood MT 12 B1
Plover WI 25 D1
Plummer ID 9 E2
Plymouth IN 26 A4
Plymouth MA 71 E2
Plymouth MI 101 E2
Plymouth MN 110 A2
Plymouth NH 29 E2
Plymouth NC 55 E2
Plymouth WI 25 F2
Pocahontas AR 51 F1
Pocahontas IA 24 A3
Pocatello ID 20 A3
Pocola OK 51 D2
Pocomoke City MD 43 D4
Pt. Clear AL 64 B3
Pt. Hope AK 74 B1
Pt. Pleasant NJ 69 E2
Pt. Pleasant WV 41 E3
Pt. Pleasant Beach NJ 69 E2
Pojoaque NM 47 F2
Polacca AZ 46 C2
Polk City IA 24 B4
Pollock Pines CA 32 A3
Polson MT 10 A2
Pomeroy WA 9 E3
Pomona CA 44 C4
Pomona NJ 69 D3
Pompano Beach FL 67 F3
Pompton Lakes NJ 70 A4
Ponca NE 23 E3
Ponca City OK 50 B1
Ponchatoula LA 63 F3
Pontiac IL 39 F1
Pontiac MI 26 C3
Pontotoc MS 52 B3
Pooler GA 66 B2
Poolesville MD 68 A4
Poplar MT 12 A1
Poplar Bluff MO 52 A1
Poplarville MS 64 A3
Poquoson VA 55 F1
Portage IN 25 F4
Portage MI 26 A3
Portage PA 42 B1
Portage WI 25 E2
Portageville MO 52 B1
Portales NM 48 C4
Port Allen LA 63 F3
Port Angeles WA 8 A2
Port Aransas TX 61 D3
Port Arthur TX 63 D4
Port Barre LA 63 E3
Port Charlotte FL 67 D3
Port Chester NY 70 B4
Port Clinton OH 26 C4
Port Edwards WI 25 D1
Porterville CA 44 B2
Port Ewen NY 70 A2
Port Gibson MS 63 F2
Port Hadlock WA 8 B2
Port Hueneme CA 44 B4
Port Huron MI 26 C3
Port Isabel TX 61 D4
Port Jefferson NY 69 F1
Port Jervis NY 28 C4
Portland CT 70 C3
Portland IN 40 C1
Portland ME 29 F2
Portland MI 26 B3
Portland ND 13 F2
Portland OR 8 B4
Portland TN 53 D1
Portland TX 61 D2
Port Lavaca TX 61 E2
Port Ludlow WA 8 B2
Port Monmouth NJ 69 E1
Port Neches TX 63 D4
Port Orange FL 67 E1
Port Orchard WA 8 B2
Port Richey FL 67 D1
Port Royal SC 66 B1
Port St. Joe FL 65 E4
Port St. John FL 67 F1
Port St. Lucie FL 67 F2
Port Salerno FL 67 F2
Portsmouth NH 29 F3

Orlando FL
Apopka
South Apopka
Casselberry
Winter Springs
Altamonte Springs
Forest City
Fern Park
Lake Apopka
Maitland
Lockhart
Fairview Shores
Winter Park
Ocoee
Winter Garden
Pine Hills
Union Park
Orlando
Azalea Park
Orlovista
Gotha
Windermere
Conway
Pine Castle
Belle Isle
Bay Hill
Doctor Phillips
Sky Lake
Tangelo Park
Orlando International Airport (MCO)
Williamsburg
Walt Disney World
Epcot
Buena Vista
Lake Nona
Buenaventura Lakes
Kissimmee
East Lake Tohopekaliga
Narcoossee
Celebration
Old Town
ORANGE CO.
OSCEOLA CO.
SEMINOLE CO.
0 1 2 3 mi
0 1 2 3 4 km

Philadelphia PA

Entries in **bold color** indicate cities with detailed inset maps.

Rome—Scott City **117**

Phoenix AZ

Thunderbird Cons. Pk. · PINNACLE PEAK RD
Hurricane Harbor Phoenix
Challenger Space Center
Deer Valley Petroglyph Pres.
Adobe Dam Reg. Park
Phoenix Deer Valley Airport (DVT)
Natl. Mem. Cem. of Arizona
Desert Ridge Marketplace

Sun City West
Peoria
Scottsdale
Grayhawk
McDowell Mountain Reg. Park
FORT McDOWELL YAVAPAI NATION

Surprise
Surprise Stadium
Sun City
Arrowhead Towne Center
Peoria Sports Complex
Turf Paradise
Musical Instruments Mus.
TPC of Scottsdale
West World of Scottsdale
Kierland Commons
Fort McDowell
Fountain Hills
The Fountain

Youngtown
El Mirage
Sahuaro Ranch
Arizona St. Univ. West
Phoenix
North Mtn. Park
Scottsdale Airport (SDL)
Taliesin West
We-Ko-Pa Casino Resort

SUNNYSLOPE
Paradise Valley
Phoenix Mountains Park and Rec. Area
McCormick-Stillman Railroad Park
Casino Ariz. at Talking Stick
The Pavilions at Talking Stick

Litchfield Park
Goodyear
Luke A.F.B.
Desert Sky Mall
McChin Pavilion
Glendale
State Farm Stadium
Grand Canyon Univ.
Wrigley Mansion
Arizona Biltmore
Biltmore Fashion Park
Camelback
SALT RIVER PIMA-MARICOPA INDIAN COMMUNITY
Granite Reef Dam

MARYVALE
American Family Fields of Phoenix
Heard Mus.
Phoenix Zoo & Desert Bot. Gdn.
Papago Park
Scottsdale Fashion Sq.
Scottsdale Center for the Perf. Arts
Contemporary Art
Huhugam Ki Mus.

Avondale
Tolleson
State Capitol
Chase Field
Phoenix Sky Harbor Intl. Airport (PHX)
Sun Devil Stad.
Sloan Riverview
Hohokam Stadium Ariz. Mus. of Nat. Hist.
Commemorative Air Force Mus.
Mesa

ASU
Gammage
Tempe Diablo Stadium
Arizona Mills
i.d.e.a. Mus.
Mesa Ariz. LDS Temple
Superstition Springs Ctr.
Superstition Freeway

Phoenix Raceway
Maricopa Village
Estrella Mountain Reg. Park
GILA RIVER INDIAN COMMUNITY
SOUTH MOUNTAIN
Guadalupe
Mystery Castle
Dobbins Lookout
South Mountain Park/Preserve
AHWATUKEE FOOTHILLS
Tempe
Gilbert
Arizona St. Univ. Polytechnic Campus
Phoenix-Mesa Gateway Arpt. (IWA)

Komatke
Gila River Vee Quiva Casino
Rawhide Western Town
Gila River Wild Horse Pass Casino
Chandler Fashion Ctr.
Lone Butte Casino
Chandler
Chandler Ctr. for the Arts

0 2 4 6 mi
0 2 4 6 8 km

Pittsburgh PA

Glenfield
Emsworth
Neville
Groveton
Camp Horne Rd.
Ben Avon Heights
West View
Ben Avon
Avalon
Neville Island
Bellevue
Evergreen
Etna
Fox Chapel
Oakmont
Verona

0 1 2 mi
0 1 2 3 km

Sharpsburg
Aspinwall
The Waterworks
Blawnox
Millvale
Allegheny Observatory
Pittsburgh Zoo & PPG Aquarium
Riverview Park
Highland Park
Sandy Creek
Penn Hills

Forest Grove
Kenmawr
West Park
McKees Rocks
Moon Run
Ingram
Pittsburgh
Acrisure Natl. Stad. & Aviary
The Rivers Casino
Point St.
PNC Park
PPG Paints Arena
UNIV. OF PITTSBURGH
Gateway Ctr.
Fort Pitt Tunnel
Carlow Univ.
Carnegie Mellon Univ.
The Carnegie
Chatham Univ.
Bot. Gdn.
Clayton
Frick Art & Frick Mus.
Wilkinsburg
Edgewood
Churchill
Forest Hills

Thornburg
Rosslyn Farms
Green Tree
Crafton
Pennsbury Village
Phipps Conservatory
Schenley Park
Squirrel Hill Tunnel
Liberty Tunnel
Swissvale

Carnegie
Green Tree Nature Ctr.
Mount Oliver
The Waterfront
Homestead
Sandcastle Water Park
Rankin
Chalfant
Braddock
North Braddock
Turtle Creek

Rennerdale
Ewingsville
Dormont
Hays Woods
West Homestead
Braddock Locks & Dam
East Pittsburgh
Kennywood

Heidelberg
Presto
Mount Lebanon
Baldwin
Munhall
Duquesne

Kirwan Heights
Galleria of Mt. Lebanon
Castle Shannon
Brentwood
White Oak
Penn State Gr. Allegheny

Sygan
Bridgeville
South Hills Village
Bethel Park
Whitehall
West Mifflin
Century III Mall
Dravosburg
McKeesport

Portland OR

(map)

Providence RI

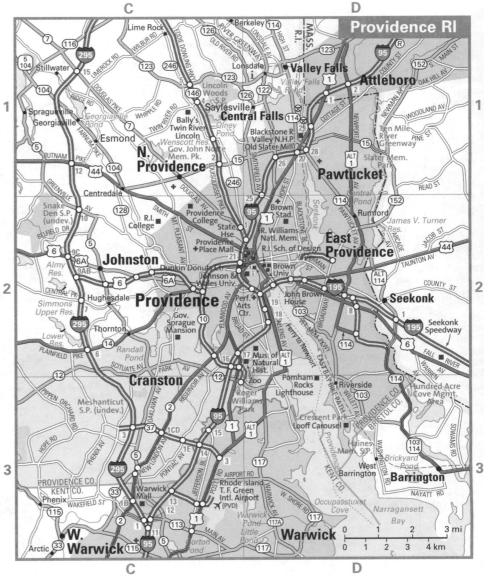

Richmond VA inset map.

Sacramento CA inset map.

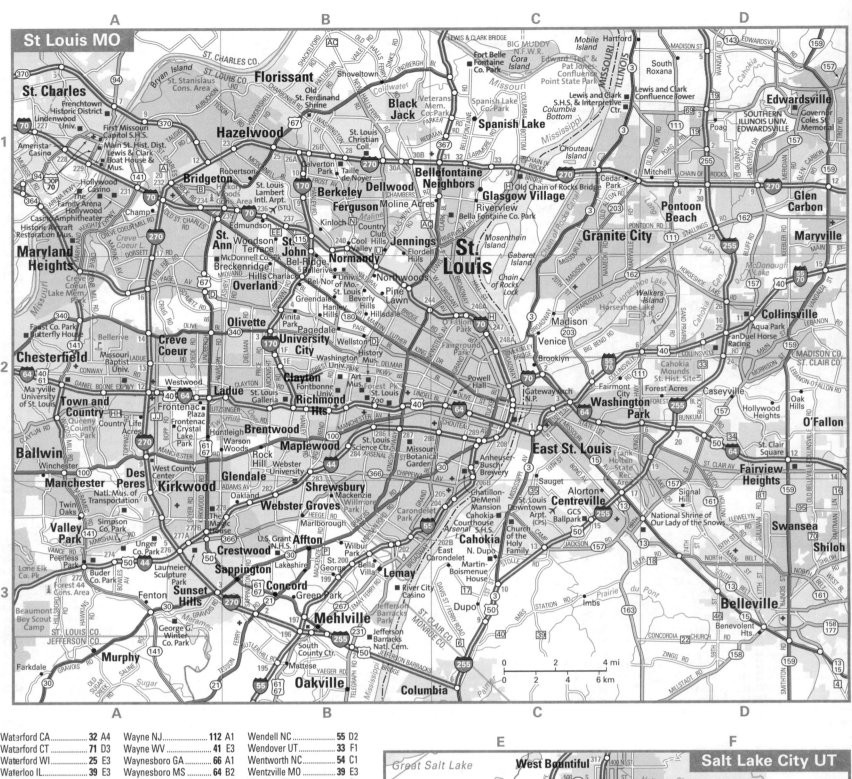

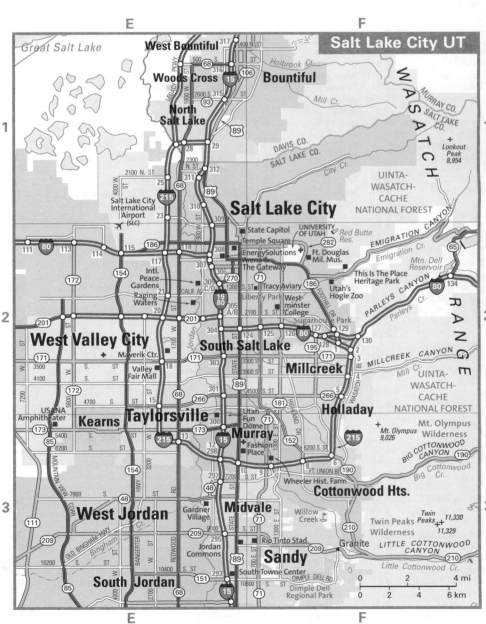

Entries in **bold color** indicate cities with detailed inset maps.

West Mifflin—Zwolle **121**

San Antonio TX

(detailed inset map)

San Diego CA

(detailed inset map)

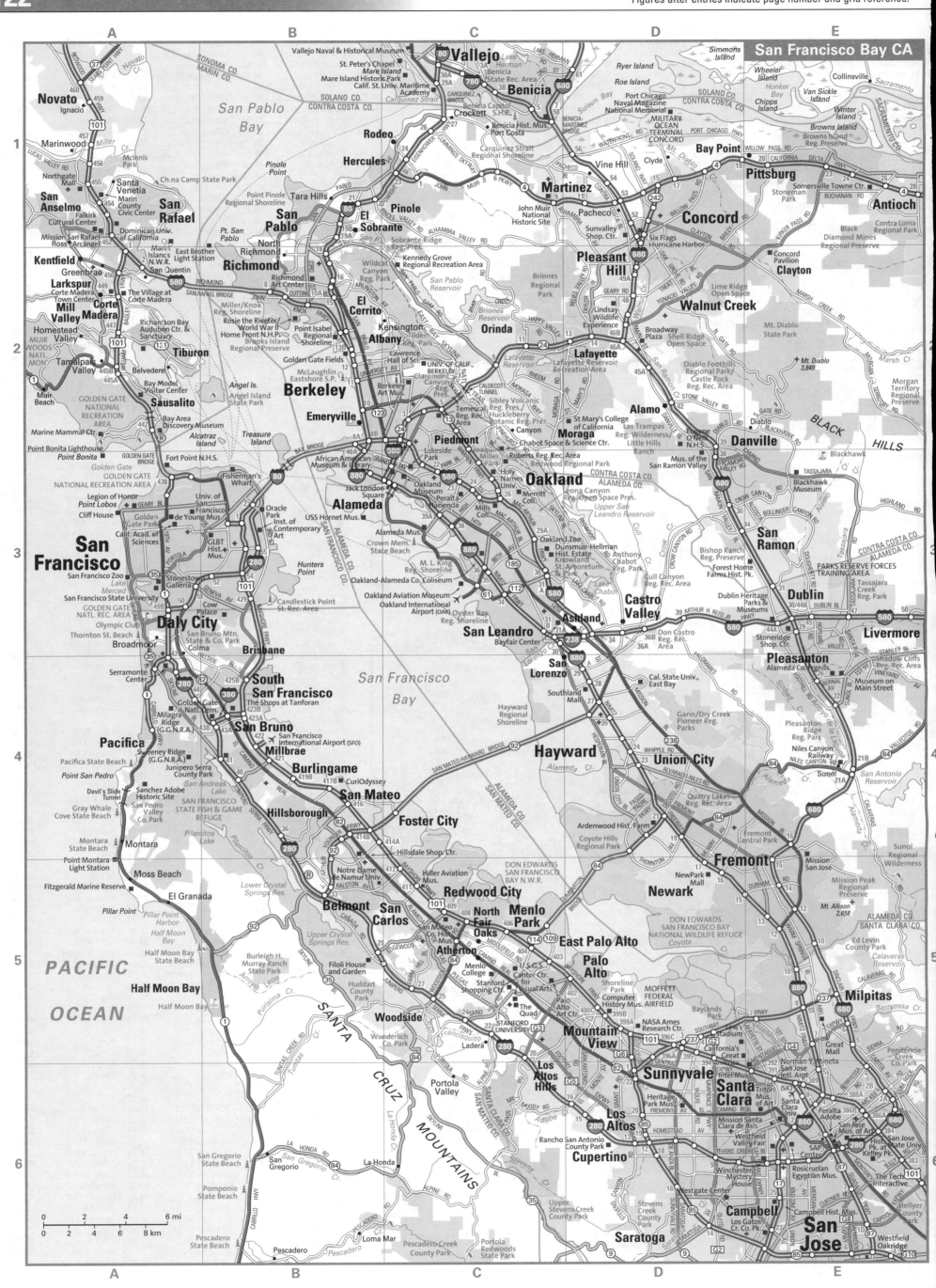

San Francisco Bay CA

Entries in **bold color** indicate cities with detailed inset maps.

Seattle / Tacoma WA

Marysville, Lake Stevens, Langley, Possession Sound, Bay View, Freeland, Clinton, Maxwelton, Hansville, Shine, Whidbey Island, Double Bluff Beach, Foulweather Bluff Preserve, Everett, Naval Station Everett, Everett Farmers Mkt., Funko Field, Angel of the Winds Arena, Mukilteo, Mukilteo Lighthouse Park, Snohomish, Snohomish Co. Airport (PAE), Glendale, Everett Mall, Mill Creek, Martha Lake, Cathcart, Lynnwood, Alderwood, Edmonds, Alderwood Manor, Maltby, Mountlake Terrace, Brier, Kenmore, Bothell, Woodinville, Shoreline, Lake Forest Park, Poulsbo, Indianola, Suquamish, Seattle, Kirkland, Redmond, Medina, Bellevue, Bainbridge Island, Bremerton, Manchester, Mercer Island, Newcastle, Port Orchard, Skyway, Renton, White Center, Burien, Tukwila, Normandy Park, SeaTac, Kent, Des Moines, Vashon, Gig Harbor, Covington, Federal Way, Auburn, University Place, Steilacoom, Tacoma, Pacific, Milton, Edgewood, Sumner, Bonney Lake, Fircrest, Lakewood, Parkland, Midland, Summit, Puyallup, South Hill

Tampa / St Petersburg FL

Tarpon Springs, Lutz, Palm Harbor, Dunedin, Oldsmar, Safety Harbor, Carrollwood, Temple Terrace, Clearwater, Town 'n Country, Tampa, Largo, Indian Rocks Beach, Seminole, Pinellas Park, Treasure Island, South Pasadena, Lealman, St. Petersburg, Gulfport, St. Pete Beach, Ruskin, Sun City Center, Sun City, Apollo Beach, Riverview, Gibsonton, Memphis, Palmetto, Bradenton, Ellenton, Oneco, Longboat Key, Bradenton Beach, Holmes Beach, Anna Maria, Sarasota, Siesta Key, Bee Ridge, Fruitville, GULF OF MEXICO, Tampa Bay

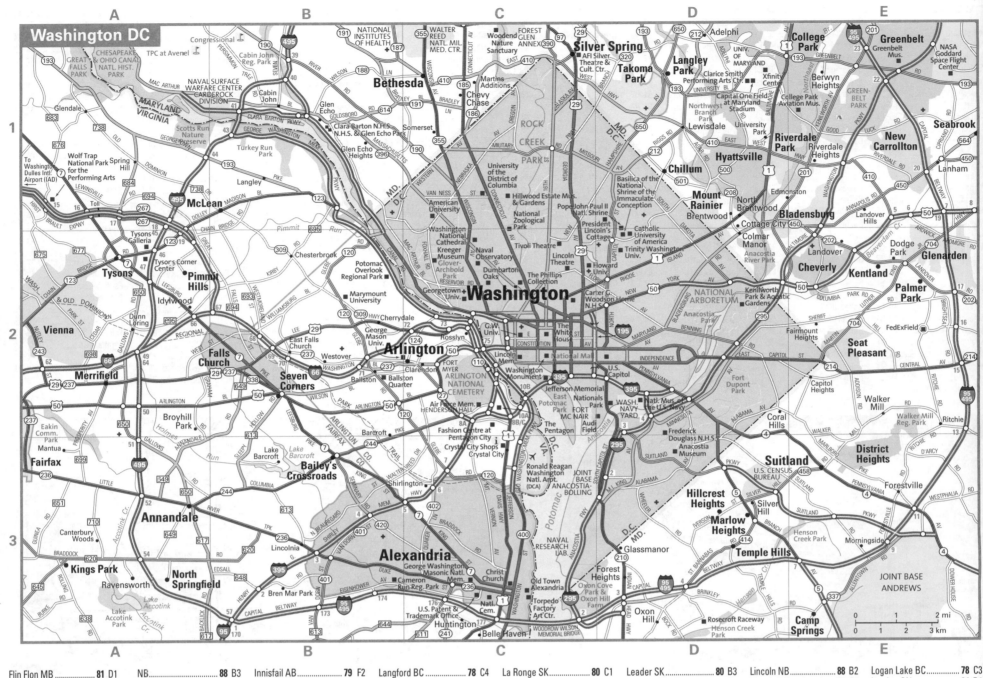

Washington DC

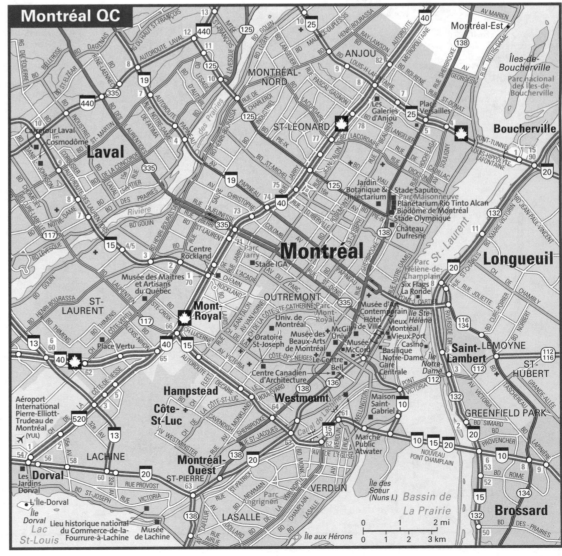

Montréal QC

Entries in **bold color** indicate cities with detailed inset maps.

Lynn Lake—Yorkton 125

Toronto ON (Vaughan, Markham, North York, Scarborough, York, East York, Etobicoke, Mississauga) — LAKE ONTARIO

Vancouver BC (West Vancouver, North Vancouver, Dist. Mun. of North Vancouver, Port Moody, Vancouver, Burnaby, New Westminster, Richmond, Surrey)

Édition 14.1 - 2024 – Éditeur : MICHELIN Éditions
Société par actions simplifiée au capital de 487 500 EUR
57 rue Gaston Tessier – 75019 Paris (France)
R.C.S. Paris 882 639 354 - DL : AVRIL 2024
Copyright © 2024 MICHELIN Éditions - Tous droits réservés
Printed by Transcontinental - Beauceville (Quebec) G5X 3P3 - April 2024 - Printed in Canada

City to City Distance Chart (diagonal labels):

- Albuquerque, NM
- Anchorage, AK
- Atlanta, GA
- Billings, MT
- Bismarck, ND
- Boise, ID
- Boston, MA
- Calgary, AB
- Charlotte, NC
- Chicago, IL
- Cleveland, OH
- Dallas, TX
- Denver, CO
- Detroit, MI
- El Paso, TX
- Halifax, NS
- Houston, TX
- Indianapolis, IN
- Kansas City, MO
- Las Vegas, NV
- Los Angeles, CA
- Memphis, TN
- México, MX
- Miami, FL
- Minneapolis, MN
- Montréal, QC
- Nashville, TN
- New Orleans, LA
- New York, NY
- Oklahoma City, OK
- Omaha, NE
- Orlando, FL
- Ottawa, ON
- Philadelphia, PA
- Phoenix, AZ
- Pittsburgh, PA
- Portland, OR
- Québec, QC
- Reno, NV
- St. Louis, MO
- Salt Lake City, UT
- San Antonio, TX
- San Diego, CA
- San Francisco, CA
- Seattle, WA
- Toronto, ON
- Vancouver, BC
- Washington, DC
- Winnipeg, MB